Love of Brothers by Katharine Tynan

Katherine Tynan was born on January 23rd 1859 into a large farming family in Clondalkin, County Dublin, and educated at a convent school in Drogheda. In her early years she suffered from eye ulcers, which left her somewhat myopic.

She first began to have her poems published in 1878. A great friend to Gerard Manley Hopkins and to WB Yeats (who it is rumoured proposed marriage but was rejected). With Yeats to encourage her, her poetry blossomed and she was equally supportive of his.

She married fellow writer and barrister Henry Albert Hinkson in 1898. They moved to England where she bore and began to raise 5 children although two were to tragically die in infancy.

In 1912 they returned to Claremorris, County Mayo when her husband was appointed magistrate there from 1912 until 1919. Sadly her husband died that year but Katherine continued to write.

Her output was prolific, some sources have her as the author of almost a 100 novels, many volumes of poetry, short stories, biography and many volumes which she edited.

Katherine died on April 2nd 1931 and she is buried at Kensal Green Cemetery in London.

Index of Contents

I0161971

INTRODUCTORY

It was a night of bright moonlight that made for pitchy shadows under wall or tree.

Patsy Kenny was looking for the goat, she having broken her tether. He had been driven forth by his fierce old grandfather with threats of the most awful nature if he should return without the goat.

The tears were not yet dry on Patsy's small face. He had kneaded them in with his knuckles, but the smears caused by the process were not visible in the moonlight, even if there had been any one to see them. It was not only the hardship of being driven out when the meal of hot potatoes was on the table, to search for that "ould divil" of a goat, and his sense of the injustice which had put the blame of the goat's straying on to his narrow shoulders. The old, in Patsy's knowledge of them, were crabbed and unjust. That was something for the young to take in the day's work. It was Patsy's fears of the supernatural that kept him creeping along in the shadow of the hedge, now and again stopping to weep a little over his troubles, or to listen fearfully like a frightened hare before going on again.

Why, close to the road by which he must go to seek the goat there was the tomb in which Captain Hercules O'Hart lay buried. People about Killesky did not take that road if they could help it. The tomb was a terror to all those who must pass the road by night, and to their horses if they were riding or driving. It was well known that no horse would pass by the tomb without endeavouring to avoid it, and if forced or cajoled into accomplishing the passage, would emerge trembling and sweating. Some unimaginative person had suggested that the terror of the horses was due to the thunder of the invisible waterfall where the river tumbled over its weir, just below the Mount on which old Hercules had chosen to be buried. The horses knew better than that. Nothing natural said the people would make a horse behave in such a way. The dumb beast knew what it saw and that was nothing good.

The anguish of Patsy's thoughts caused him suddenly to "bawl" as he would have put it himself.

"Isn't it an awful thing?" he asked, addressing the quiet bog-world under the moon, "to think of a little lad like me havin' to be out in the night facin' all them ghosts and that ould heart-scald of a man burnin' his knees at home be the fire? What'll I do at all if that tormint of a goat is up strayin' on the Mount? It would be like what the divil 'ud do to climb up there, unless it was to be the churchyard below, and all them ould bones stickin' up through the clay.

"There isn't wan out this night but meself," he went on. "It's awful to think of every wan inside their houses an' me wanderin' about be me lone. It isn't wan ghost but twinty I might meet betune this an' the cross-roads, let alone fairies and pookas. Won't I just welt the divil out o' the oul' goat when I ketch her?"

A little whinny close to him made him look round with a fearful hope. He saw neither pooka nor fairy, but the long horns of the animal he was in search of.

He snatched joyfully at her chain, forgetting all his anger. Indeed none knew better than the goat Patsy's gentleness with all living creatures. Her mouth was full of grass. He remembered his grandfather's speech as he tethered the little goat on the bare hillside above the house.

"My poor girl," he had said, "you've got little enough to ate, but then you've a beautiful view."

"Sure she strayed," said Patsy in extenuation, "because she was hungry, the creature."

So he had not had to leave the brightly lit bog-road for that black tunnel of trees just beyond which led to old Hercules' tomb, and the well where the woman fell in and the fields where old Michael Halloran, who had been steward and general overseer to the O'Harts, was reputed to be seen night after night, hedging and fencing the lands and he years dead.

"You was a good little goat," said Patsy in his great relief. "Come home now and I'll milk you: and maybe that cross ould man would let me have a sup o' tay for my supper."

He had pulled the goat down the bank into the dry ditch. It was a good thing he had stopped to "bawl," else maybe he'd have missed the goat who had been having her fill of Mrs. McEnroe's after-grass. Still he wondered now at his temerity since the bawlin' might have brought them upon him disturbin' their sleep that way.

He suddenly caught the sound of horses' feet coming along the bog-road towards him. He stopped and listened, holding firmly on to the goat. The bog-road was light as day. Two people were walking their horses side by side, a dog at their heels. "It'll be Mr. Terence Comerford, an' Sir Shawn O'Gara, comin' home together," Patsy said to himself. "What at all would be keepin' them out till this hour of the night, unless it was to be talkin' to Bridyeen Sweeney? Quare ways young gentlemen has that they'd be talkin' to a poor girl an' maybe turnin' her head, let alone settin' the neighbours to talkin' about her. God help her."

In this musing, be it said, Patsy was but repeating the talk of his elders, although he was naturally what is called an old-fashioned child.

He crouched low in the ditch while the horses came on at a walking pace. The riders were talking, one in a low voice, so low that Patsy could not make out what he said. This one was slender and young. The other, young also, but big and burly, was riding a horse which apparently did not like the walking pace. She, it was a mare, curveted and caracoled in the road, which was one reason why Patsy could not hear what was being said. The boy peered out, with fear in his heart. The knowledge of horses was born in him. His father had been stud-groom to Mr. Comerford of Inch. By and by Patsy meant to escape from his old tyrant and become a stable-boy at Inch or at Castle Talbot. Perhaps in time he might come to be stud-groom, though that was a dizzy height towards which as yet his imagination hardly carried him.

"Mr. Terence has drink taken," said Patsy, in his own mind. "He's not steady in the saddle. An', glory be to goodness, it's Spitfire he's ridin'." Patsy was at home in many stables where the grooms and stable-helpers condescended to accept his willing aid in running messages or the like. "What would the Misthress or Miss Mary say if they was to see him now? Look well to him, Sir Shawn, look well to him, or it's killin' himself he'll be!"

This apostrophe was unspoken. Mr. Terence Comerford had brought Spitfire under control and she walked more soberly. The talk had ceased for moment. It broke out again. As the riders went on their way Sir Shawn's voice sounded as though he was pleading hard with his friend. They had always been the most attached and devoted friends from boyhood.

Terence Comerford's laugh came back borne upon a little wind.

"It'll be," said Patsy in his thoughts, "that Sir Shawn'll be biddin' Mr. Terence to have sinse. A quare thing it is, and he all but promised to Miss Mary that he'd be down at Dowd's every night since she and the Misthress went to Dublin, talking to poor Bridyeen. 'Tis sorrow the crathur'll have, no less, if she goes listenin' to Mr. Terence. 'Tis a wonder Sir Shawn wouldn't be givin' him better advice. Unless it was to be, there's some do be sayin' he's fond of Miss Mary too."

All gossip of his elders, told round the turf-fire at night when Patsy was supposed to be fast asleep in the settle bed, instead of "cockin' his ears" for grown people's talk.

He peered out with wide eyes in the direction the riders had taken. His small bullet head and narrow shoulders threw a shadow on the moonlit road.

"Sir Shawn 'ud have a right to be seein' Mr. Terence home to Inch itself," he thought. "It isn't alone ould Hercules an' the river tumblin' over the weir an' the terrible dark road, but there's ould Halloran's ghost on the long avenue to Inch, and there's the ghost of the minister's wife by the churchyard. And Spitfire, that would take fright at a pinkeen much less a ghost, under him, and Mr. Terence be the way of him none too steady."

Mr. Terence's laughter came back on the wind, and was caught up and repeated by something that lurked in the Wood of the Echoes, as the people called it, which grew on a spit of solid land that reached out into the bog. Those echoes were difficult to explain. Why should a little wood of slender trees within a low wall catch and fling back human voices?

The echo repeating that mocking laughter, out there in the bog, was a new element of terror to Patsy. He had better be getting away from this queer unlucky place before the riders were out of hearing. The little old grandfather, with his blazing eyes of wrath and the stick concealed somewhere behind his coat-tails, his most familiar aspect to Patsy, was better than this solitude, with that old Echo across the bog there cackling in that unchancy way. Soon, very soon, the lower road, overhung with trees, pitch-black, where one had to pass by old Hercules' tomb, just above the fall of the river over its weir, would swallow Mr. Terence, while Sir Shawn's way would wind upwards towards the mountains. Unless indeed Sir Shawn was to go home to Inch with Mr. Terence, seeing he was riding Spitfire and so many perils to be passed, and him not too steady by the look of him.

Patsy trotted along in the wake of the riders, his bare feet making a soft padding noise in the dust of the road. His way was Sir Shawn's way. The wealth of the world would not have induced Patsy to go down under the black shade of the trees into the assemblage of all the ghosts.

The little goat followed with docility at his heels, uttering now and again a plaintive bleat of protest at the pace.

Suddenly there came a sound which, filling Patsy's heart with a concrete terror, banished all the shadowy terrors. It was the sharp slash of a whip, followed by the sound of a horse in mad flight.

"It's Spitfire, it's Spitfire!" cried Patsy to the moon and the stars. "She'll kill Mr. Terence. The world knows she'd never take the whip."

It seemed to him as though there were two horses in the headlong flight, but he could not be sure. He stumbled along, sobbing in his haste and calling out inarticulate appeals to Heaven, to Sir Shawn, to save Mr. Terence, while the clatter of the horses' feet died in the distance. He even forgot his terror of the dark road which closed about him as he followed on Spitfire's track. It might be that Sir Shawn was catching up with the runaway horse, ready to snatch at the bridle if only he could be in time.

Suddenly Patsy, sobbing and shaking, cannoned into some one, something, in the darkness of the trees. A man's voice cursed him low and deep, no ghostly voice, nor that of the countryside, an unfamiliar voice and speech to Patsy. His slender little body was caught in a fierce grip. He was lifted and dashed on to the road. If it had been a stony road, instead of the yielding bog, there would have been an end of Patsy's story. As it was he lay very quietly, while the little goat went home without him.

CHAPTER I

O'GARAS OF CASTLE TALBOT

Patsy Kenny, stud-groom to Sir Shawn O'Gara, a quiet man, devoted to his horses and having a wonderful way with them, sometimes allowed his mind to wander back to the night Mr. Terence Comerford was killed and the days that followed.

He could recall the inquest on poor Mr. Terence, himself, with a bandaged head, keeping the one eye he had available fixed on the gentleman who asked him questions. He knew that Sir Shawn O'Gara was present, his face marble pale and his eyes full of a strange anguish. Well, that was not to be wondered at. The gentleman who asked the questions made sympathetic references to the unusual friendship between Sir Shawn and Mr. Comerford. Patsy had been aware of the nervous tension in Sir Shawn's face, the occasional quiver of a nostril, "Like as if he was a horse, a spirity one, aisy frightened, like Spitfire," Patsy had thought.

He remembered that tense anguish of Sir Shawn's face now, as he sat on the trunk of a fallen tree in the paddock of the foals at Castle Talbot. The foals were running with their mothers, exquisite creatures, of the most delicate slenderness. The paddock was full of the lush grass of June. The mares were contentedly grazing. Now and again one lifted her head and sniffed the air with the wind in her mane, as if at the lightest sound she would take fright.

Patsy had had a hard tussle that morning with an ill-tempered horse he was breaking, and he felt tired out. He had no idea of compelling a horse with a whip. Sir Shawn had bought this horse at a fair a short time before. He was jet-black and they had called him Mustapha. That was Master Terry's name for him, a queer heathenish name to Patsy's mind, but all Master Terry did and all the mistress, Master Terry's mother did, was right in Patsy's eyes, so Mustapha the horse was called.

He was certainly an ill-tempered brute, with a lot of the devil in him, but Patsy Kenny was never angry with a horse; it was an invaluable quality in a stud-groom. Patsy was wont to say that when he found a horse wicked he looked for the man. There was no evidence of the man so far as their record of Mustapha went. He had been bought from a little old man as pink as a baby and with a smiling innocence of aspect, so small that when Mustapha tossed his head the little man, hanging on by the rope-bridle, was lifted in the air and dropped again.

"That crathur," said Patsy to himself, "would never have done the horse a wrong. I wonder where he got him from an' who had the rearin' of him. I'm surprised the master cared to handle him. He's as like as two pins to Spitfire. Where was it they said Spitfire went? Some mountainy man bought her for a five-pound note I've heard tell."

He pulled out a fine red handkerchief and mopped his forehead with it. He'd had two hours of it trying to "insinse some rayson" into Mustapha's head. He had not made much progress. Mustapha was still kicking and squealing in his loose-box. The sounds reached Patsy Kenny where he sat on his log and made him sad. Gentle as he was he thought he had an understanding of even Mustapha. The ears back, the whites of the eyes showing, the wild nostrils, the tense muscles under the skin of black satin, were something of an unhappiness in his mind. Some time or other Mustapha must have been ill-treated.

He put his head down on his hand. He was really tired out. So he was unaware of the approach over the grass towards him of two people till their shadows fell upon him and he looked up.

"That brute has taken it out of you, Patsy," said the elder man, who had a curious elegance of face and figure. Years had not coarsened Sir Shawn O'Gara. He was still slight and active. His white hair was in almost startling contrast with the darkly foreign face, the small black moustache, the dark eyes, almost too large and soft and heavily lashed for a man's eyes.

The boy who was with him was very unlike his father. He had taken after his mother, who had once been Mary Creagh, of whom some one had said she had the colour of the foxes. The boy had his mother's reddish brown eyes and hair, something of the same colour underlying his fair skin as it did hers. He had the white, even teeth, the flashing and radiant smile. Mary Creagh had been a beautiful girl, with a look of motherliness even in her immature girlhood. As a wife and mother that aspect of her beauty had developed. Many a strange confidence had been brought to Mary Creagh, and later to Lady O'Gara. She had a way of opening hearts and lips with that soft, steadfast glance of hers. Her full bosom looked as though it were made for a child's head or a man's to rest upon.

"He'll come round, he'll come round," said Patsy. "He'll have been hurted some time or another. Whin he gets to know me he'll be biddable enough."

"Oh, I know your theories," Sir Shawn said, a smile breaking over the melancholy of his face. "You'll never give in that a horse could be cursed with a natural ill-temper. But there are ill-tempered people: why not ill-tempered horses?"

"Bedad, I dunno!" said Patsy, scratching his head thoughtfully. He stood up with a jerk. It had occurred to him suddenly that he was sitting while the gentlemen were standing. "I never could see inside a human. I don't know how it is at all that I can see the mind of a horse."

"You're a wonderful man, Patsy," said the boy gaily. "You are wasted as our stud-groom. The scientific beggars would like to get hold of a man who could see into the mind of a horse. Only we couldn't spare you. I'm afraid Mustapha would only listen to reason from you, and I've set my heart on riding him this Autumn."

"You won't do that, Master Terry, till I've had a good many more talks with the horse. I'd be sorry to see you ridin' him yet, sir."

Terry O'Gara, brilliant in white flannels, he had been playing tennis with his mother's distant young cousin, Eileen Creagh, seemed to draw the afternoon sun on to his spotlessness. Patsy Kenny, a little dazed with fatigue, blinked at his whiteness against the green grass.

A mare came trotting up to them with her foal. The mare allowed herself to be fondled, but the little foal was very wild and cantered away when they tried to stroke him.

The big paddock was a pleasant sight with the mares and their foals wandering over the young grass. The trees surrounding the paddock had not yet lost their first fresh green: and the white red-roofed stabling, newly built to accommodate the racing stud, made a vivid high light against the coppices.

The three wandered on from one mare and foal to another. Patsy, chewing a straw, offered the opinion that Magda's foal was the best of the lot. Magda belonged to her Ladyship.

"There won't be a foal in it like that little wan," said Patsy, looking at a tall chestnut foal, the slender legs of which seemed as though they might break with a little pressure, so delicate were they. "The filly won't be in it, Master Terry, wid your Mamma's horse. I've never seen a better foal. He'll win the Derby yet. Woa, Magda, woa, my beauty."

He was trying to get close to the mare, she being restive. Suddenly she uttered a joyous whinny and started off down the field, the little foal at her heels, the long manes of both flying in the wind.

"She knows her Ladyship has sugar for her. An' there's Miss Eileen. I never knew a young lady as much afraid of a horse as Miss Eileen. You should tache her better, Master Terry."

They stood by a gate to look at the horses which at a little distance beyond a small enclosure hung their long sleek noses across a five-foot paling. The points of the horses had to be discussed. Patsy had quite forgotten his fatigue. He opened the gate and they crossed the narrow strip between that and the paling. A second gate was opened and they passed through.

While they were looking at the horses they were joined by Lady O'Gara and Miss Creagh, the latter, a delicately fair girl with a mass of fine golden hair caught up with many hairpins a-top of her small head, keeping close to Lady O'Gara.

Lady O'Gara was laughing. Her husband sometimes called her the Laughing Goddess. She had two aspects to her beauty, one when she was soft and motherly, the other when she rallied those she loved and sparkled with merriment. Her still beautiful copper-coloured hair had hardly a white thread in it. She was very charming to look at in her matronly beauty.

"I've had to defend poor Eileen from the mares," she said. "They were impudent, crowding around me for sugar and sticking their noses in my pocket. Magda and Brunette nearly came to blows. I had to push them off with my whip. Poor Eileen!"

"I'm so sorry you were frightened," Terry O'Gara said, drawing a little nearer to the girl and looking into her blue eyes.

The others had gone on.

"You won't be afraid with me," said the boy, who had just passed out of Sandhurst; and was feeling immensely proud of his commission and his sword and all they betokened, although he talked lazily about "cutlery" and the pleasure of getting into mufti, making his mother's eyes dance.

"If you like, we will keep behind," he said. "If you are not accustomed to it, it is rather alarming to be caught into a herd of horses. My mother is so used to them that she cannot imagine any one being afraid."

The horses were coming in a long string from the other end of the paddock, whinnying and neighing, shaking the ground as they came. The girl drew back towards the hedge.

"It's only rough love," the boy said. "Patsy Kenny can do anything with the horses. They quarrel if he takes more notice of one than another."

"They won't hurt your mother?" the girl said anxiously. "There she is in the midst of them. Is it safe?"

"Quite safe. Nothing will happen to Mother while Father and Patsy Kenny are there. What a frightened child you are!"

Miss Creagh's soft red mouth widened into a smile which had amusement in it. She was six years older than the boy who called her a frightened child. The smile was gone before he could see it.

"I'm afraid I'm rather a coward," she said meekly. "Father has always said that it was absurd for a soldier's daughter to be alarmed of so many things."

Terry O'Gara thought at the moment that it was the most beautiful and appealing thing in the world for a girl to be frightened of many things, when the girl happened to be as pretty as Eileen Creagh, and he was the valiant youth who was to protect her from her terrors. Although he liked the feeling of protecting her he fell in with her suggestion that they should go back and talk to the foals. Miss Creagh was certainly a coward, for she cried out when a horse showed any evidence of friendliness; but when Terry suggested that they should go to the garden and look for strawberries she did not fall in with the suggestion.

"Let us wait for your mother here," she said, having gained the safe shelter of the space between the palings and the gate. "You are sure she is quite safe? Just look at her among those wild horses! There couldn't be ... an accident?"

He laughed at her terrors.

"Mother was born in a stable, so to speak," he said. "She has a way with the horses. But how fond you are of her! I am so grateful to you for appreciating my mother as she deserves."

"She is an angel," said the girl fervently.

"Well, I think so." He laughed rather shyly. "It would not be easy for a boy to have better parents. Father is quite unlike Mother, of course ... but ... I have a tremendous admiration for him, all the same. I'll tell you a secret. I believe up to this time I have wanted more than anything else to please my father. When I had to work for exams. I hated, or any stunt of that kind, when I, oh, I oughtn't to be talking about myself. It isn't that I love Mother less, but Mother is so happy. She would always find something good in my failures. But, to see Father's face light up...!"

"He looks rather sad," Miss Creagh said wistfully.

"Yes, though he can be uncommonly jolly. We have had such rags together in London. Why, here is Shot." He stooped to fondle the head of a beautiful red setter. "He must have got shut up in the garden. What I can't understand about Shot is his indifference to you."

"He knows that in my secret heart I'm afraid of dogs, a dreadful admission, isn't it? I think it was our old nurse. I can always remember her driving a dog out of the nursery. 'Nasty thing!' she used to say. 'You shall not come near my baby.' I suppose I got the idea quite in babyhood that a dog was something noxious. Not that the others minded. The house was always full of dogs."

"Oh, you'll get over that. Won't she, Shot? Do you think his hair and eyes are like my Mother's?"

"Like?" Miss Creagh was puzzled. "Oh, surely not! How could a dog's hair and eyes be like a person's. Your beautiful mother! It seems such an odd comparison."

"Oh, well. Shot is beautiful too."

Despite his infatuation Terry felt a little disappointed in Miss Creagh.

Sir Shawn and Lady O'Gara had gone on into the next paddock, which belonged to the young mares. There was a momentary excitement. One of the horses had got through after them and was racing up and down between the hurdles whinnying loudly. By the time he was secured and put back in his proper quarters the young people were out of sight.

CHAPTER II

PATSY REMEMBERS

"Shot's a good dog," Patsy Kenny was wont to observe in his slow way, "an' his father before him was a good dog. Yet I wouldn't be sayin' but what ould Shot, the grandfather, wasn't the pick o' the basket."

Old Shot had lived for five years after Sir Shawn O'Gara's marriage to Mary Creagh, which had sorely offended and alienated Mrs. Comerford, who had brought up the girl from childhood and loved her like a daughter. When he had died it was by Lady O'Gara's wish that the dog was buried in the grass-plot just outside the drawing-room window. She could see the mound from the window recess, where she sat to write her letters, in which she kept her work-table, the book she was reading, and various other belongings; she had screened it off so that the deep recess was like a little room to itself.

"When I look up and see the mound instead of Shot it always hurts me," she had said in early days. "But then I feel that he likes to be near."

"He was so fond of you, Mary," her husband often said, "fonder even, I believe, than he was of me."

"Oh, no, Shawn, not that. No one could take your place with Shot. But he accepted me, dear old dog, and I am very proud of it."

That was before Shot's son had aspired to take his father's place, while he was still indeed one of a likely litter of puppies in the stable-yard, just beginning to be cast off by Judy who had other things to do in a sporting Autumn besides looking after a lot of sprawling, big-pawed puppies, who were quite independent of her and becoming rather unmanageable.

It was also before old Shot had begun to return to his friends as nothing more tangible than a padding of soft paws on the stairs, a movement under the dining-table, where he had been accustomed to lie in life, a sound of a dog lying down with a sigh, or getting up from the hearthrug before the billiard-room fire.

These manifestations had sometimes perturbed visitors to Castle Talbot; but intimates at the house had come to accept as its owners did these sounds of a presence that was never seen. No one was any longer incommoded by it except young Shot, who would get up uncomfortably and lie at a distance, his nose on his paws, regarding with a wistful melancholy the place from which he had been driven forth.

"Meself an' ould Shot'll never lave the Master till we have to," Patsy Kenny had said to Lady O'Gara, to whom he was as much attached as old Shot had been.

"Me an' Shot'll stick by the Master," he had often said in his own mind, and sometimes aloud, when he was out in the paddocks with the horses and there was no human ear to listen to him. Then he would have a vision of a young man in a grey suit, slender and elegant, face downward on the grass and he calling out to someone to forgive him. "Sure God help him, he has suffered," he would add as the memory came to him.

Patsy, who had been taking a short cut by the wood to the stable-yard when he had come upon that sight, it was long ago, had gone away terrified and aching with pity for the misery he had surprised. Sir Shawn O'Gara had interfered once to save little Patsy from a beating and had been rewarded disproportionately by a silent ardent devotion, at which no one, he himself least of all, had ever guessed. Patsy had liked Mr. Terence Comerford too. He was handsomer, the people thought, than Sir Shawn, being golden-haired, blue-eyed and ruddy, and very big and broad-shouldered, with a jolly greeting for everyone. Many a time he had let Patsy hold his horse and flung him a sixpence for it. The peasants had no eye for the beauty and distinction of Sir Shawn O'Gara's looks, his elegant slenderness, the somewhat mournful depths of his eyes which were of so dark a grey that they were almost black. Too foreign looking, the people pronounced him, their idea of foreigners being bounded by their knowledge of a greatly-daring Italian organ-grinder who had once come over the mountains to Killesky with a little red-coated monkey sitting a-top of the organ, to the great joy of the children. That had been a record rainy season, and the organ-grinder and the monkey had both sickened for the sun, and would have died if old Lady O'Gara, who was half-Italian herself, had not heard the tale and sent the man back to his own country.

"He'd be askin' Mr. Terence to forgive him because maybe he was vexed wid him about poor Bridyeen," Patsy had often thought since. "An' maybe because Miss Mary Creagh had always liked him better than Mr. Terence, though she was too much afraid of Mrs. Comerford, to say it. Or maybe 'twas that he couldn't save him from Spitfire. Not but what she was kind enough, the crathur, if he hadn't took to floggin' her."

Very rarely Patsy thought on the man who had cursed him in the ditch that night long ago. He was only an accidental terror of the night crowded with terrors, from which Patsy had reached his grandfather's door and tumbled in "about the flure" in a fainting condition. He had queer hazy memories that the old man was kind, that the two little eyes which had often blazed fury at him, were dim with tears. He did not know if he dreamt it or not that he had heard his grandfather telling the other old men around the turf fire that he, Patsy, was a good little lad, but that he had to be strict with him to keep him good.

When he had got about again he had heard that Sir Shawn O'Gara had been very ill, that the shock of his friend's death had been too much for him. Then one day the old Lady O'Gara had come to the cottage on the edge of the bog to ask for him. It had got out that Patsy had seen something of the terrible happening of that night, and she had been very gentle and friendly with him, and had asked him if he would not like to go to school; and afterwards what he would like to do.

He could see her delicate profile now if he closed his eyes, the olive skin, the deep velvety eyes, the red lips. Even the country people did not deny Lady O'Gara beauty, of a foreign sort. Though they would never admire her as they admired Miss Mary Creagh.

Soon after Patsy had gone to school Lady O'Gara died, and a year later Sir Shawn and Miss Mary Creagh were married. By this time Patsy had become a favourite pupil with Mr. O'Connell, at the National Schools, who thought that in time he might qualify for a "vit," seeing his love for animals; but perhaps Mr. O'Connell's liking for Patsy was only because he found in him an equal mind with his own about animals, Mr. O'Connell's attachment to his dog, Sambo, being a cause of laughter to most of his pupils. Patsy had a happy time with Mr. O'Connell; but the necessary education for the veterinary profession in the matter of mere book-learning he seemed either unable or unwilling to acquire, so he went in time to the stables at Castle Talbot to qualify as he had coveted for the hereditary position of stud-groom. Sir Shawn, since he had married Miss Creagh, had taken to keeping racehorses; and Patsy Kenny had a way with horses. He was a natural solitary as regarded his kind. Many a pretty girl had looked Patsy's way invitingly, seeing in him a steady, sober boy who might be trusted not to spend his wages in drink, whose dreamy eyes and soft slow voice promised gentleness with a woman; but Patsy never thought of the girls apparently. He was very fond of his master, but his great devotion was for Lady O'Gara who, as Miss Mary Creagh, had dazzled him when she came and went at Castle Talbot, not forgetting if she met Patsy to stop and speak with him. That devotion to Miss Mary, continued to Lady O'Gara, had perhaps spoilt Patsy's chances of being happy after the manner of other men. He would have said himself, perhaps, that with the horses to think of he had no time to think about getting married. Certainly he did not seem to find his bachelor state amiss. His little house, in the new block of stabling, white walled, red-roofed, painted with cross beams to its pointed gable, was kept with meticulous care. Patsy did his own work. Lady O'Gara was right perhaps when she called him a natural celibate.

Long, long ago old Judy Dowd and her granddaughter, Bridyeen, had left Killesky, for America. They had not gone away with the drafts of boys and girls who went week after week during the Spring weather, leaving Beragh station on their way to Liverpool with a great send-off from friends and relatives, ending, as the train went, with cries of lamentation that brought the other passengers to their carriage windows, curious or sympathetic, according to their natures.

No: Judy Dowd and Bridyeen had gone off in an underhand manner, leaving Mr. Casey, the solicitor, to dispose of the public-house and effects. The neighbours had been rather indignant about it, and had made up their minds as to the reason of this unsportsmanlike flitting. But by the time they were saying to each other that Judy Dowd had a right not to be spoiling her grand-daughter, making her pretty for the eyes of gentlemen; that what could a girl want more than Barney Killeen, who had a farm and an outside car, if he was sixty itself? that there was no use humouring the fancies of girls: that they'd always known how it would end: finally that it was well Bridyeen should be taken away before she made a scandal in the parish, by that time the Dowds were no more than a name and a memory.

Few people now remembered the old unhappy far-off things. Judy Dowd's public-house in Killesky, which had been a very small affair, had made way for Conneely's Hotel. There was not much hotel about it, but there was quite a thriving shop, divided into two parts, one, general store, the other public. If you were a person of importance and called at Conneely's for refreshment you had it in "the drawing-room" upstairs, where the Misses Conneely's drawings in chalk hung on the walls, and their photographs adorned the chimney-piece, while their school prizes were arranged neatly on the round table in the middle of the room, flanking the wax flowers under a glass shade which made the centre piece.

The Miss Conneelys had done well in the Intermediate. Their elder brother was a priest. Father Tom's photograph was in the centre of the chimney-piece a-top of the clock. They could play the piano and violin and had fortunes when the time came for them to marry. Their mother would never have permitted them to serve in the bar nor even behind the drapery counter. They were black-haired, rosy, buxom girls, who set the fashions in Killesky. There had been a sensation when Nora Conneely came back from Dublin with a walking-stick, but after an amazed pause Killesky, the young ladies of it, broke out in walking-sticks.

There was enough positive about the Conneelys, the priest, the prosperous self-satisfied girls, the managing capable mother, to make people feel that there had always been Conneely's Hotel in Killesky. If the old people remembered Julia Dowd's little public-house with its thatched roof, the low ceiling and the fire of turf to which you could draw a chair while you had your drink, the little parlour beyond which was reserved for customers of a superior station, they did not talk about it.

Inch too was shut up. Mrs. Comerford had gone away after Mary Creagh's engagement to Sir Shawn O'Gara. She had taken it very ill, as a slur to her dead son's memory. She had always been an austere, somewhat severe woman, but she had taken Mary Creagh from her dying mother's arms, a child of a few weeks old, had reared her as her own and been tender to her, with the surprising precious tenderness of a reserved, apparently cold nature. Mrs. Comerford had gone to Italy and had never since returned. Perhaps she would never come now, although the place was kept from going to rack and ruin by James Clinch, the butler, and Mrs. Clinch, who had been cook and had married the butler after Mrs. Comerford had gone away.

All these things came back to Patsy Kenny in his solitary hours. He was very fond of sitting on a log or a stone between his strenuous working times, going over old days in his mind.

This June afternoon, rather wearied still by his struggle with Mustapha, he was sitting on a block in front of his little house in the stable-yard. Judy, a half-bred setter, the names of the animals at Castle Talbot were hereditary, was lying at his feet. The pigeons were pecking about him daintily. Only Judy's watchful, jealous eye prevented their flying on to his knee or his shoulder.

The memories unfolded themselves like the scenes of a cinematograph, slipping past his mind. He remembered Bridyeen Sweeney, whose delicate beauty used to draw the gentlemen to Dowd's long ago. He contrasted her in his mind with Nora Conneely whom he had met that morning as he went to the post-office, wearing what he had heard called a Merry Widow hat, and a tight skirt, displaying open-work stockings and high-heeled shoes, a string of pearls about a neck generously displayed by the low blouse she was wearing, her right hand twirling the famous walking-stick.

"I dunno what at all came to Bridyeen," he murmured to himself. "She was as pretty as a picture, like a little rose she was, and so modest in all her ways. Even my grandfather used to say there was nothing against Bridyeen. I wouldn't have thought it of Mr. Terence either that he'd be tryin' to turn the little girl's head and he the Mistress's cousin an' they as good as promised. I only hope Master Terence had time to repent, if the stories were true itself that the people told. Sure maybe there was nothin' in it."

He had perhaps dozed off. He came awake suddenly to Judy's snarling. Judy never gave the alarm for nothing. A man had come into the stable-yard, quite obviously a tramp. Behind him came a woman and a child of the same fraternity. The woman stood humbly in the wake of the man, and the boy kept close to her. The man was a bad-looking fellow, Patsy said to himself. Half-consciously he noticed the man's hands, wicked-looking hands, covered with hair, the nails stubby and broken. The long arms were like the arms of a monkey. His tattered coat was velveteen. Patsy remembered to have seen the material on the game-keepers of a big estate in the next county.

"'Ullo, matey," said this uninviting person, with an attempt at jocularity. "'Ave you anythink to give a poor man out of a job?"

The truculent voice, with its attempt at oiliness, the small red eyes under the shock of hair, the thick purple lips, had an extraordinary effect on Patsy. He hated the tramp, yet he felt a queer sick fear of him. Once, when Sir Shawn had taken him to England for a big race, he had seen a dog destroy an adder, with the same mixture of half-terrified rage and loathing he was feeling now.

"There's nothing for you here," he said gruffly. "You don't look as if you had much taste for work."

Then he looked beyond the tramp to the woman and child. She was decent, the poor creature, he thought. Her poor rags were clean and mended. She had a shrinking, suffering air. The boy, who was about nine years old, seemed to cling to her as though in terror of the burly ruffian. He was pale and thin and even on this beautiful June day he looked cold.

Patsy was suddenly gentle. He saw the glare in the tramp's eyes.

"Here's a shillin' for you," he said. "I've no job you'd care about. But the woman and the child might like a cup of tay."

"All right," said the tramp, placated. "Tea's not in my way. I'll be back in 'arf a mo'. Don't you be makin' love to my ol' woman."

He flicked his thumb and finger at the woman with an ugly jocularity: then went, with the tramp's shambling trot, out of the stable-yard the way he had come, down the back avenue which opened on to the road to Killesky.

CHAPTER III

A TEA PARTY

"I've seen that man of yours before," said Patsy, turning round and gazing at the woman.

He felt the most extraordinary pity for her. She must have been a pretty girl once, he thought, noticing the small pure outlines of the face. The child was like her, not like the ruffian who had just set off in the direction of Conneely's Hotel. A pretty boy, with soft, pale silken hair and blue eyes that looked scared. Patsy remembered his own childhood with the terrible old grandfather, and his heart was soft with compassion.

"I don't think so, sir," said the woman. She was English by her voice. "He hasn't been in these parts before."

Patsy noticed with the same sharp pity which seemed to hurt him, that she trembled. She was tired and hungry, perhaps; not cold, surely, in this glorious June sunshine.

"Sit down," he said, "sit down." He indicated a stone seat by the open door of the house. "You are tired, my poor girl. I've put the kettle on. It'll be boilin' by this time. I'll wet the cup of tay and it'll do you good."

There was no one in the stable-yard to observe the strange sight of the stud-groom giving a meal to the tramping woman and her child. He brought out a little cloth and spread it on the stone seat. Then he fetched the cups and saucers, one by one.

"Let me help you, sir," said the woman. "I was a servant in a good house before I had the misfortune to marry."

There had been some strange delicacy in Patsy's mind which had induced him to have the outdoor tea rather than a less troublesome arrangement within doors. Perhaps he had an instinctive knowledge of what the woman's husband might be capable of in the way of thought or speech.

"Sit down there, Georgie," said the woman to the child, with a kind of passionate tenderness. "He's too little, so he is," she addressed Patsy Kenny, "for the load o' cans and pots he has to carry. His bones are but soft yet."

"Cans and pots?"

"There, beyond the gate. We sell them as we go along. When they're sold we buy more. We had a donkey-cart, but ... we had to sell it. We only take now what Georgie and me can carry."

"And your husband?"

"He carries nought. He doesn't hold with a man carrying things."

Patsy said nothing. What was the matter with him that he felt such a pain of pity and such a rage of anger? He had felt the like before for an ill-treated animal. Ill-treated humans had not often entered his experience, since he lived so much to himself.

He went to the gate leading to the back avenue and looked out. Hidden by the gate-post were a number of pots and pans and bright glittering new cans. A little away lay another heap. He stooped. There was a contrivance, something like a yoke for the shoulders, to which the cans were attached. He had seen, also in England, gipsy carts covered with such wares. He had not known that human shoulders could be adapted to this burden.

"God help ye," he said, coming back. "'Tis too much for you, let alone the child. The polis should see to it."

"He takes the load from the boy before we come to a village," she said, nodding her head the way the man had gone.

It was wonderful to see how quickly and deftly the woman set out the tea-things, made the tea, using much less than Patsy's liberal allowance, and cut bread and butter. Patsy found a few new-laid eggs and put them on to boil. The child sat in the shade: Patsy had found him a chair, made of ropes of straw, to rest on instead of the cold stone. He sat in a relaxed way as though all his muscles were limp, taking no heed of the dog that sniffed about him. Dead-tired, Patsy thought, and loathed the muscular ruffian who went free while a child and a woman bore the burdens.

It was pretty to see the woman coaxing the child to eat, forgetting herself. Patsy looked about the familiar place and saw it strange with an appearance of domesticity. The creature was very gentle, he said to himself, and she was decent. Her poor clothes were tidy, and the boy's likewise. Their boots caused a queer pang in Patsy's heart. They were disgraceful boots, bulging at the sides, broken: he had noticed that the boy shuffled as he walked.

The woman sat holding her tea-cup in her hand, looking around the yard. Patsy's house had a little yard to itself off the stable-yard proper. In the middle was a bed in which there was a rose-tree with pinks and pansies growing about its roots, Patsy's garden, of which he was very proud.

"It's a nice little spot you have here," she said, with a sigh. The canary, which hung by the door in a cage, sent out a hard bright runlet of song. The dog lay on her side with one brown eye fixed on her master. One of the big cats, which kept the stables free of rats and made company for the horses in winter, came delicately and rubbed himself against Patsy's blue hand-knitted stockings. Her eyes roved enviously about, taking in the quiet peacefulness of the scene.

"I'll be washin' up for you before I go," she said.

"Sure I'm used to doin' for myself," returned Patsy.

"You've no wife?" she said; and looked down at the boy where he lay back wearily in the straw chair.

"I'm a bachelor boy," said Patsy.

Her eye considered her host in a way that caused Patsy a curious internal shyness, not altogether unpleasant.

"A pity," said she. "It would be a nice little place for a woman and a child."

Then she straightened herself and stood up. She had made a very good meal.

"I saw where the basin was in the scullery," she said. "Don't you trouble. It's a woman's work, not a man's. You stay here and talk to Georgie."

He carried in the tray when she had piled it with cups and saucers. Otherwise he obeyed her. Better if that ruffian came back he should find him talking to Georgie rather than helping the woman to wash up.

But Georgie was very uncommunicative. He seemed too tired to talk. He too had not done so badly with the meal once he had begun. After a while his head fell a little to one side and he slept.

Patsy sat where he was. He could hear the noise of water flowing inside the house and the chink of cups and saucers in process of washing up. Not for worlds would he have entered the house. He was thinking strange thoughts. For the first time he was touched by a woman, this poor, ill-clad, tramping woman, the wife of an evident scoundrel, touched to the heart for her and her child. The happy, pretty girls who had looked shy invitation at him had not appealed. They had, one by one, put him down as a dry old bachelor and taken their charms elsewhere. Patsy had never missed wife or child. He would have said himself that he had enough to think of, with her Ladyship and the Master and Mr. Terry, enough to fill his heart.

Not that he felt anything beyond an immense compassion for these poor victims of man's cruelty. Perhaps with such a person as Patsy Kenny compassion would serve for love always. "The creatures!" he said to himself, "the creatures! Sure it isn't the hard ways of the world they're fit for at all."

The woman emerged from the cottage, moving with a gentle softness. There was nothing of the tramp about her beyond the broken boots, the hat which had obviously been under the weather, the poor clothes. She sat down beside Patsy Kenny and spoke in a low voice for fear of waking the sleeping child.

"It is a hard road he has to travel for one so young," she said, and he noticed that she looked quickly towards the gate.

"It is," said Patsy Kenny. "Too hard. He had no right to be carryin' all that tinker's stuff. That man of yours, my girl, oughtn't to be let do it."

A little colour came to the woman's cheek.

"We've run away from him over and over," she said. "He's always tracked us down. Time and time again I was doin' well and Georgie at school, but he always found us: I used to say my prayers to be delivered from him, but I never was: I don't suppose I ever will be now. I can't hide from him. I wouldn't mind for myself, if it wasn't for Georgie. He'll kill Georgie."

"How long have you been at it?" Patsy Kenny asked quietly.

"This sort of life? He found us in Leicestershire three months ago. I was in a place with one lady. She was kind and let me have Georgie. She always said she'd never have known there was a child in the house. Georgie went to school and came home of afternoons. It was a quiet, peaceful spot. Baker found me again. It wasn't the first time by many he dragged us out on the road. He sold all my clothes as well as takin' my savin's. He said there was money for him over here. I don't see no sign of it. The life will kill Georgie. We tramped from Dublin: with the last of my money Baker bought the tins to keep us goin' on the road. It was bad in the cold, wet weather last month."

"Have you no one at all belongin' to you?" Patsy asked in a low voice.

"Sisters and brothers, all respectable. My parents are dead. When I took Baker I turned my back on them all."

Patsy's mind was working hard. There must be some help for the woman's case. It could not be law that this ruffian should have the power to drag his wife and child after him, loading them with burdens they were not fit to carry. The creature knew no better than to yield to him. The Master was a magistrate and a kindly one. He was always settling disputes of one kind or another. Patsy thought of bidding her wait where she was till the Master could be found.

He looked up from his thoughts and saw that Mr. Baker had come back. His face was very red and shiny. He wore a truculent look.

"'Ullo!" he said thickly. "'Ere's quite a family party. 'Ope you've been enjoyin' of yourselves as I 'ave, subjec' to restrictions. A bob don't go fur in liquor now-a-days. You might ha' made it two."

"One seems to have been quite enough for you," said Patsy, with a light of battle in eyes no longer dreamy.

"I don't deny as I 'ad a bob myself to spend," said the ruffian. "'Ere, you, Georgie! You wake up, you lazy young devil! 'Tis time we was on the road."

Patsy stepped between the man and the child who had come out of his sleep with a cry of fear. He put a open hand on Mr. Baker's chest and pushed him backward. Somewhat contrary to his expectations the man did not resent his action, beyond remarking that no one had the right to interfere between a man and his kid.

"Now it comes to that," he said, with a sudden change to jocularity, "if so be as you've a fancy for 'er I'd sell her for five quid an' throw in the kid. It's no catch draggin' 'em round an' me 'avin' to carry the cans 'arf the time because o' your blasted coppers."

The full enormity of the speech seemed to reveal itself only gradually to Patsy's mind. He turned red and then pale. The poor woman was quivering as though a lash had struck her.

"You're a bad brute," said Patsy quietly. "The woman's too good for you."

"You can 'ave her for nothink if you like. She never was much good to me."

He sat down suddenly in the chair Georgie had left empty.

"I want to see your boss," he said: and his tone was bullying.

"I was thinkin' about that myself," said Patsy.

"You go along the road an' wait for me," he said with a sudden ferocity which made the woman start. "Off with ye now. I'll come up with ye: unless this gentleman 'ud make it a matter of a five-pun' note."

"Hold your dirty tongue," said Patsy, and landed Mr. Baker one in the chest.

The man rushed at him with his head down, a shower of foul words coming from his lips. Before anything could happen someone intervened, Terry O'Gara, dazzlingly clean as he always looked.

"Here, you keep quiet, you ruffian!" he said, delivering a very neat blow just under the man's chin. "What is it all about, Patsy? Hadn't I better send for the police?"

Mr. Baker had fallen back against the stone bench and subsided on to it, feeling his jaw bone.

"I'll make you pay for this yere conduck to an 'armless man wot was doin' nothink," he growled.

Something floated into Patsy's mind, vague, terrible. Before he could grasp it another person joined the group, Sir Shawn O'Gara.

"What's the matter?" he asked. "Who is this person?"

His face changed. Patsy Kenny, who was watching him, saw the change. He had grown livid, his lips blue. Was he ill? Was he going to fall?

Before Patsy could do anything he recovered himself and spoke.

"You have business with me?" he said to the tramp.

"Yes, sir." Mr. Baker was suddenly cringingly respectful. "I came 'ere to talk business an' was set upon by this yere man o' yourn somethink crool. I'd sack him if I was you. Your 'orses wouldn't be safe with 'im, 'im bein' so 'ot-tempered."

Sir Shawn still looked very ill. Patsy had once seen a person in a bad heart-seizure. Was Sir Shawn's heart affected? Small mottled patches of a purple colour had come out on the smooth darkness of his skin. Angina. That was what the doctor called it in the case of that other person. Had that mysterious, terrible disease laid hold on the Master? He had not looked well for many a day. Patsy had wondered that the Mistress did not see it, was not disturbed by it, seeing how fond a wife she was. His heart sank with fear for the Master.

"Let me deal with him, father," said Terry, looking like a young god in contrast with the unpleasant Mr. Baker.

"I know this man," Sir Shawn said, quietly. "He once rendered me a service."

"When I were gamekeeper over to Ashbridge 'All," said Mr. Baker eagerly, "you'd a bin shot but for me. Some gents will never learn 'ow 'to 'old their guns. I knocked the barrel up just in the nick. That Mr. Lascelles, 'e weren't safe."

Ashbridge! Oh, so the man had been employed at Ashbridge Hall, Lord Trentham's place, some thirty miles away on the edge of Lough Aske. How long ago? Patsy kept asking himself the question. He looked after Sir Shawn and Mr. Baker as they went away in the direction of the house. Sir Shawn had an official room with a door opening out on to the grounds, so that the many people who came to consult him on one business or another need not enter through the house.

"That fellow's face would hang him anywhere," said Terry O'Gara. "I wonder what amount of villainy lies between a gamekeeper's place at Ashbridge and the brute he is to-day?"

"God help them that are in his power," Patsy Kenny said fervently. Then he went to the gate and looked out. The pots and pans and cans had disappeared. Down the long straight road there was no one in sight. The woman and child had vanished.

Oddly enough he was disturbed by the noise Mustapha was still making in his box-stall.

"I shouldn't be surprised now if he was to be a foal of Spitfire," he said. "I did hear she was bought by a man somewhere about Lewy mountain. The little man we bought him from was a mountainy man, if he wasn't a fairy."

CHAPTER IV

FROM THE PAST

The morning after these happenings Lady O'Gara, turning over the pile of letters on the breakfast table, changed colour at the sight of one which bore an Italian postmark. It was addressed in a large firm handwriting in which only very keen observation could have discovered any sign of weakening. After that momentary glance she laid away the letter with the superscription turned downwards while she read the rest of her correspondence.

When she had finished breakfast she followed her husband into his office, as that special room was called. The windows had not been opened, they were French windows and they served as a door out on to the gravel sweep which ran around the house, and she thought she detected a faint disagreeable smell, as of drugs. She unbolted a window and flung it wide and the warm June air came flowing in, banishing the unpleasant sharp odour.

"You haven't been taking anything, Shawn?" she asked, looking at him a little anxiously. "I thought I smelt something peculiar. You are not looking well."

"I am very well, Mary," he answered. "Perhaps it was the person I had here yesterday evening. I believe I closed the window after he went out. He had been drinking. There was a horrible smell."

"I came to the door while you were talking to him and I heard you say, 'What do you mean by coming here?' Who was he, Shawn?"

Again Sir Shawn was suddenly pale. She was looking down at the letter she had extracted from the pile, and he turned his back to the window, so that when she looked at him again with her frank ingenuous gaze, his face was in shadow.

"He was a man who saved my life, or thinks he did, at a shooting-party at Ashbridge. There was a fellow there who had never handled a gun before. He would have put a whole charge of shot into me if this chap, Baker, hadn't knocked up his gun in time. I don't think it would have killed me, although it might have been rather unpleasant. Baker likes to think, for his own purposes," he spoke with a weary air, "that he saved my life. He may have saved my beauty. He considers himself my pensioner."

"Ah!" Lady O'Gara was satisfied with the explanation. "What a pity he should drink! Can we do nothing for him?"

"I'm afraid not. He would like to be my game-keeper, but that is out of the question. He had not much character when he left Ashbridge. He has had more than one job in England since then, and has lost them all. He has come down very much in the world even since I saw him last."

"A pity," said Lady O'Gara, "since he rendered you a service."

"I gave him some money and got rid of him: it was the only thing to do."

Once again Lady O'Gara's frank eyes turned upon her husband.

"I don't think you ever told me about that thing before," she said. "I should have remembered if you had told me."

"No," he said with an averted face. "It happened, the winter you were in Florence. I came home and was met by the news that you were away. The sun dropped out of my skies."

She blushed suddenly and brightly. Her husband had turned from his gloomy contemplation of the lawn outside, on which a tiny Kerry cow was feeding. He said to himself that she was more beautiful in her mature womanhood than the day he married her. She had been soft and flowing even in her girlhood, with a promise of matronly beauty. Now, with a greater amplitude, she was not less but more gracious. Her bronze hair which had the faintest dust upon it went back from her temples and ears in lovely waves which no art could have produced. It was live hair, full of lights and shadows. Her husband had said that it was like a brown Venetian glass with powdered gold inside its brownness. There were a few brown freckles on the milk-white neck. Her eyes were kind and faithful and set widely apart: her nose straight and short: and she had a delightful smile.

She came now and put her arms about his neck. They were in curious contrast, she so soft, fair and motherly: he slender and dark, with weary eyes and a look as though he had suffered.

"Shawn!" she said, "Shawn!" and there was a passionate tenderness in her voice, as she pressed his head against her heart.

Then she let her arms fall and turned away, looking as though some sadness had clouded her joy.

"Poor Terence!" she said.

There was the same thought between them, but they left it unspoken. She had chosen Shawn O'Gara in her own heart even while she was expected to marry Terence Comerford.

"Why do you talk of Terence now?" he asked.

"I have had a letter from Aunt Grace after all these years." She held the letter towards him.

"She has forgiven you?" he asked, making no movement to take the letter.

"She is coming back to Inch. She writes that Stella, her adopted daughter, is growing up. She has forgiven us. She is pleased that we named our son after poor Terence. You remember you were rather opposed to it, Shawn."

"I did not wish to be reminded of the loss of my friend at every moment," he said. "The tragedy was too new."

Still he showed no indication of taking the letter from her hand.

"Read it to me," he said, in his weary voice. "I wonder how Stella will like Inch after Italy. There is so much rain and cloud. One has to be born to it to like it."

"When I was in Italy I simply longed for a day of Irish rain," Mary O'Gara said: "it is good for us. We need it. We grow parched in the dry climates."

"It has held the secret of perpetual youth and beauty for you, Mary," her husband said, looking at her with loving admiration.

She laughed and blushed. She was not beyond blushing at a compliment even from her husband.

"We must make things as gay for the child as possible," she said. Then she added:

"I wonder if Aunt Grace realizes that Terry is now a young man. He seems épris with Eileen, so I suppose he will not fall in love with Stella?"

Sir Shawn looked startled.

"I hope not," he said. "Eileen seems to have him very securely in her chains."

Lady O'Gara frowned ever so slightly. "I wish our children did not grow away from us so soon," she said. "Terry might have continued a little longer being in love only with his mother."

Sir Shawn lifted his eyebrows in a manner which accentuated his foreign look.

"Jealous, Mary?" he asked.

"Not of Eileen. She allures him, but, I come first."

"You would always have your place. You are of the women who are adored by their sons. You would not care for Eileen for a daughter-in-law, though she has been almost your adopted daughter these ten years back?"

"She would not suit Terry."

"She is very fond of you."

"Yes, I think she is fond of me." Her voice was cold.

"I hardly know you, Mary, in this mood towards Eileen. You are usually so sweetly reasonable."

"It is the privilege of a woman to be unreasonable sometimes."

The sunshine came back to her face, laughed in the depths of her eyes and brought a dimple to either cheek.

"I suppose I am a little jealous of Terry," she said. "You see he is very like you, Shawn. And I am fond of Eileen, really. Only, I suppose all mothers are critical of the girls their sons fall in love with, especially if it is an only son. It is odd how it has come suddenly to Terry that Eileen is a pretty girl. Of course he has only seen her in her vacations. Sit down now, Shawn, and I will read you Aunt Grace's letter."

He sat down obediently in the revolving chair in front of his desk and she came and stood by him. Her voice was a little disturbed as she read the letter.

"MY DEAR MARY, You will be surprised to hear that I am coming back again to Inch. The years bring their dust, as some poet says: they certainly soften griefs and asperities. When I left Inch I was broken-hearted for my one boy. It was a poisoning of the grief at that time to know that you and Shawn O'Gara were going to be married. I felt that you had forgotten my beautiful boy, that his friend had forgotten him: but that I acknowledge now to have been a morbid and unreasonable way of looking at things. My boy never thought of any girl but you, yet I could not expect you to go unmarried for his sake: indeed I would not have wished it. You and Shawn must forgive that old unreasonable bitterness of mine, the bitterness of a mother distraught by grief.

"I have left you alone all these years, but I have not been without knowledge of you. I know that your son is called Terence after my son. I appreciate that fact, which indicates to me that you keep him in loving remembrance.

"After all these years I am suddenly weary for home, so weary that I wonder now how I could have kept away so long. Whether I shall end my days at Inch depends on Stella. My wild experiment of adopting this child, as some of my friends thought it at the time, has turned out very well. Stella is a dear child. I send you a photograph which hardly does her justice. As she is entirely mine she goes by my name, although her father was French. I should like to say to you that though I shall provide for Stella it will not be to your detriment. I have a sense of justice towards my kin.

"I trust to you to receive Stella and me in a manner which will prove that you have blotted out any memories of the past that are otherwise than happy.

"Your affectionate cousin-aunt, "GRACE COMERFORD.

"PS. Stella has something of your colouring."

"Here is the photograph," said Lady O'Gara, handing it to her husband. "Stella is very pretty, is she not?"

He twisted his chair so that the light from the window might fall on the photograph. The face was in profile. It was tilted delicately upwards. There was a little straight nose, a round chin, a mouth softly opened, one of those mouths which do not quite close. The large eyes looked upward; the hair was short and curled in little rings.

He looked at it and said nothing, but his eyes were tragic in the shadow.

"The profile is quite French," said Lady O'Gara. "I remember the young man who I think must have been Stella's father. He was a lieutenant of Chasseurs. He was killed in Algiers, afterwards. I saw it in a newspaper about four years after our marriage. He was going to be married when he came to Inch. His mother, who was as poor as a church mouse, had written a bitter complaint to Aunt Grace that Gaston was about to marry a poor Irish girl, a governess, whose part he had taken when he thought her unfairly treated. I think Stella must be Gaston de St. Maur's child."

"Odd, not leaving the child her own name," Sir Shawn said, handing back the photograph.

"Aunt Grace would want her so entirely for her own. She always had a fierce way of loving. If she had loved me more reasonably and less jealously she would not have quarrelled with me as she did. She was always rather terrible in anger."

She gathered together a bundle of letters which she had laid down on the table.

"I must go and write to Aunt Grace," she said. "She must not wait for a letter telling her how glad I shall be to see her back at Inch, how glad we shall all be. She was very good to me, Shawn." She sent a wistful look towards her husband who sat with his back to her. "If she had been the aunt she called herself, instead of a somewhat remote cousin, she could not have been kinder. She treated us very generously, despite her anger at our marriage."

"You brought me too much," said Shawn O'Gara, not turning his head, "and it has prospered. You should have brought me nothing but yourself. You were a rich gift enough for any man."

Lady O'Gara looked well-pleased as she came and kissed the top of her husband's head, dusted over its darkness with an effect of powder as contrasted with the dark moustache and dark eyes.

"I am glad for Terry's sake I did not," she said; and went out of the room.

"Mr. Kenny wishes to see your Ladyship," said a servant, meeting her in the hall. Patsy, perhaps by reason of his friendly aloofness, had come to be treated with unusual respect by the other servants. "He is at the hall-door. He would not come inside."

She found Patsy, playing with Shot's son and daughter, they were the fourth generation from "Ould Shot" on the gravel sweep.

"Come in, Patsy," she said, and led the way into an octagonal room, lit by a skylight overhead and walled around with ancient books which were very seldom taken from their shelves.

"Sit down," she said, "and tell me what is troubling you."

Patsy sat down on the extreme edge of one of the chairs, which were upholstered in scarlet damask. He looked up at her with blinking eyes of worship, like the eyes of the dogs. The room, painted white above the bookshelves, was full of light. He turned his cap about in his hands. Obviously there was something more here than the business on which he usually consulted Lady O'Gara.

"'Tis," he began, "a little bit of a woman, an' a child, no bigger nor a robin an' as wake as a wran...."

With this opening he began the story of the woman and child, who had come with the disreputable person the afternoon before. It appeared that Mr. Baker had deserted his wife and son, flinging them the pots and pans with a scornful generosity. He had apparently arrived at the possession of money some way or other, and overtaking them on the road at some considerable distance away he had bidden them, with threats, to take themselves out of his sight, since he had no further use for them.

"He was full of drink," Patsy said, looking down. "Your Ladyship, his tratement of them was something onnatural. She said she'd run away from him often, but he'd always found her when she was doin' well an' earnin' for herself an' the child. The people she lived with were often kind and ready to stand by her, but sure, as she says, the kindest will get tired out. He'd broken the spirit in her, maybe, for she showed me his marks on the poor child. She said nothin' about herself, but I could guess, the poor girl! The man that could lay his heavy hand on a woman or a child is a black villain. I wouldn't be comparin' him to the dumb bastes, for they've nature in them. The poor little woman, she's dacent. It would break your heart to see how thin she is an' how fretted-lookin' an' the little lad wid the scare in his eyes."

"Has the woman come back?"

"Wasn't that what I was tellin' your Ladyship? Lasteways, she didn't come back exactly. I found her on the road an' she not knowin' where to turn to, in a strange country. There they were, when I found them, hugging aich other an' cryin'. And the cans beside them in the ditch."

"What cans?"

"Wasn't I tellin' your Ladyship, the pots and pans and the few little bright cans among them, and not a penny betune the two poor souls, nor they knowing where to turn to!"

"Where are they now?" Lady O'Gara asked quietly.

"They're in my house, your Ladyship. I brought them back there last night an' I gev it up to them. I slep' in the loft over the stables myself."

"Oh, but, Patsy, they can't stay in your house! The people would talk."

"Sure I know they'd talk, if it was an angel in Heaven. That's why I kem to your Ladyship."

"I'll come and see the woman, Patsy, and we'll decide what is best to be done."

Patsy's face cleared amazingly.

"I knew you'd come," he said. "It'll be all right when your Ladyship sees them, God help them."

CHAPTER V

THE HAVEN

Lady O'Gara came in by way of a little-used gate a few days later. She had been to Inch, where the house was being turned out of doors and everything aired and swept and dusted and repolished, for a home-coming so long delayed that people had forgotten to look for it. Castle Talbot had six entrance gates, each with its lodge: and this one was rarely used.

Susan, as Mrs. Baker preferred to be called, Susan Horridge: she seemed to wish to drop the "Mrs. Baker" came out with a key to open the gate, which was padlocked.

Such a different Susan! The old Susan might have been dropped with "Mrs. Baker." She had been just ten days at the South lodge, and now, in her neat print dress, her silken hair braided tidily, her small face filling out, she looked as she dropped a curtsey just as might the Susan Horridge of a score years earlier.

"You keep the gate padlocked, Susan?" Lady O'Gara asked, with a little surprise. "This is a quiet, honest place. I hardly think you need fear any disagreeable visitors."

"Oh, but, m'lady, you never know." Susan had admitted her by this time. "A lone woman and a little boy, and him that nervous through being frightened!" She hurried on as though she did not wish to make any reference to the cause of Georgie's fright. "I heard men singin' along the road the night before last it was. It fair gave me the jumps. Glad I was to have that gate between me and them and the strong padlock on it."

"This lodge is perhaps a little lonely for you. It's a very quiet road. The people don't use it much. It runs down to a road where they think there's a ghost. You're not afraid of ghosts?"

"No, m'lady. If but they'd keep the people from the road."

"Ah! you will find the people friendly and kindly after a time. You're new to the place."

"Maybe so, m'lady. I always was one for keeping myself to myself. My Granny brought me up strict. I wish I hadn't lost her when I did." She heaved a deep sigh. "We had a sweet little place at home in Warwickshire. Such a pretty cottage, and an orchard, and the roses climbin' about my window."

What matter that she said "winder"! Her eyes, the pale large eyes, had light in them as though she beheld a vision.

"'Twere all peace with my Granny and me," she went on. "And her Ladyship at the Court, Mr. Neville was our Squire and her Ladyship was Lady Frances Neville, used to drop in to see Granny, and she used to say what a good girl I was, always busy with my needle and my book. And our Rector's wife, Mrs. Farmiloe, she gave me a silver thimble when I was nine, a prize for needlework. Lady Frances used to say, 'Don't you keep her too close to work, Mrs. Horridge. A child must play with other children.' But my Granny she'd up and say: 'She's all I have, and I'd rather bury her than see her trapesin' about with boys like some I know.' And there was Miss Sylvia peepin' at me from behind her Ladyship and me peepin' at her from behind my Granny. I went to the Court at sixteen as sewing maid, and at twenty I was Miss Sylvia's own maid. She married Lord Southwater, and I'd have gone with her only I couldn't leave my Granny. She was failin', poor old soul!"

She paused and again she heaved the deepest of sighs.

"Beggin' your pardon, m'lady, for talkin' so much. You'd maybe take a look at the little place?" she said.

Lady O'Gara turned aside. She was in no great hurry home and she was interested in Susan. Susan had padlocked the gate again and held the key swinging from her finger, while she looked up at Lady O'Gara as though her saying "yes" or "no" meant a great deal to her.

"I wonder what would happen if we wanted to get in or out by that gate at night time," Lady O'Gara said. "We don't use it much. Still we might want to and you might be in bed."

"I'd get up at any hour, m'lady," Susan said eagerly. "I'm a light sleeper: and it would only be to throw on something in a hurry."

She looked scared, as though her peace of mind was threatened, and Lady O'Gara felt a pity for such manifest nervousness. Susan would forget her terror presently as she got further and further away from the bad days. Obviously she was very nervous. Her eyes dilated and her breath came and went as she gazed imploringly at Lady O'Gara.

"Don't look like that, Susan," Lady O'Gara said, almost sharply. "You look as though I were judge and executioner. You shall keep your padlocked gate. After all it is a bad road, I don't think Sir Shawn will want to take it, though it is the shortest way to Inch. You did not find the gate padlocked when you came?"

"No, m'lady. 'Twas Mr. Kenny. He guessed I'd be frightened, so he brought the padlock and put it on himself."

The finest little line showed itself in Lady O'Gara's smooth forehead. Her skin was extraordinarily unfretted for her forty-five years of life. But now the little crease came, deepened and extended itself to a line, where its presence had been unsuspected.

"Patsy is very kind," she said, with a penetrating glance at Susan. What a pretty girl Susan must have been, so soft and pale and appealing, a little human wood-anemone! She would be very pretty again when she had got over the scared look and the thinness which was almost emaciation. And how well that print suited her! Lady O'Gara had sent down a bundle of things to the South lodge, so that Susan might not appear as a scarecrow to the people. The print had pale green leaves sprinkled over a white surface. It suggested a snowdrop, perished by the winter, as a comparison for Susan rather than the wood-anemone one.

"Indeed he's very kind," said Susan; and dropped a curtsey. "The clothes fitted Georgie as though they were made for him. I'll be able to use all you sent, m'lady, I'm such a good needlewoman. I hope I may mend your Ladyship's lace or any fine embroideries. Once we're settled, with Georgie away at school all day, I'll have a deal o' time on my hands. I'd like to do something for you, m'lady."

"So you shall, Susan. Margaret McKeon, who has been with me since I was a child, is no longer able for work that tries the eyes. I promise I'll keep you busy as soon as you get settled in here."

"Oh, m'lady! Thank you, m'lady!" said Susan, colouring as though Lady O'Gara had promised her something very delightful. "I do love fine needle-work, m'lady. Any fine damask cloths or the like I'll darn so you'd hardly know. I'm never happier than when I'm sewin' an' my Georgie reads a bit to me. He's a good scholar, is my Georgie, although he's but nine."

"You've made a pretty place of it," Lady O'Gara said, looking round the lodge with satisfaction. "I was afraid it was going to be a grimy place for you, for it had been empty since old Mrs. Veldon died. You see we didn't know you were coming. You've had it whitewashed."

"Yes, m'lady. Mr. Kenny came and whitewashed it. He was very good, better than ever I can repay. He cleaned out the little place for me. The pots and pans turned in well. And he lent me a few things till, maybe I could earn a bit, washin' or mendin' or sewin'; I'm a good dressmaker. Maybe I could get work that way."

"There hasn't been a dressmaker in the village since the last one went to America. I'll ask the parish priest and the nuns to tell the women you can dressmake. You'll have your hands full."

Again Susan flushed delicately.

"I'm never so happy as when I've no time for thinkin'," she said. "Any work pleases me, but fine work best of all. I can do lovely work tuckin' and veinin'. When I'm at it I'm happy. 'Tis like what drink is to some people; it makes me forget."

The lodge was indeed altered from what Lady O'Gara remembered it, when Mrs. Veldon lived there. Mrs. Veldon had been so piteously sure than any washing or whitewashing would kill her with rheumatism that she had been left to her murky gloom. Now, with a few gaily coloured pictures of the Saints and Irish patriots on the walls, the dresser filled with bright crockery, including a whole shelf of lustre jugs, the pots and pans set out to advantage, to say nothing of the cans, a clean scrubbed table, a few chairs, a strip of matting in front of the fireplace, flowers in a jug on the table which also bore Susan's few implements of sewing and a pile of white stuff, the place was homelike and pretty.

Lady O'Gara decided that Susan was one of the women who have the gift of creating a home wherever they may be. So much the worse, she added in her own mind, not particularizing what it was that was so much the worse. Round Susan, standing meekly by the table while her Ladyship sat, floated the mysterious aura which draws men and children as to a warm hearth-fire.

So much the worse, thought Lady O'Gara, and commented to herself that Patsy must have stripped his own house bare. Those jugs were his, the gay crockery, and the pictures of the Saints and patriots, she wondered what appeal these might have for Susan, and that shelf of books in the corner. Patsy had a taste, laughed at by his fellows, for book-buying, whenever the occasion arose. He was well-known at auctions round about the country, where he bought miscellaneous lots of books, with some few ornaments as well. She could see the backs of two books Patsy had a great admiration for, "Fardarougha the Miser" and "Charles O'Malley"; and, on the chimney-piece, there were two large pink shells and a weather house which she had often seen on Patsy's chimney-piece. The more solid pieces of furniture and some of the plain crockery had been sent down from Castle Talbot.

"I see Patsy's been lending you his treasures," she said.

"Yes, indeed, m'lady. I asked him not to, but he wouldn't take any notice of me. He said he'd no use for the things. He's stripped himself bare, m'lady. I didn't know men were like that. Small wonder the dumb beasts love him. I wonder he has anything left to give."

She spoke with such fervour that Lady O'Gara was touched.

"You've had a sad experience of men, my poor Susan," she said. "But you are quite right about Patsy. There are few men as gentle as he is. We all look on Patsy as a dear and valued friend. I must find him some other things to keep him from missing these. Not books, I know his house is piled with books. He won't miss those, though he has given you the ones he like best. I wonder whether I could find pictures like those. I think I have seen that Robert Emmet, or something like it, in a shop-window in Galway."

"I don't know who the gentlemen are," Susan said, looking from one patriot to another, "and I didn't want to have them taken from his walls. I expect they've left a mark on the wall-paper where they were taken down, for he said he'd got to do some papering for himself."

It was on Lady O'Gara's tongue to utter a gentle warning that Patsy must not be too much about the South lodge, but the warning remained unspoken.

"He's the best man I ever knew," said Susan, "I didn't know there was his like in the world. It's a strange thing, m'lady, that men can be so different. Listen, m'lady, if Baker was to come back, you wouldn't let him claim me? The Master wouldn't let him claim me? I'd drown myself and the child before we'd go back to him. He did knock us about something cruel. And my Georgie, so gentle that he'd move a heart of stone. I frightened Baker from laying a hand on Georgie; I told him I'd kill him if I was to be hanged for it."

The woman's eyes, no longer gentle, blazed at Lady O'Gara.

"Hush! Hush!" she said. "He shall not trouble you. If he should come back..."

"He's found us out no matter where we've been. Even good Christians got tired at last of Baker comin' and askin' for his wife and son and makin' a row and the police fetched, and it gettin' in the papers. They give us up. Oh, Lord, if they knew what they was givin' us up to! They'd better have shot us."

"If he comes back he will be prosecuted for deserting you. We shall not give you up to him. You may be sure of that. Here is my hand on it."

She held out a firm white hand which showed a couple of beautiful rings. Susan looked at it for a moment in amazement before she took it. The colour flooded back into her face. Her eyes became quieter. Then she took the hand and kissed it, hard.

"Thank you, m'lady," she said. "I trust you."

Lady O'Gara walked to the door and paused to ask for news of Georgie, who was already at school. He was doing very well. It was so easy for him to reach the school by this gate, and he was beginning to get on well with the boys; and Mr. McGroarty, Mr. O'Connell's successor, gave a very favourable report of him.

"We feel so safe inside the big wall, me and Georgie," said Susan Horridge. "It isn't likely he'd come on us from the Park." She looked a little apprehensively over the beautiful prospect of trees in their early Summer beauty, and the shining greensward; with the hills beyond. Through an opening in the trees there was a glimpse of a deer feeding.

"No one here associates you with that man. Patsy and I have taken care of that," Lady O'Gara assured her. "If he came back looking for you no one could tell him where you were. Would you like a dog for company? There is a litter of puppies of Shot's breed in the stable-yard. You shall have one, if you like it."

"Is it like it?" asked Susan, her face lighting up, "I should be very pleased to have it. So would Georgie. That boy's fair gone on animals."

"Those dogs make very good watch-dogs, though they are so gentle. You should see how Shot keeps walking before and behind me if he thinks he sees a suspicious character when we are out walking! I shall send down a puppy, then."

Susan Horridge stood in her doorway shading her eyes with her hand, as she looked after Lady O'Gara. There were tears in her eyes. "The Lord didn't forget us," she said to herself.

"I shall have to speak to Patsy," Lady O'Gara was thinking as she hurried along. She was a little late for lunch. "Poor Patsy! It would be a thousand pities if his heart should open to that poor creature for the first time."

CHAPTER VI

STELLA

Mrs. Comerford and Stella arrived unexpectedly. They found Lady O'Gara at Inch. She had gone over, taking Susan with her, to give the finishing touch to the preparations. There was a new staff of servants under Clinch and Mrs. Clinch. There were things the new servants might have forgotten: and Mrs. Clinch was old and rheumatic now, not equal to much climbing of stairs. Lady O'Gara remembered many things which most people would have forgotten, little things about the arrangement of rooms and furniture, the choice of flowers, the way Mrs. Comerford had liked the blinds drawn, all the trifling things which mean so much to certain orderly minds.

She was in the bedroom which had been Mrs. Comerford's, was to be hers again. The room which had been Mary Creagh's was prepared for Stella. The pink curtains which she remembered as faded had been laid away and new pink curtains hung up. The old ones were riddled with holes. She hoped Aunt Grace, she went back to the familiar name, would not miss them, would be satisfied with the room, which looked so fresh with its clean white paper and the pink carpet and cushions and curtains. She was filling bowls and vases with red and white roses, setting them where the tired eyes of the travellers might rest upon them when they came. Probably they would arrive about ten o'clock.

The room looked over the lawns and paddocks at the back of the house. She had not heard any sounds of arrival, but the bedroom door opened suddenly and Mrs. Comerford came in.

"Clinch told me I should find you here, Mary," she said: and the two who had loved each other and parted, with cold resentment on one side, tears on the other, were looking into each other's eyes.

Lady O'Gara had often wondered, she had been wondering, wondering, during the last few days, how they should greet each other, what should be the first words to pass between them. The half-dreaded, half-looked-for moment had come, and the greeting was of the tritest.

"We have arrived, you see," said Mrs. Comerford. "We caught the Irish Mail last night instead of staying the night in London."

"Oh, did no one meet you?"

"We left the luggage and came up on Farrell's car. It was Farrell's car, just as muddy and disreputable as I remember it. It was driven by old Johnny's son. I am sorry Johnny is dead. Perhaps the car is not the same, but there is nothing to choose between that and the old one."

The meeting had taken place. The great moment had come and gone: and there was Aunt Grace talking about Farrell's car as though all that lay between them had been but a dream.

Lady O'Gara's eyes suddenly filled with tears.

"Ah, you are tired," she said with soft tenderness, "you are tired!"

The change the years had wrought in the tall handsome woman who had been queenly to her young mind overwhelmed her. She forgot the dread she had had of the meeting, which had destroyed any happy anticipation. "Come and sit down," she said. "Let me help you off with your cloak. You will have breakfast? What a long journey for you!"

Mrs. Comerford allowed herself to be put into the softest of the easy chairs. A look of gratification, of pleasure, came to her face. She allowed Lady O'Gara to take off her hat and long travelling cloak, to unlace her shoes.

"You were always a kind creature," she said, "and it is nice to be home again. How beautiful the cloudy skies are! Many and many a time during those years I have wanted grey skies. I've been sick even for a whole wet day. Do you think, Mary, that if we Westerners get to Heaven we will want a wet day now and again?"

So the old resentment had gone. How strange it was after all the grief and estrangement to have Aunt Grace talking like this. It encouraged Lady O'Gara, sitting on the floor at Mrs. Comerford's feet, to pat the foot from which she had drawn off the shoe, with a tender furtive caress.

"You'd better get up, Mary. I hear Clinch coming. You have hardly changed from the girl of twenty-five years ago. Of course you are plumper, more matronly. You have a boy of twenty-one."

Clinch came in with the bag, followed by Mrs. Clinch with a tea-tray, smiling broadly.

"The young lady said she'd have a bath before her breakfast, ma'am," she said, and there was a radiance about her old face which had not been there for many a day.

"Breakfast, we had breakfast in the train. Miss Stella cannot want breakfast." Mrs. Comerford smiled as she said it. "She made a very good breakfast in the train."

"She's young and the young want food. 'Tis a good day that's in it, ma'am, to see you home again, with such a beautiful young lady too. She'll make the house lively. The first thing she did was to fling her arms about Shot's neck, Lady O'Gara's dog, ma'am. For all he's a proud, stand-off dog, he licked her face."

"Now, don't spoil Miss Stella. Every one spoils her, so I suppose there's no use expecting you to be the exception."

"She brings her love with her," said Mrs. Clinch. "She's so delighted with all she sees, and making friends with everyone. They'll be won over by her: even old Tom Kane will give her the key of his garden, as he calls it, before she's an hour in the place. She'll be into his strawberry beds that he's so jealous about, you'll see."

Mrs. Clinch went off. Lady O'Gara poured out a cup of tea, remembering, over all the years, that Mrs. Comerford liked only a little sugar. She found her slippers and put them on and brought a footstool for feet to rest upon. She was thinking that this Stella, the young adopted daughter, explained the change in the woman before her. Mrs. Comerford had grown much softer. She was still a remarkable-looking woman, the wreck of stately beauty. In her black garments, which fell about her in flowing lines, she had the air of a priestess. Her age showed in her thinness, which was almost emaciation, and her face was wrinkled and heavily lined. Yet her smile was more ready than

Lady O'Gara remembered and her eyes quieter. They had been very blue eyes once upon a time, her son had had such blue eyes, now, they had faded almost to lavender, and they were almost gentle. Yet there was something in the face, some suggestion of burnt-out fires, which forbade the idea of a gentle nature, and the lips were too thin for softness.

"Am I a wreck, Mary?" she asked. "Yes, I know I am. Some one took me for a Duchess the other day, addressing me as 'Your Grace.' Italy has dried up my skin. It will hardly revive at my time of life. But I am happy: you cannot imagine how Stella makes for happiness. Stella and age between them have broken me down. A child could play with me."

She laughed as she said it. Grace Comerford had not laughed much in the old days. Mary had adored her, with an adoration tinged with awe. She had always felt in those days that it would be an awful thing to offend Aunt Grace. She had offended her and it had been awful.

"I am longing to see Stella," she said.

"She is very joyous. I was becoming morose when I found her, like a rogue elephant. I was wrong, Mary, to make such a grievance of your marriage. You were a good child to me, and you would have pleased me if you could. I know better now than to be angry with you for caring more for Shawn O'Gara than for my son. You should have told me at the time. You shouldn't have let me believe that you cared for Terence. Was I an ogre? Perhaps I was. I must have been."

"I wanted to please you dreadfully in those days. You had been everything to me."

"You and Terence were everything to me. Still, I should not have been so unreasonable as to expect you to marry Terence to please me when you liked Shawn O'Gara better. I ought to have known that love does not grow up like that. You and Terence were almost brother and sister."

"Yes," said Lady O'Gara. "We were so used to each other. I was eighteen when I first saw Shawn and we fell in love at first sight." She blushed, with a startling effect of youth. "Terence and I were like brother and sister. It would not have worked. We were very fond of each other, but no more than that. You were wrong when you thought Terence would have cared."

She had expected some disclaimer, remembering Mrs. Comerford's bitter anger because her son had been supplanted by his friend, even while he was yet in the world; but no disclaimer came.

"Yes, I was wrong. I see it now. I ought to have come back long ago and said I was wrong. I could not bring myself to do it, and, there were other reasons. It is very good to come back and to see you so bonny, Mary, and to feel that we may live in love and peace as long as I am here."

She drank her tea and looked round the room, with a sigh as though her heart rested on what she saw.

"You have made the old room very sweet, Mary," she went on, "and you have remembered my tastes. Dear me, see those old things on the chimney-piece! Those crockery dogs, how fond Terence was of them when he was a child! And that piece of agate, and the Rockingham lambs! I had almost forgotten them."

"You, had better come over to Castle Talbot to lunch," Lady O'Gara said. "I want you to see my boy. He has just passed out of Sandhurst."

"A soldier? How strange that I should have had to ask! I left your letters unanswered, but I always read them. That was how I knew that you had called your boy after my son."

"Yes, Terence has chosen to be a soldier, for some years, at least. There is not very much doing now. After a few years his father thinks he might take to politics."

"I want to see him. And I want you to see my girl."

She glanced towards the door as though she expected it to open.

"Eileen Creagh is with us. You remember her father, Anthony Creagh. He came here once or twice in old days. She has lived with us for a long time. Terry was always at school. It would have been lonely for me without Eileen."

"Yes, I remember I did not like Anthony Creagh because I thought he came for your sake. He married a fair girl, very unlike you. I've forgotten her name."

"Eileen is very pretty, like her mother. Beautiful soft silver-gold hair and greyish blue eyes: she is very gentle."

"Characterless?"

Lady O'Gara smiled ever so slightly. "Oh, she has character, I think."

"No one will look at her when Stella is by. You will see. She has no animation; I know her kind. By the way, you have Patsy Kenny still with you? You told me about Patsy in the letters I did not answer."

"Still with us. He is an institution, like the Shots. I have a Shot still, the great-grandson of old Shot. I don't know what we should do without Patsy. He has such a wonderful way with the horses, with all animals, indeed."

"He'll adore Stella. She's so fearless with animals. Many a fright she gave me when she was a child. But the animals, even when they were savage with others, never hurt her. There was an awful day when we found her with the boarhound puppies at Prince Valetti's Villa in her arms, and the mother looking on well-pleased. She was a savage brute to other people. The Prince was ready to shoot her if she had turned nasty with Stella: but there was no occasion. Stella scrambled through the barrier when we called her name."

"Is she like a French girl?"

"No: why should she be?"

"I suppose I was wrong. I thought she was the child of Gaston de St. Maur, who used to visit us here."

"Her mother was Irish," Mrs. Comerford said.

"And she is like her mother?"

Before Mrs. Comerford could answer there came a knocking as of knuckles on the door.

"Come in, my darling," Mrs. Comerford said, her face lighting up.

A charming girlish face looked in at the open door.

"May I? Is it Lady O'Gara whom my dearest Mamma so greatly loves?"

There was the slightest foreign intonation in the voice, something of deliberate utterance, as though English was not the language of the speaker.

The girl came into the room and towards them. She was charming. Her hair curled in rings of reddish brown on her little head. Her eyes were grey with something of brown in the iris: her eyebrows strongly marked. She had a straight beautiful little nose, lips softly opening, a chin like that of the Irish poet's "Mary Donnelly," "round as a china cup." There was something softly graceful about her as she came into the room. She looked down, then up again. Her eyes, were they grey? They were brown surely, almost gold. Her little head was held as though she courted a caress.

"I am so glad you have come back, Stella," Lady O'Gara said, fascinated straight off by this charming vision.

"I wonder how Mamma stayed away so long," Stella returned. "The sweet house, the beautiful grey country." She took Lady O'Gara's hand and kissed it lightly; yet with an air of reverence, "the beloved people."

"The country will not prove too grey for you, I hope, Stella," Lady O'Gara said, feeling touched and pleased by the girl's air of homage. "My husband's mother, who was an Italian, said that the grey skies made her weep when first she came to Ireland. They were so unlike Italian skies."

"I must be Irish then," said the girl, "for I adore them. Even when it rains I shall not weep."

"She has something of your colouring, Mary; don't you think so?" Mrs. Comerford asked.

"Yes, perhaps more golden."

She was feeling surprised at herself. This girl made more appeal to her than Eileen Creagh whom she had had with her from childhood. This girl touched some motherly chord in her which Eileen had never awakened. She wanted to stroke her dear curls, to be good to her. Yet she had been telling herself all those years, that she had no need for a daughter, having Terry.

CHAPTER VII

BRADY'S BULL

The meeting between Eileen Creagh and Stella Comerford brought the flying dimple to Lady O'Gara's cheek. She watched them as though they were young children meeting in the shy yet uncompromising atmosphere of the nursery.

Stella was inclined to be friendly and then drew back, chilled by something she detected in Eileen's manner. Eileen was indifferently polite.

Terry and his father were out when the party arrived for luncheon, but they returned very soon afterwards. Lady O'Gara's attention was otherwise absorbed so that she did not notice the sudden delighted friendliness in Terry towards Stella nor the quick withdrawal into sullenness which spoilt Eileen's looks for the luncheon-hour.

Lady O'Gara was wondering about her husband. Why should he have looked so startled when his eye fell on Stella? He had known that she was coming. To Lady O'Gara's anxious eye Sir Shawn looked pale. He had been pale of late, with curious shadows about his face, but when she had asked him if he was not feeling well he had answered with an air of lightness that he felt as well as ever he had felt.

At the luncheon table he sat with his back to the light. The persistence of those shadows in his face worried her loving heart. She wondered if Mrs. Comerford saw a great change in him. It ought to have been a very happy occasion. Mrs. Comerford had met Shawn with an air of affection mingled with deprecation, as though she asked pardon for the old unreason. If she saw that the years had changed him she made no sign.

"I have stayed away a long time from you and Mary," she said. "I had made it difficult for myself to come back: but I have wanted to come back. Now I hope we shall remain neighbours to the end."

Sir Shawn had not responded as he ought to have done. He had worn a queer look. After a while his wife had found the proper adjective for it: his eyes were haunted. He might have seen a ghost. It distracted her from her talk across the table with Mrs. Comerford, happy talk of friends long parted and re-united, full of "Don't you remember?" and "Have you forgotten?": arrears of talk in which so much had to be explained, so many fates elucidated. It might have been so happy if only Shawn had not worn that odd look.

Once Lady O'Gara thought she caught his eyes fixed with a gloomy intentness on the group of young people at the other end of the table. She glanced that way, and the ready smile came. Terry was making himself very agreeable to the two pretty girls. It was obvious, even at a glance, that Eileen had little chance against the new-comer's vivacity. She sat with her lips pursed a little and something of gloom on her face. Terry, between his sallies with Stella, who was at once shy and bright, full of those charming glances out of the eyes which were grey at one moment, golden brown at another, sent now and again a tenderly apologetic look Eileen's way, trying to draw the sulking beauty into the conversation. There was nothing for Shawn to be gloomy about in this little comedy. Terry was always so sweetly amiable.

In the days that followed the comedy unfolded itself. Stella was very often at Castle Talbot, or they were at Inch. Terry was evidently drawn towards Stella, while loyally endeavouring to keep up his former attitude towards Eileen. If Eileen wished to keep him she went the worst possible way about it, for she sulked, and sulkiness did not become her. Her fair skin took on a leaden look. She repulsed Stella's advances till Stella was hurt and vexed.

"Eileen will not be friends with me," she complained to Lady O'Gara. "She is so cold. That lovely pale hair of hers I took it in my hands one day when it was undone, and it was cold as ice. Her heart is like her hair. Why will she not like me?"

Why not, indeed? Apart from the fact that Stella chattered, pretty chatter like the singing of a bird, and was so quickly intelligent about everything, and so interested in the new life that the slower Eileen was rather left out of things, her attitude towards Eileen was most disarming. She admired her greatly and was evidently quite unaware of her own good looks. She tried to win her over with gifts, which Eileen accepted, while she was not propitiated.

"She will not like me," Stella complained with a flash of tears in her eyes, "if I was to give her my heart she would not like me."

"You should not have given her your seed-pearls," said Lady O'Gara. "It is too valuable a gift to pass from one girl to another."

It was beginning to dawn on her that Eileen was greedy and selfish. Perhaps she had had intuitions of it when Eileen had disappointed her. Eileen was only friendly to Stella when she wanted something. Once she had obtained it she relapsed into her former coldness. Lady O'Gara realized that Eileen had always been greedy. She had laid Terry under heavy toll for small attentions and such gifts as he might give her. Eileen's incessant eating of chocolate had made Lady O'Gara wonder how she could give so good an account of herself at meal-times. She smoked, it was a new fashion of which Lady O'Gara did not altogether approve, a cigarette now and again and Terry supplied the gold-tipped, scented kind which Eileen took from a cigarette case of platinum with her name in turquoise at the corner. The cigarette case was a new possession. Lady O'Gara supposed that it came from Terry. She had not asked. A violet scent, so good that on its first introduction Lady O'Gara had cried out that someone was wearing wet violets, now always heralded Miss Creagh's coming into a room.

There were some things which had not come from Terry. When Lady O'Gara had noticed them Eileen had said carelessly that they were given her by Robin Gillespie, the son of the doctor at Inver, and a doctor himself in the Indian Army. Anthony Creagh and his wife had an overflowing quiverful. Lady O'Gara made excuses for the girl who must have had it in her blood to do without. Still, Robin Gillespie, the doctor's son at Inver, could not have much to spare, but apparently he had given Eileen a good many trinkets.

"When does Terry join his regiment?" Sir Shawn asked his wife one day with a certain sharpness.

"Not till September."

"And it is now August. A pity he should waste his time philandering."

"Does he philander?"

Lady O'Gara's voice had a hurt sound in it. She found nothing amiss in her one child.

"He philandered with Eileen till Stella came. Now apparently he inclines to Stella. He mustn't play fast and loose with girls."

"It sounds so ugly, Shawn. Terry is incapable of such a thing, as incapable as you yourself. He is not the flirting sort. He is just a simple boy."

There was something piteous in her voice.

Her husband lifted her face by the chin till he looked down into her eyes.

"If he were like me he would only have one love," he said. "You made your own of me, Mary, altogether, from the first moment I saw you."

Stella had made friends with every one round about her. She was in and out of the cottages. She knew all about the old people's ailments and nursed all the children. Eileen complained with a fastidious disgust that Stella did not seem to know whether the children were dirty or clean. She kissed and hugged them all the same. In likewise she loved and petted the animals and so commended herself hugely to Patsy Kenny.

"She's worth twenty of Miss Eileen," he said. "All I'm afeard of is she'll run herself into danger. She doesn't know what fear is. She ups and says to me the other day whin I bid her not make too free with the mares that the only rayson the crathurs ever was wicked was that men wasn't good to them."

"I've heard you say the same yourself, Mr. Kenny," said Susan Horridge, over the half-door of whose lodge he was leaning. He often paid Susan a visit in this uncomfortable fashion, refusing a chair in the kitchen or even one outside.

"So you have," Patsy acknowledged, and made as if to go; but lingered to ask what Mrs. Horridge thought of Miss Stella.

"I like fair hair best myself," he said, with a shy glance at Susan's hair, neatly braided around a face that began to have soft, even plump, contours once more.

"Miss Eileen has a lovely head of hair," Susan acknowledged.

"And yet," said Patsy, "Miss Stella's my choice. Did you ever take notice of her side-face? It's the purtiest, softest thing I ever seen. I think I seen somethin' like it wance, but where I disremimber."

"Which of the young ladies is Mr. Terry sweet on, Mr. Kenny?"

"Bedad, I don't know, ma'am." Patsy scratched his head. "I wouldn't be sure he's not sweet on the two o' them."

A day came when the two girls, crossing the fields by a short cut, found themselves face to face with a very fine bull. They had not noticed him till they came quite near him. Their path wound round by a little wood which, since it belonged to the paddock of the mares, was surrounded by high hurdles. The bull must have broken into the field, for he had no right to be there. The piece of rope hanging from his neck showed that he had escaped from bondage.

The path curved gently by the edges of the coppice. They came upon the bull unawares. He was grazing when they first saw him, his fine curled head half-buried in the long grass.

"It is Brady's bull," Eileen said in a whisper. "He is not to be trusted. And he sees your red cloak."

The bull lifted his head and stared at them. Eileen had slipped behind Stella and had begun to retreat backwards.

The bull stamped with his foot and emitted a low roar. Stella did not seem to feel afraid. She kept her eye steadily on the bull. The day was chilly and Lady O'Gara had wrapped the girls up in Connemara cloaks of red and blue flannel. She had put the blue one about Eileen's shoulders, remarking that it matched her eyes.

"Run, Eileen, run," Stella said quietly without taking her eyes from the bull. "Keep the gate open for me."

Eileen ran with a will, never looking back to see what was happening.

Stella took off the red cloak. The bull had put his head to the earth as though about to charge. He roared, a roar that seemed to shake the ground. As he came on she flung the offending garment on to his horns and stepped to one side.

She did not wait to see the result. She could run like Atalanta. It was a pretty good sprint to the gate, which closed and opened by an iron switch. As she ran, the roars of the bull followed her. He was rending Lady O'Gara's Connemara cloak. Presently he would discover that the perpetrator of this outrage upon his dignity was yet in sight.

She was some distance from the gate when she heard the thudding of the bull behind her. For a second or two she did not discover that Eileen was not holding the gate open for her. It was apparently shut to. Would she have time to open it before the bull came up! The switch, which was new, took some pressure to move. Would she have time?

She had just a wild hope that Eileen might have left the gate unfastened. She flung herself against it. No, the switch had fallen into its place: there was no time, no time even to climb the gate. The bull was upon her with a rush. She felt the wind of his approach. She closed her eyes and clung to the gate. Her mind was never clearer. She saw herself trampled and gored, flung in the air and to earth again a helpless thing for the bull to wreak his wrath upon.

Suddenly there was a shout, close at hand, almost at her ear. Something hurtled through the air, a stone flung with an unerring aim which struck the bull in the forehead. The gate opened with her and she felt herself drawn through the opening while the switch fell with a sharp click.

"I say, that was a near thing!" said Terry O'Gara. "You're not going to faint, are you? Just look at that chap tearing up my old football blazer. Thank God, it isn't you."

"Where is Eileen?" she asked. "She was terribly frightened."

"I know," he answered, somewhat grimly. "I dare say she has done a faint. I left her over there by the stile. She was sitting down, recovering herself. Lucky I heard the roars of the bull and was so close at hand. I suppose it was Eileen who shut the gate. She made some sort of explanation, but there was no time to listen. What a fright you've had, you poor child!"

The bull, having reduced the blazer to rags like the Connemara cloak, had trotted away and was grazing quietly, some of the tattered pieces still hanging to his horns, with an odd effect of absurdity.

"I never thought an animal could be so alarming," said Stella.

"You must be more careful in future," he answered. "Not that I want you to be afraid, like Eileen. This brute had no business here. He must have broken through the hedge. He might have got into the foals' paddock. There's a way in for anything very determined where the water runs in that far ditch."

"Oh, I'm glad he didn't get in among the pretty foals."

"It would have been a horrible thing, but better the foals than you."

He looked at her with a simple boyish tenderness. There was something childish about her beauty, something boyish about the slight figure and the curly head, borne out by her frank gaze.

"I wish I had killed the brute," he said, with a vengeful glance in the direction of the quietly-feeding bull.

"You probably cut him with that stone, poor beast."

"Yes: it had a good sharp edge. How lucky I found it just there!"

He noticed that she turned very pale. Quickly his arm went round her to give her support.

"You poor little thing!" he said. "I am so sorry. Are you better now?"

The colour came back to her face. She withdrew gently from his arm.

"I am all right," she said. "It was splendid how you came to my rescue."

Her frank eyes thanked him in a way he found bewildering. He was very goodly in his flannels, with his alert slender darkness and his bright eyes, softened now as his gaze rested upon her.

"It won't make you afraid?" he asked anxiously. "I mean, of course, you must be cautious; but any one would be afraid of Brady's bull. Don't be timid like Eileen, who screams if a foal trots up to her, and is afraid even of Shot."

He had quite forgotten the time when he had found Eileen's timidity pleasing.

"Oh, I shall not be afraid of Shot, or the foals," she said, and laughed. "After all," she lifted her eyes to him as though she asked for pardon, "any one might be afraid of a bull. I'm not a coward for that."

"Of course you're not," he answered, with a sound in his voice as though she was very pleasant to him. "Bulls are treacherous brutes."

They went back slowly to where Eileen sat watching their approach gloomily.

"Well!" she said. "You've been a long time. Wasn't that a horrid brute? I never ran such danger in my life before."

"Stella ran a greater because you had taken care to slam the gate after you," Terry said, with young condemning eyes. "I was only just in time to save her from that brute."

"Oh well, I was frightened. I only thought of getting away as far as I could from him. I shan't walk in the fields again in a hurry. If it isn't horses, it's bulls."

Eileen's face kept its unbecoming gloom on the homeward way, even though she pressed very close to Terry for protection whenever they came near the feeding horses, or one of them trotted up to be petted and stroked. She knew she was disapproved of, and the knowledge was unpleasant to her, although it did not cause her any searchings of conscience. Eileen always took the line of least resistance, as her clever sister, Paula, who was a B.A. of Dublin University, had said.

CHAPTER VIII

SIR SHAWN SEES A GHOST

"There's a blast o' talk goin' through the place like an earthquake," said Patsy Kenny to Sir Shawn, "that the little cottage down by the waterfall is took by a stranger woman."

There was "a blast of talk" even about trifles among the country-people, from whom Patsy kept his distance with an abhorrence of gossip and curiosity about other people's business. Many a one had tried to pump Patsy, the people had an inordinate curiosity about their "betters" and of late tongues had been very busy with the return of Mrs. Comerford and the reconciliation with Lady O'Gara: also with Miss Stella and her parentage. Those who tried to pump Patsy Kenny about these matters embarked, and they knew it, on perilous seas. Patsy's stiff face as he repelled the gossips was a sight to see. He had also to keep at bay many questions about Susan Horridge and her boy, in doing which he showed some asperity and thereby gave a handle to the gossips.

"I should have thought the cottage by the waterfall a damp place," said Sir Shawn, indifferently. He was not much interested in the petty happenings of the neighbourhood.

"She won't stay," Patsy went on with a shake of his head. "They'll get at her about ould Hercules. A lone woman like that will be scared out of her life. I saw her in Dunphy's shop buyin' her little bits of food. She's not the common sort. She was all in black, with a veil about her face. She'll have no truck with them long-tongued people about here."

"Oh, a superior class?" said Sir Shawn, now faintly interested. The Waterfall Cottage was his property. He supposed Norman, who lived in the town and did his legal business, had let it.

"Not to say a lady," said Patsy, "but nigh hand one. She have the little place rale snug and comfortable. She'll keep herself to herself. There's two lone women in it now, herself and Mrs. Horridge. Mrs. Horridge do be drawin' the water from the well behind the Waterfall Cottage, and this Mrs. Wade kem out an' spoke to her. She took great notice of Georgie. The schoolmaster's well contint with Georgie. He takes to the Irish like a duck to water. The master do be sayin' he's better at the language nor them that should be spakin' it be rights. He'll have him doin' a trifle o' poetry in it by the Christmas holidays."

"Oh! So the two lonesome women have made friends with each other. Between them they'll be a match for Hercules' ghost," Sir Shawn said, faintly smiling.

By this time Terry had joined his regiment, and Eileen had gone for a time to her parents. She usually went home rather unwillingly, complaining of the discomfort of the tightly packed house. Apparently she did not add to the joy of her family during those periodic visits and she made no pretence of eagerness about going. But this time, for some reason, she was quite pleased to go. She even set about refurbishing her wardrobe, and was not above accepting help from Stella, who was very quick with her needle and possessed a Frenchwoman's art in making excellent use of what materials came her way. These preparations somewhat mystified Lady O'Gara, for usually Eileen took only her less reputable garments when she went home, because she had to live in her trunk, or share a wardrobe with two sisters, who would hang their roughest garments over her evening frocks if she were to bring them.

Lady O'Gara sometimes wondered if she had chosen wisely in selecting Eileen from Anthony Creagh's quiverful to be her companion during the years Terry was at school and college. The others had been tumbling over each other like frolicsome young puppies when the choice was made; Eileen had been sitting placidly eating bread and honey. She remembered that Anne Creagh had said that Eileen would always get the best of things! To Lady O'Gara's eyes, the demure little girl, with a golden plait hanging down each side of her face, and the large blue eyes, had looked like a little Blessed Mary in the Temple of Albrecht Dürer.

Perhaps she had not chosen. Perhaps Eileen had chosen her, when she said to Anne Creagh, "Dear Anne, you have so many girls. Lend me one for company. I shall be very good to her and shall only keep her during your pleasure."

Eileen had heard the speech, and had seized on Lady O'Gara, not to be detached. When it had come to longer and longer visits, so that Eileen was oftener at Castle Talbot than at home, Anne Creagh had said, "Ah, well, Eileen knows what is good for her. The others don't. They've no worldly wisdom. There is Hilary, who runs away from every school we send him to. They are all like Hilary, except Eileen. She's a changeling."

With Terry gone, Eileen had put off her sulkiness. Lady O'Gara came on the two girls one day at work on a pink billowy stuff, which was evidently going to be an evening-frock. At least Stella was at work, and Eileen was looking on. Eileen usually commandeered some one to her service when any sewing was to be done. She had confessed that she could not endure to have her forefinger pricked by the needle.

"You are going to be very smart, Eileen," Lady O'Gara said. "This looks like gaieties at Inver."

"There may be some," answered Eileen, colouring slightly. "There are some soldiers under canvas at Inver Hill."

Lady O'Gara referred to Eileen's preparations a little later in talking with her husband. Sir Shawn had got a bee in his bonnet about Terry and Eileen. For the first time during all their years of love he had been irritable with his wife about Terry, Terry, who had given them so little trouble in his twenty years of life.

"I am glad she has the spirit," he said. "A pretty girl like Eileen need not go wasting her charms on a young ass who doesn't know his own mind."

"Oh, Shawn! Poor Terry!"

"Terry has been playing fast and loose with Eileen."

"He would not like to hear you say so," Lady O'Gara said, with a proud and wounded air.

"There you go, Mary, getting your back up! Your one son can do no wrong. Do you deny that he was philandering after Eileen before Stella came, and that he has been philandering after Stella since?"

"Do you know, Shawn," Lady O'Gara said, with sudden energy, "that, fond as I am of Eileen, I think she has not the stuff in her to hold a boy like Terry. There is something lethargic in her. I'm afraid she is a little selfish. She can be very sweet when she likes, but I think at heart she is cold."

"This is a late discovery, Mary."

Lady O'Gara laughed, a little ruefully.

"I think it is a very old discovery," she said. "Anne said to me once, she never pretended that she loved Eileen as well as some of the others, that Eileen had a way of looking at her when she was in high spirits or something of the sort that was like a douche of cold water. I have had the lame experience myself. Eileen said something the other day about 'at your age.' I felt ninety, all of a sudden."

"Nonsense, Mary! Eileen adores you."

Lady O'Gara said no more. She let pass, with a shrug of her shoulders, her husband's accusation that she was fickle like Terry, putting away the old love for the new.

Suddenly Sir Shawn asked a direct question.

"Are you quite certain about Stella's parentage, Mary? She is the child of that French soldier, St. Maur, was it? and the Irish governess?"

"Of course, Shawn."

It had never occurred to Lady O'Gara to doubt it.

She looked at her husband with wondering eyes. The lights in her brown eyes were as deep and quiet now as when she was in her young beauty. She had a sudden illumination. Was that the bee in Shawn's bonnet? There had been a certain silence about Stella's parentage. She thought she understood it. Mrs. Comerford had always been jealous of her loves. She did not wish it recalled that Stella, whom she adored, had not belonged to her by any tie of blood. Shawn must have got it into his head that the mystery might cover something disgraceful.

"You may be quite sure, Shawn," she said, her candid eyes fixed on him: "There was nothing to conceal. Aunt Grace has told me everything."

His face cleared. "Then I confess," he said almost gaily, "that Stella is a young angel. Perhaps I was too hard on Terry."

The evenings began to draw in. Sir Shawn missed his boy. The hunting season was at hand. The opening meet was to be at Dunmara Cross-Roads in a fortnight's time. Lady O'Gara went out perhaps once a week. The other days Sir Shawn would miss Terry jogging along beside him, on the way to the meet in the morning, full of cheerful anticipation; riding homewards, tired and happy, in the dusk. Stella had never ridden to hounds. She had done little riding, indeed, since the days at the advanced Roman Convent when the girls went out on the Campagna in a flock, in charge of a discreet riding master, of unimpeachable age and plainness.

He was thinking as he rode home one evening, with the dusk closing in, that it would be pleasant to have Stella with him when Mary was not available. It was one tangible thing against Eileen that she did not like horses. Anthony Creagh's daughter! It seemed incredible to Sir Shawn, as it did to Patsy Kenny, that any one should not like horses.

There was a little mare not quite up to racing standard which he thought would just do for Stella. Indeed, though he did not know it, Patsy Kenny had put the idea into his head.

"That wan 'ud carry a lady in less than no time," Patsy had said, "A lady about the size of Miss Stella. She'd take the ditches like a bird."

But Patsy was always talking in his slow way, and Sir Shawn was not always listening to him, or he seemed not to listen. He had a way of forgetting his surroundings and travelling off to a distance where even she who loved him best could not follow. But sometimes he heard when he did not seem to hear and was unconscious of having heard. He was going to ride Mustapha this Winter as soon, he said with his slow smile, as Patsy Kenny would permit it. Mustapha, although a beautiful creature to look at, had not yet been "whispered" by Patsy. He had still an uncommonly nasty temper, and indeed most of the tricks a horse could possess. Sir Shawn thought some hard work would improve Mustapha's temper, but Patsy remained oddly unwilling. "Give me a week or two longer to get over him," he would say when Sir Shawn proposed to ride Mustapha.

He had lunched one day with Sir James Dillon, fourteen miles off, and had waited for tea, and on the way home his horse had lost a shoe. He hoped Mary would not be anxious. He had said he would be home by five, and had meant it; but Lady Dillon, who was, her friends said, the wittiest woman in Ireland, had so beguiled the time in the billiard-room after lunch that he had not noticed it passing. And, since he was not the man to ride a horse who had lost a shoe, he had walked the last six Irish miles of the road.

Very seldom did he take the road on which Terence Comerford had been killed, more than twenty years back. One could avoid it by a détour, so he had only taken it when necessity called for the short road, and he had always found it an ordeal. But he was not going to put an extra mile on to the tired horse because of his own feelings.

He had come near the dreaded spot where Terence Comerford had been flung on to the convenient heap of shingle. Already he could hear the roar of the water where it tumbled over the weir like long green hair. Above it on either side the banks of the river rose steeply. On the side nearest to him was the Mount, in the heart of which Admiral Hercules O'Hart had chosen to be buried. It was covered thickly with trees. In Spring it was beautiful with primroses which showed not a leaf between, a primrose sea which seemed in places as though a wave had run forward into the lower slopes of green grass and retreated leaving a foam of primroses behind.

The horse pulled up sharply at the sound of the waterfall and stood quivering in the darkness. There was a glimmer of light overhead, but because of the thick trees this road was very dark.

"It is only the water falling over the weir, you foolish thing!" he said, caressing the long brown nose of the little horse.

The horse answered with a whinny and, talking to him to distract his attention, Sir Shawn got him along. Perhaps the horse knew that his master's heart was cold. It was a well-nigh unendurable pain to Sir Shawn to pass the place where the friend of his youth and boyhood had been killed.

Suddenly the horse jibbed again. A long ray of light had streamed out on to the darkness of the road. At first Sir Shawn thought it was a hooded lantern. Few came this road, unless it might be a stranger who did not know the countryside traditions. But the light was steady; it did not move as a lantern carried in the hand would have done.

It flashed upon him what it was. The woman in the Waterfall Cottage must have lit her lamp, forgetting to shutter her window which looked upon the road. The cottage turned a gable to the road, from which a paling divided it. Otherwise the little place was hidden away behind a wall, approached by a short avenue from a gate some distance away. A pretty place, with a garden that looked on to the fields, but very lonely for one woman, and too near the water.

The light remained steady. As though it gave him confidence, the horse went on quietly, feeling his master's hand upon him. Just opposite the gable of the cottage a wall of loose stones led into the O'Hart park. The house had been long derelict and was going to be pulled down, now that the Congested Board, as the people called it, had acquired the O'Hart property.

Anyone who wanted to go that way knocked down a stone from the wall. There was a little cairn there always, though the employees of the Board were constantly putting back the stones.

The light from the cottage fell full on the cairn. Sir Shawn's eyes rested on it and were quickly averted. There the heap of stones for mending the road had lain that night long ago when Spitfire, had run away with Terence Comerford and thrown him. There had been blood on the stones, blood and ... and ... brains. Horrible!

Sir Shawn had come level now with the long ray of light. At the edge of it he paused. He could see plainly the interior of the room. The unshaded lamp threw its bright light into every corner of the room. It was comfortable and homelike. The furniture had belonged to the previous tenant of the cottage and had been taken over by the estate. It was good, old-fashioned furniture of a certain dignity. The grandfather clock by the wall, the tall mahogany bookcase, the sofa and chairs covered in red damask, were all good. There was a round convex mirror above the fireplace and some pictures on the wall. The fire burned brightly, toning down somewhat the hard unshaded lamplight.

A woman was sitting by the fire. She was in black with a white collar and cuffs. Her hair was braided about her head. She sat with her cheek resting in her hand, a pensive figure.

As though she knew she was being watched she started, turning her face sharply towards the window. Evidently she had forgotten to pull down the blind. As she turned, her face was in the full lamplight.

"My God!" Sir Shawn said to himself. "My God!"

He stood for a few seconds as though in pain, leaning against the horse's side, before he went on. When he lifted his head darkness had come again. The window had been shuttered.

CHAPTER IX

THE LETTER

From the pile of her letters one morning a month or so later, Lady O'Gara picked out one and eyed it with distaste. It looked mean. The envelope of flimsy paper was dirty. Some emanation came from the thing like a warning of evil: she laid it on one side, away from her honest respectable letters.

While she read through one or two of these the disreputable letter awaiting her attention worried her. It was something importunate, disagreeable, like a debased face thrust in at her door. With a sigh she turned to it, to get it out of the way before she opened Terry's letter, clean and dandyish, written on the delicate paper the Regiment affected.

She held the thing gingerly by the edge, and, going away from the table, she stood by the fire while she opened it. A smell of turf-smoke came out of it, nothing worse than that. Perhaps, after all, it was only one of the many appeals for help which came to her pretty constantly.

"HONOURED MADAM, This is from one who wishes you no harm, but onley good. There is a woman lives in the Waterfall Cottage your husband goes to see often. Such doins ought not to be Aloud.

"From your sinceer Well-Wisher, XXX."

If it had been a longer letter she would not have read it. It was so short and written so legibly that the whole disgraceful thing leaped at her in a single glance.

As though it had been a noxious reptile which had bitten her she flung it from her into the heart of the brightly burning fire of wood and turf. A little flame sprang up and it was gone, just as Sir Shawn came into the room.

They had the breakfast room to themselves now that there were no visitors, but Lady O'Gara hesitated to speak. She had no intention of keeping the matter of the anonymous letter from her husband, but she wanted to let him eat his breakfast in peace, and to talk later on, secure from possible interruptions.

She gave him scraps of news from her letters, and from The Times of the preceding day, which reached them at their breakfast table. She felt disturbed and agitated, but only as one does who has received an insult. She would be better when she had told Shawn about the horrid thing.

Her restlessness, so unlike her usual benign placidity, at last attracted her husband's notice.

"Any disturbing news, Mary?" he asked.

"Nothing." Her hand hovered over Terry's letter. "Terry thinks he can get a few days' leave next week for the pheasants and bring a couple of brother-officers with him."

"H'm!" Sir Shawn said, a little grimly. "He hasn't been away very long. I suppose Eileen is coming back."

"She comes on Monday."

"I expect he knows it."

"Perhaps he does. Have you finished, Shawn? Another cup of tea? No? I want to talk to you, dear. Will you come out to the Robin's Seat. It is really a beautiful morning."

"Let me get my pipe."

Unsuspiciously he found his pipe and tobacco pouch and followed her. The Robin's Seat was a wooden seat below a little hooded arch, under a high wall over which had grown all manner of climbing wall-plants. The arbour and the seat were on the edge of a path which formed the uppermost of three terraces: below the lowest the country swept away to the bog. The wall, made to copy one in a famous Roman garden, was beautiful at all times of the year, with its strange clinging and climbing plants that flourished so well in this mild soft air. In Autumn it was particularly beautiful with its deep reds and golds and purples and bronzes. The Robin's Seat was a favourite resting-place of these two married lovers, who fed the robins that came strutting about their feet, and even perched on their knees, asking a crumb.

Despite the disturbance of her mind Lady O'Gara had not forgotten her feathered pensioners. She threw crumbs to them as she talked, and the robins picked them up and flirted their little heads and bodies daintily, turning a bright inquiring eye on her when the supply ceased.

"Well, Mary?"

"I hate to tell you, Shawn." She brushed away the last crumbs from her lap. "I did not tell you the truth when I said there was nothing disturbing among my letters."

"I knew there was something. We have not lived so long together for me not to know you through and through. And you are as open as the day."

"It was a horrid thing, a creeping, lying thing."

"An anonymous letter." His eyes fluttered nervously under the droop of the long lashes. "You should have put it in the fire, darling."

"I did. There was so little of it that unfortunately I saw it all at a glance. It is horrid to think that anyone about here could do such a thing."

Suddenly she laughed. She had a peculiarly joyous laugh.

"They, whoever wrote it, should have said something more likely to be believed. They said, I beg your pardon for telling you, Shawn, that you were visiting a lady at the Waterfall Cottage."

She was looking at him and suddenly she saw the shadows come in his face which had had the power to disturb her before: or she thought she did. The upper part of his face was in shadow from the balsam that dropped its trails like a fringe over the arch.

"You did not believe it, Mary?"

"What do you think? Would you believe such a story of me?"

"Don't!" he said, and there was something sharp, like a cry, in the protest. "No reptile would be base enough to spit at you."

They were alone together. Below them the terraces fell to the coloured bogs. A river winding through the bog showed as a darkly blue ribbon, reflecting the cloud of indigo which hung above the bog. Beyond was the Wood of the Echoes, the trees apparently with their feet in the water in which other trees showed inverted. Not a creature to see them, but the robins.

Suddenly he put his head down on her shoulder, with the air of a tired child.

"Your correspondent was not a liar, Mary," he said. "I have visited Mrs. Wade at Waterfall Cottage, at night too, and only not by stealth because I thought that Hercules' ghost." he shivered a little, "would have kept spies and onlookers from that place."

Lady O'Gara shifted his head slightly with the greatest gentleness, so that she might caress him, stroking his hair with her fingers.

"Well, and why not?" she asked, with her air of gaiety.

"There never was such a wife as you, Mary," he said. "Go on stroking my hair. It draws the pain out."

"You have neuralgia?" she asked with quick alarm.

"No: it is a duller pain than that. It is a sort of congestion caused by keeping secrets from you."

"Secrets!" Her voice was quite unsuspicious. "You could not keep them long."

He sat up and looked at her, and she saw that there was pain in his eyes.

"I have been keeping secrets from you all our wedded life together, Mary."

She uttered a little sound of dismay, of grief. Then she said, with an assumption of an easy manner:

"And if you have, Shawn, well, they must be things I had no right to know. There are reticences I can respect. Other people's secrets might be involved...."

"That was it," he said eagerly. "There was another person's secret involved. I kept it back when it would have rested my heart to tell you."

"I shall not ask you to tell me now unless the time has come to tell. I can trust you, Shawn."

"The time may have come," he answered, drawing down her caressing hand to kiss it. "Another man might have told it to win you the more completely, Mary. He might have found justification for betraying his friend. I thought at one time you must have cared for Terence Comerford and not for me. It was the strangest thing in the world that you should have cared for me. Terence was so splendid, so big, so handsome and pleasant with everyone. How could you have preferred me before him? And I knew he wasn't fit for you, Mary. I knew there was another girl, yet I held my peace. It tortured me, to keep silence. And there was the other girl to be thought of. He owed reparation to the other girl. But his mother had her heart set on you for a daughter-in-law. I believe he would have done the right thing if he had lived, in spite of all it would have meant to his mother. He had a good heart, but, oh, my God! he should not have lifted his eyes to you when there was that other poor girl!"

He spoke in a voice as though he were being tortured, and her caressing hand felt the cold sweat ooze out on his forehead. How sensitive he was! How he grieved for his friend after all those years!

"He did not really lift his eyes to me as you say," she said. "His mother wanted it. He never did. A woman is not deceived."

"But you cared for him, to some extent?" he asked jealously.

"I never cared for any man but one," she answered. "I used to think you would never ask me. Perhaps you never would have only that I came to you when you were so broken down after your illness; and you had not strength enough to resist me."

She finished with a certain pathetic gaiety. With all his deep love for her she had not brought him joyfulness. Many people had noticed it. Her own well-spring of Joy had never run dry. It had survived even his sadness, and had made the house bright for their one child, but there had been moments, hours, when she had felt oddly exhausted, as though she had to bear a double strain of living.

"You saved me from utter despair, 'an angel beautiful and bright.' That is what you seemed to me when you showed me your exquisite pity."

"Poor Terence!" she said softly. "Do you know, Shawn, I believe he was often on the edge of telling me his secret. Over and over again he began and was interrupted, or he drew back."

"Hardly, Mary. Men do not tell such things to the ladies of their family."

"Oh!" She coloured like a girl. "It was, that. I thought it was … a lady … someone he knew in Dublin perhaps."

"It was a girl in Killesky. Her grandmother kept a little public-house. She looked like an old Gipsy-Queen, the grandmother. And the girl, the girl was like a dark rose. All the men in the county raved about her, the gentlemen, I mean. It was extraordinary how many roads led through Killesky. The girl was as modest as she was beautiful. Terence was mad about her. He knocked down a Connaught Ranger man who made a joke about her. That last leave, before he was killed, he was never out of the place. She had been at a convent school, the old woman had brought her up well, and she used to go on visits to school friends in Dublin. Terence told me he met her in Dublin when we were at the Royal Barracks. I implored him to let her alone, but he was angry and told me to mind my own business. That last time it was more serious. Poor little Bridyeen! I told him he ought to marry her. I think he knew it. It made him short-tempered with me. But … I hope … I hope…" the strange anguish came back to his voice "that he would have married her."

"I remember now," Lady O'Gara said. "I remember the girl. Aunt Grace thought very well of her; she told the old woman she ought not to have Bridyeen serving in the bar. She was a beautiful little creature, like a moss rosebud, such dark hair and the beautiful colour and the ardent look in her eyes. Old Mrs. Dowd answered Aunt Grace with a haughtiness equal to her own. Aunt Grace was very angry: she said the old woman was insolent. I did not learn exactly what Mrs. Dowd had said, but I gathered that she said she knew how to keep her girl as well as Aunt Grace did."

"I sometimes thought the old woman was ambitious," Sir Shawn went on, dreamily. "She used to watch Bridyeen while all those fellows were hanging about her and paying her compliments. I have sometimes thought she meant Bridyeen to marry a gentleman. Several were infatuated enough for that. The old woman was always about watching and listening. I don't think any of them was ever rude to the little girl. She was so innocent to look at. If any man had forgotten himself so far he would have had to answer to the others."

"What became of them, afterwards? Killesky seldom came in my path. I did not know that the picturesque old woman and the little granddaughter had gone till after we were married, when I drove that way and saw the garish new shop going up.

"It was like the old woman to carry off poor Bridyeen from all the scandal and the talk. You remember how ill I was. I thought that as soon as I was well enough I would go and see them, the old woman and the poor child. I would have done what I could. They were gone. No one knew what had become of them. They had gone away quietly and mysteriously. The little place was shut up one morning. You remember how pretty it was, the little thatched house behind its long garden. They had gone to America. Fortunately the people had not begun to talk."

"That poor little thing!" Lady O'Gara said softly. "She looked as shy as a fawn. I wonder what became of her."

"Don't you understand, Mary? She has come back. She is ... Mrs. Wade."

"Oh! She married then? Of course you would want to be kind to her. I suppose she is a widow!"

"I don't think she married. I don't know what brings her back here, unless it is the desire to return which afflicts the Irish wherever they go. She has fixed herself in such a lonely spot. After all, she is my tenant. It is my business to see that she wants for nothing. I recognized her one night I came that way, when I was late and had to take that road. I saw her through the unshuttered window with a strong light on her face. I went back there in daylight and came upon her drawing water from the well. She was frightened at first, but afterwards she seemed glad to see me. She is very lonely. No one goes to see her but Mrs. Horridge, a good creature, but Bridyeen is a natural lady. I must not go there again though she is a grey-haired woman older than her years, it was strange that I recognized her after twenty years; there are beasts who will talk."

"I shall come with you, Shawn," said Lady O'Gara. "That will be the best way to prevent their talking."

CHAPTER X

MRS. WADE

A friendship had sprung up between Mrs. Horridge and Mrs. Wade, as Sir Shawn had said, a curious friendship, not altogether equal, for Mrs. Wade had a certain amount of education and was curiously refined, America had not altered her even to the extent of affecting her speech; and that was a very exceptional thing, for the returned Americans usually came with a speech altered out of all recognition.

When Lady O'Gara came into the little sitting-room at the cottage, having knocked with her knuckles and obtained no answer, she found Susan Horridge there. Susan stood up, making a little dip, took the boy's garment she had been mending and went away, while Mrs. Wade received her visitor with a curious air of equality. It was not such an equality as she might have learnt in the United States. There was nothing assertive about it. It was quite unconscious.

She seemed profoundly agitated by Lady O'Gara's visit, her colour coming and going, her eyes dilated. She had put out a hand as Susan Horridge went away, almost as though she would have detained her by force.

"Please forgive my coming in like this," Lady O'Gara said. "I was knocking for some time, but you did not hear me. My husband, Sir Shawn O'Gara, has told me about his tenant, and I thought I would like to come and see you."

"Thank you very much, Lady O'Gara. I am sorry you had to wait at the door. Won't you sit down?"

"May I sit here? I don't like facing the light. My eyes are not over-strong."

"Dear me. They look so beautiful too."

The naïve compliment seemed to ease the strain in the situation. Lady O'Gara laughed. She had sometimes said that she laughed when she felt like to die with trouble. People had taken it for an exaggerated statement. What cause could Mary O'Gara have to feel like dying with trouble? Even though Shawn O'Gara was a melancholy gentleman, Mary seemed very well able to enjoy life.

"How kind of you!" she said merrily. "I might return the compliment. What a pretty place you have made of this!"

"I brought a few little things with me. I knew nothing was to be bought here. And the things I found here already were good."

"It is a damp place down here under the trees. Now that you have made it so pretty it would be hard to leave it. Else I should suggest another cottage. There is a nice dry one on the upper road."

"Oh! I shouldn't think of leaving this," Mrs. Wade said, nervously. Still her colour kept coming and going. America had not yellowed her as it usually had the revenants. Her dark skin was smooth and richly coloured: her eyes soft and still brilliant. Only the greying of her hair told that she was well on towards middle age.

"But it is very lonely. You are not nervous?"

"I like the loneliness."

"You should have a dog."

Her tongue had nearly slipped into saying that a dog was the kind of company that did not ask questions.

"I should have to exercise a dog."

A queer look of fear came into her eyes. Lady O'Gara could have imagined that she looked stealthily from one side to another.

"But you must go out sometimes," she said.

Again the look of fear cowered away from her. What was it that Mrs. Wade was afraid of?

"I was never one for walking," she said, lamely.

"You don't like to tear yourself from this pretty room?"

It was very pretty. The walls had been thickly whitewashed and the curtains at the window were of a deep rose-colour. A few cushions in the white chairs and sofa repeated the rose-colour. The room seemed to glow within the shadow of the many trees, overhanging too heavily outside.

"You have too many trees here," Lady O'Gara went on. "It must be pitchy towards nightfall. I shall ask my husband to cut down some of them."

She was wondering at her own way with this woman. Gentle and kindly as she was, she had approached the visit with something of shrinking, the unconscious, uncontrollable shrinking of the woman whose ways have always been honourable and tenderly guarded, from the woman who has slipped on the way, however pitiable and forgivable her fault. It is the feeling with which the nun, however much a lover of her kind, approaches the penitent committed to her care.

She suddenly realized that in this case she did not shrink. Whatever difference there might be between her and Mrs. Wade there was not that difference. They met as one honourable woman meets another. Lady O'Gara was glad that she had forgotten to shrink.

"Thank you very much," said Mrs. Wade. "It is kind of you to think of it. But, I like the trees. You are very kind, Lady O'Gara. About the dog, if I had a little gentle one, who would stay with me while I gardened and not want too much exercise, I should like it."

"I believe I can get you such a one. My cousin, Mrs. Comerford, or rather her adopted daughter, has Poms. There is a little one, rather lame, in the last litter. His leg got hurt somehow. I am sure I can have him. You will be good to him."

Mrs. Wade had drawn back into the shadow. The one window lit the space across by the fireside to the door and the other portion of the room was rather dark. But Lady O'Gara had an idea that the woman's eyes leaped at her.

"I saw the young lady," she said. "She came to Mrs. Horridge's lodge one day I was there. She was so pretty, and the little dogs with her were jumping upon her. Little goldy-coloured dogs they were."

"Yes, that would be Stella. She loves her dogs: I know she would be so glad to give you one, because you would be good to it."

"Maybe she'd bring it to me one day? She's a pretty thing. It would be nice to see her in this house."

The voice was low, but there was something hurried and eager about it. Lady O'Gara imagined that she could see the heave of the woman's breast.

"Certainly. We shall bring the puppy together. I shall tell Stella."

A sudden misgiving came to her when she had said it. Perhaps she ought to be too careful of Stella to bring her into touch with a woman who had slipped from virtue, however innocently and pitiably. It was a scruple which might not have troubled her if Stella had been her own child. There was another thing. Would Grace Comerford, if she knew all, be willing that her adopted daughter should be friends with Mrs. Wade?

Again something leaped at her from the woman's eyes, something of a gratitude which took Lady O'Gara's breath away.

"It will be nice to have a little dog of my own," she said. "It will be great company in the house at night. A little dog like that would be almost like a child. And in the daytime he'd give me word if any one was coming."

Suddenly she seemed to have a new thought. She leant forward and said in the same agitated way:

"You wouldn't be bringing Mrs. Comerford?"

"No, no," said Lady O'Gara. "I shall not bring Mrs. Comerford."

"I knew her long ago. She was kind, but she was very proud," Mrs. Wade said, dropping back into the shadow from which she had emerged.

So it was of Mrs. Comerford she was afraid! What was it? Conscience? Did she think Terence Comerford's mother could have heard anything in that far away time?

"I shall not bring Mrs. Comerford," she said. "Stella is much with me at Castle Talbot."

Again she wondered why she had said "Stella." It would have been "Miss Stella" to another woman of Mrs. Wade's class.

"Might I be making you a cup of tea, Lady O'Gara?" Mrs. Wade asked with a curiously brightening face. "I had put on the kettle in the kitchen for Mrs. Horridge. It will be boiling by this time."

Lady O'Gara was about to refuse. Then she changed her mind. A refusal might hurt Mrs. Wade. Beyond that she had a sudden curiosity, her husband had often said that she had a touch of the gamin, as to how Mrs. Wade would give her tea. Would she sit down with her in the equality of an afternoon call? There was a little twitch at the corners of her lips as she answered that she would like tea. Sir Shawn was away shooting wild duck, and she would be alone at tea if she went home.

While she waited, still with that half-delighted feeling of curiosity, she went and stood before the old-fashioned bookcase which contained Mrs. Wade's library. Very good, she said to herself. There were odd volumes of Thackeray and Dickens, Mrs. Gaskell and Charlotte Brontë. Her dimples came and were reflected as she turned about in the convex glass, with an eagle atop, over the fireplace. Outside a couple of stone eagles perched on the low roof, after the fashion of a bygone day. Far away in the silvery distance of the convex mirror a miniature Lady O'Gara dimpled.

She was remembering a pretentious lady who had called on her a few days earlier, the wife of a newly rich man who had taken Ardnavalley, a place in the neighbourhood, for the shooting. Sir Robert Smith, the multi-millionaire, was very simple. Not so Lady Smith, who had remarked that Bront was always readable.

There were also a few volumes of poetry, not very exacting, Tennyson, Adelaide Procter, Longfellow, and some Irish books, "The Spirit of the Nation," "Lady Wilde's Poems," Davis, Moore: a few devotional books.

Ah well, it was very good, gentle and innocent reading. And there was Mrs. Wade's prayer-book, The Key of Heaven, on a small table, the "Imitation of Christ" beside it. By these lay one or two oddly bound books in garish colourings, Lady O'Gara opened one. She saw it was in French, an innocuous French romance suitable for the reading of convent-school girls.

Mechanically she looked at the flyleaf. It bore an inscription; Miss Bride Sweeney, Enfant de Marie, had received this book for proficiency in Italian, some twenty-two years earlier at St. Mary's Convent.

She held the book in her hand when Mrs. Wade appeared, carrying a little tray of unpainted wood, on which was set out a tea for one person, all very dainty, from the small china cup and saucer on its white damask napkin to the thinly cut bread and butter.

Lady O'Gara had been thinking that if Mrs. Wade did not wish to be identified with Bride Sweeney, she should not leave her school-prizes about.

"Ah, you are looking at that old book," Mrs. Wade said, setting down her little tray, while she spread a tea-cloth on the table. "They are very dull stories. Even a convent-school girl could not extract much from them. I'm sorry it's so plain a tea. If I'd known your Ladyship was coming I'd have had some cakes made."

"This home-made bread is delicious," Lady O'Gara said. "But, won't you have some tea too?"

"No, thank you. I am not one for tea at every hour of the day like Mrs. Horridge. I take my tea when you are taking your dinner. You wouldn't like a boiled egg now? I've one little hen laying."

Her voice was coaxing. Now that Lady O'Gara could see the face in full light she thought it an innocent and gentle face. The eyes still looked upward with a kind of passion in their depths. She remembered her husband's epithet, "ardent." It well described Mrs. Wade's eyes. Just now the ardour was for herself. She wondered why.

"Thank you so very much," she said sweetly. "I don't think I could eat an egg, though. Your tea is delicious."

"The cream is from your own Kerries. Mrs. Horridge arranged it for me that I could get the milk from your dairy. It would make any tea good. She brings me the milk twice daily, or her little lad does."

"Susan seldom ventures out, I think," Lady O'Gara said, while she sipped her tea. "I am glad you get her beyond her own gate."

"She's a scared creature. She dreads the road. Mr. Kenny gets her all she wants from the village. She comes to me across the Mount. She doesn't mind that way even in the dark, though the people about here wouldn't take it on any account. Perhaps she doesn't know the stories. Perhaps, like myself, she thinks a ghost is better company than humans sometimes."

"Ah; you are not afraid of ghosts!"

"If I was," Mrs. Wade's eyes suddenly filled with tears, "would I be settled here? It's not thinking of the Admiral's ghost I'd be. Maybe there's some you'd welcome back from the grave, if you loved them well enough. I can't imagine anyone not wanting the dead back, if so be that you loved them."

Her voice died off in a wail, and suddenly it came to Lady O'Gara that just outside, where the water fell over the weir, Terence Comerford had met with his death.

"No," she said softly, "I cannot imagine any one being afraid of the dear dead."

As she said it she remembered the shadows about her husband's face and her heart was cold.

It was only later that she wondered if Mrs. Wade had chosen that lonely spot to return to because there Terence Comerford's handsome head had lain in its blood. It occurred to her at the same time that not one word had passed between them which could indicate that she knew anything of Mrs. Wade beyond that she had been a dweller in these parts long before she had come to be a tenant of Sir Shawn O'Gara at the Waterfall Cottage.

A curious thing that there should be there side by side, thrown into an odd companionship, two women who had reason to be afraid and had chosen these lonely places to hide. Poor Susan! The reason for her hiding was obvious. With Mrs. Wade it was another matter. Why need she have come back if she so dreaded her past? Or was it the memory of Terence Comerford that drew her, the thought of the old tragedy and the old passion?

CHAPTER XI

THE ONLY PRETTY RING-TIME

Castle Talbot took on new lightness and brightness when Terry came home. His mother said fondly that it was like the Palace of the Sleeping Beauty where life hung in suspense between his goings and comings. The mere presence of this one young man seemed to put all the servants on their mettle. The cook sent up such meals as she did not at any other time. "Sure Sir Shawn and her Ladyship never minded what they would be atin'," she said. The gardener, a gruff old cynic usually, gave his best grapes and peaches for "Master Terry"; even the small sewing maid who sat in a slip of a room at a remote corner of the house, mending the house-linen under the supervision of the housekeeper, was known to have said that though she never saw Master Terry she felt he was there.

The dogs were aware of his coming before he came. They had their own intuitions of the joyful expectancy in the house and what it meant. Shot would take to lying in the hall, with one wistful eye fixed on the open hall door, while Lady O'Gara's two Poms became quite hysterical, rushing out when there was no one at all or someone they were well accustomed to, assailing them with foolish shrieks.

"It is all right when Terence is coming home," Lady O'Gara said, smiling. "I can forgive Chloë and Cupid for yapping. It is when he is gone and they rush out at every sound that I find it unbearable."

"You will kill the fatted calf for Terry," Sir Shawn grumbled, "as though he had been a year away. The youngster does nothing but amuse himself. When I was his age we got in some hard work at soldiering."

"Every generation says the same of the one that comes after it," Lady O'Gara rejoined. "Terry loves his work, though he manages to enjoy himself."

"Too much of a golden youth," grumbled his father. "You spoil the boy, Mary!" But his eyes were glad all the time, and the grumbling was only a pretence.

"You'll see what the golden boys are capable of if the war they are always talking about comes in our time," Lady O'Gara said, and a swift shadow passed over her face. "I hope there will be no more wars, even to vindicate them. I suffered enough in those years of the South African War when you were out and Terry and I were alone."

Eileen arrived a few hours earlier than Terry. She clapped her hands to her ears when she arrived, and the Poms broke out into shrill chorus. Shot, who began already to be very dim-sighted, came to the door to see what the clamour was about, and with the most indifferent movement of his tail returned to his place on the rug before the fire.

"Little beasts!" said Eileen, poking viciously at the Poms with her umbrella. "I don't know how you endure them, Cousin Mary; I can hardly tell which is the worst, Chloë or Cupid."

Eileen had never liked the dogs any more than she liked the horses. She was fond of cats and had a favourite smoke-blue Persian, between whom and the Poms there was an armed neutrality. The cat's name was Cleopatra, and she deserved it. Her green eyes shone like emeralds when she curled boa-fashion about her mistress's white neck and looked down at the Poms.

Lady O'Gara had come out on the steps to meet Eileen and had kissed her on each cold satin cheek, making a tender fuss about removing her wraps. Her coldnesses were easily dispelled.

"Come right in, darling, and have some tea," she said fondly. "Why, you are perished! It is very cold. We shall have a frost to-night. And how are all at home?"

"Oh, much the same as usual. Mother has rheumatism. Dad is grumbling over his large and expensive family and the bad year it has been for everything. It is always a bad year with farmers, isn't it? The house is tight-packed, as usual. They always have visitors. I was glad to escape to this delicious roominess. They are all outrageously well and hungry, as Dad says. And some of them will love to come after Christmas, if you can really have them. They must be at home for Christmas, they say. I am sure some of them could well be spared."

A momentary vision passed before Lady O'Gara's inner eyes. It was of Mrs. Anthony Creagh and the quiverful, three boys and five girls then, to be increased later. Mrs. Anthony sat in her armchair, one child on her lap, a second with its face buried in her trailing, somewhat shabby silk skirt, two others peeping from behind her chair. The boys were at a table with books open before them. Eileen, aged eight, and already the beauty of the family, stood by her mother's knee, eating an apple.

"Cousin Mary wants one of my little girls to go home with her," Mrs. Creagh had said, rather tearfully. She was an incurably motherly person, whose heart expanded with the quiver, "She wants one of my little girls to play with her Terry. Who will go?"

The boys had looked indifferent. The child whose face was buried in her mother's skirts seemed to burrow a little further in, while the two standing behind the chair disappeared. The baby on its mother's knee only gurgled cheerfully, as though at the best joke in the world.

Then Eileen had laid down her half-eaten apple, and turning, had thrust her moist little hand into Lady O'Gara's, warm from her muff. Dear friendly thing! Lady O'Gara had brought her back in triumph to Castle Talbot, feeling that she could never do enough to make up to the child for forsaking for her that long family, happy and happy-go-lucky. Eileen had become conventional in her growing-up, not much like the others, who frolicked like puppies and grew up pretty well at their own sweet will.

"I told Mother she should not fill the house with visitors in addition to her long family, if Dad had had a bad year," said Eileen, putting off her furs in the hall. "She said that what people ate never counted. Isn't it just like Mother? What a jolly fire, darling Cousin Mary! And how sweet to see you again!"

She took up Lady O'Gara's hand and kissed it. She had done the same thing that evening long ago when she had come for the first time to Castle Talbot, and had snuggled against Lady O'Gara in the brougham, warming her heart, which was chilly because in a very short time Terry was to go off to his preparatory school for Eton. It was his father's will and she had not grumbled, but she had often felt in her own heart that she had had very little of Terry since he was eight years old.

"Come and eat something," she said, leading the girl into the drawing-room, where the lamps had been lit and the tea-table drawn near the fire. "I told Cook to send up an extra good tea, knowing you would be cold and hungry after your journey."

"How delicious!" Miss Creagh said, lifting off one cover after another. "I haven't had a decent tea since I went away. We are such a hungry family, to say nothing of the visitors."

"Terry will be here in time for dinner," Lady O'Gara said, her eyes joyful. "So put on your best bib-and-tucker. We don't get many occasions to wear our finery. I shall wear my Limerick lace and emeralds."

"And Terry won't see them because he will be thinking only of yourself," Eileen said, devouring sandwiches and hot cakes. For a girl of her slender delicacy she had a very good appetite and usually indulged it, although there were moments when she tried to hold it in check, having detected, as she said, a tendency to embonpoint.

"I can really afford to be greedy, Cousin Mary," she said, with a laughing apology. "I've been starved at Inver. How the stacks of food went! They have such healthy appetites. I couldn't eat potato-cakes, soaked in butter, nor doorsteps as the boys called them, of bread and jam and honey. Fearfully fattening food."

"You remind me of when you came to me and started to grow out of your clothes with such alarming rapidity. When your white satin, long-waisted frock grew too small for you, you said, for you did not like giving it up, 'I can really get into it if I hold myself in like this. And anyhow I've given up pudding!'"

"Ah, that was the worst of me," said Eileen mournfully. "I could never continue long doing without pudding."

She came down to dinner wearing a pale green frock with a prim fichu of chiffon and lace. Terry had already arrived and was in the drawing-room, standing on the hearthrug with his back to the fire.

"Hullo, Eileen!" he shouted, "How stunning you look! You grow prettier every day!"

The compliment was too brotherly in its easy candour to please her altogether: but she knew very well she was "stunning." She could see herself in a long old-fashioned mirror on the wall. Her hair was like gold floss. There was no sign of the embonpoint she feared in the slender grace of her figure. The pearls about her neck became her mightily, as did the green ribbon, the same shade as her dress, snooded in her hair.

She lifted her eyes to the boy's frank gaze in a way which she had usually found very effective. She had been able to do anything with Terry when she looked at him like that, and she had tried the same allurement on others than Terry.

"You're only just back," he went on. "Jolly nice of you to come for me. The mater must have missed you."

"They insist on my presence at Inver now and again. I don't know why. It is very unreasonable of them!"

She put out a satin slipper and stirred Shot with it.

"The only drawback to this dear house," she said, "is that there are dogs everywhere."

Shot growled in his sleep. Perhaps she had not touched him in quite the right way. She withdrew her foot in alarm, more alarm that she felt, and turned eyes of a child-like fear upon Terry. "Oh! Shot is cross," she said innocently. The man in Terry answered. He bent towards her as though drawn irresistibly.

There was a flutter of feminine garments in the doorway of the room. Someone looked in and withdrew. Sir Shawn, coming down the stairs, did not notice the small figure by the fire in the hall, fast fading to ashes, the centre of a circle of adoring dogs, who had withdrawn themselves from Miss Creagh's unfriendliness.

He went on to the drawing-room door. He too was attracted by the tableau. Nothing could have been prettier than the boy's bold advance, the girl's withdrawal. They were too engrossed in each other, or appeared to be, to notice his face in the doorway.

With a deep sigh, as of relief, he turned away. Then he caught sight of the pink blob by the fireplace in the hall. Stella was down on her knees feeding the dying fire with sods of turf. Her rose geranium frock made what the children call a "cheese" about her. Her golden brown head was charming against the audacious colour of her frock. The dogs had taken advantage of her position to press about her. Now and again she pushed off Cupid, who was the bold one, with the sod of turf in her hand.

Sir Shawn felt particularly kind towards the girl.

"Hullo, Stella," he said: "I didn't know you had come."

"Some little time ago," she replied. "Grannie is with Lady O'Gara. Do you mind my making up the fire?"

"Not a bit." His heart was light within him, almost to the extent of taking Stella into his confidence. Discreet little thing! She, too, had surprised the pretty picture in the drawing-room, and had withdrawn, leaving the lovers to themselves.

"The lovers." He said the words over to himself, mouthing them as though they were sweet. He had been unnecessarily alarmed. Things were arranging themselves beautifully. He believed in early marriages. The happiness of the youngsters would keep him young. He would get away from his shadows. After a while Terry must come home and settle down somewhere near. A few years of soldiering in these piping times of peace were as much as the boy need do.

So his mind ran on into the happy future while he sat on the arm of one of the red-leather chairs and beamed at Stella, who had always been rather alarmed of Sir Shawn, and came out now as prettily as a flower in the warm sun.

He looked at his watch. It was a quarter to eight. Dinner-time. A pity the youngsters had not more time to settle their pretty affair. He began to think of what gift he would give Eileen. His mother's pearl cross, large pearls set en cabochon. Mary had so many things. She would not grudge that to Terry's wife.

There were Mary and Grace Comerford coming down the staircase, talking as though they did not see each other constantly. How well Mary looked in the brown silk! It brought out the dear shades of red in her hair and eyes.

He went over and joined the two ladies.

"Only just in time!" he said, in rather a loud voice, as he opened the drawing-room door.

He intended it as a warning, but it was apparently not necessary. Terry was sitting in a chair at one side of the fireplace with Shot's head on his knee. Miss Creagh, a cloud on her face, was in the opposite chair, caressing Cleopatra. Sir Shawn's heart sank. Had they been quarrelling, silly children? He began to tremble for his dream.

"Cleopatra scratched Shot's nose," said Terry, holding up the liver-coloured nose for inspection. "See, it has bled. Eileen will have it that it was Shot's fault. Of course it was not. Shot is so gentle."

He stood up to meet the ladies and, swift as an arrow from the bow, he went to Stella's side.

Poor Sir Shawn! Poor gentleman! The fabric of his rosy dreams had faded to ashes. He looked almost piteously towards Eileen: and, unreasonably, was angry with her because with that sullenness of expression her beauty had departed: she was almost plain. Under his breath he damned Cleopatra.

CHAPTER XII

MOTHER-LOVE

Somehow or other Lady O'Gara found it difficult to get Stella to herself in the days that followed. There were times when she almost thought that Stella deliberately kept away. Sir Shawn had often said, rallying his wife, that Mary never saw further than her own nose. She was a little bewildered about the young people. Terry and Eileen seemed to have quarrelled. Eileen found occupations that kept her in her own room. She had suddenly developed a desire to make herself a coat and skirt, and Lady O'Gara had gone in many times, to find her pinning and fitting on the lay-figure which occupied the centre of the room, surrounded by all manner of snippets and pieces.

This ridiculous pre-occupation of Eileen's gave Lady O'Gara something she did not complain of. She had more of her son than otherwise she would have had. Terry had never looked for better companionship than his mother's, but he grumbled about Eileen nevertheless.

"She used to be always ready to come anywhere," he said. "I know I can't always have you, because Father needs you so much. We have always torn you in pieces between the two of us. I asked Eileen to come out shooting on the bog with me and she wouldn't. She just opened her door and I saw a horrid thing, an indecent thing that pretended to look like a woman's body, taking up the middle of her room."

"It's for fitting dresses on, you ridiculous boy!" Lady O'Gara said laughing.

"It gave me a shock. A horrid, stuffed thing. I shall not be able to look at Eileen again without seeing that. Why does she want to make her dresses? Can't your maid do it? Industry in Eileen is quite a new thing. Not that she's half as good a companion on the bog as you are, darling. I've always had to carry her over the pools. She said she couldn't jump."

Lady O'Gara's face at this frankness was a study.

"She's so helpless. Not like a country girl, at all. You remember that day with the bull. She left Stella to be gored by the bull and expected to be admired for it."

There was certainly a change in Terry's attitude towards Eileen. Lady O'Gara sighed, because of what she knew was in her husband's mind rather than for any disappointment in herself. Eileen was not her ideal wife for Terry.

"Eileen will go with you all right," she said. They were standing in front of the house on the gravel-sweep. "I've just told her she was injuring her complexion by staying indoors. She has gone to put on her hat. I did not like to tell her that Margaret McKeon lamented to me that Eileen was cutting out that beautiful Foxford tweed so badly. We'll go and rout out Stella. She has not been over here for five days."

Terry's face lit up.

"I don't know why Stella's out with me," he said. "She is always hiding behind your skirts or Mrs. Comerford's when I am about and want to talk to her."

His mother looked at him, with the yearning tenderness of the woman who would give all the world to her beloved man if she only might.

"You like Stella?"

"Yes: she's a little darling. Don't you?"

"I am very fond of Stella. Perhaps ... she thinks ... You like Eileen very much?"

After all, if her boy wanted Stella, why should even his father's preferences prevail? She had surprised a glance in Stella's eyes when they rested on Terry for a brief moment before they quickly veiled themselves. The child had something Southern in her. So, for the matter of that, had Terry. She was fond of Eileen, but, simple as she was, she had not had Eileen with her pretty constantly for many years without being aware of a certain shallowness in the girl. The blood under the fair skin ran thinly, coldly.

His face lit up with such a light that she was alarmed at what she had done. What would Shawn say if he knew? But, after all, Shawn had married where he loved. Why should not the boy have the same felicity? Stella had been pushing her small soft way into Mary O'Gara's heart. She knew now that Eileen could never have been the little daughter she wanted.

"You think she would mind that?" His eyes leaped at her.

She felt like one who had burnt her boats. She would not look before or behind. Shawn was wrong, she said vehemently to herself. Eileen was not the girl for Terry.

"I will tell you a secret, Terry," she said. "The first evening you came back, in the drawing-room before dinner, there was something that might have passed for a love-scene between you and Eileen. Your father opened the door and withdrew. Then he discovered that Stella had come downstairs before him and was playing with the dogs in the hall by the dying fire. He supposed that she had surprised that scene before he did."

Oh, poor Shawn! What a use she was making of his confidence! But men never knew about their sons as mothers did. She would give anything, except her own soul, to procure Terry the joy he desired. And it was a good joy. She loved Stella. Of course, she would be very good to Eileen, but she did not want Eileen for a daughter-in-law. Shawn did not look very deeply. He had hardly considered Eileen except as something pretty and gentle, who was pleasant in the house and sang him Moore's Melodies of evenings in a small sweet voice. He missed her when she returned to her own people.

"I was an idiot for a second," the boy said, shamefacedly. "I don't suppose you understand, Mother, but men are like that. Eileen can be very alluring when she likes and..."

"Don't tell me anymore. I can imagine," Lady O'Gara said and laughed, a laugh which had a certain shyness in it.

"Then we fell out over the cat and dog," he said. "Eileen was rather rude. Perhaps I was a little rough with Cleopatra, but she had scratched Shot's nose. You know what Shot is! It was an entirely unprovoked attack. I believe I did say that Cleopatra should be sent to the Cats' Home."

Eileen appeared at this point, coming with an unwilling air. It was true that her staying within-doors so much had not improved her looks. She had not a very good circulation at any time. That, or her mood, had given her rose and white a dull, leaden look. Her discontented little face was lifted towards the dappled sky. It was really a beautiful day of Autumn. There was a little wind, and the last yellow leaves on the branches tinkled like so many small golden cymbals. A pale gold sun was going low amid oceans of amber touched with rose, and above dappled clouds were floating as though the day was February.

"It is so cold," said Eileen, and shivered. "I don't see how Margaret can get on without fitting me. She had made up such a nice fire in my room. I cannot see why any one wants to go out in such weather."

"Oh, come along, you little grumbler!" Lady O'Gara said with her infectious gaiety. "Come for a good trot. I know what will happen to you: you'll get chilblains if you sit by the fire in cold weather. Your hands will be dreadful to look at, and your feet will be a torture."

Eileen looked down at her feet and then at her hands, childishly. She had very pretty feet and hands.

"They are all right so far," she said.

"You and Terry had better race each other to the bridge," Lady O'Gara said. "I want to see the colour in your face, child."

"Come along," said Terry, and caught at Eileen's hand. Half-unwillingly she ran with him, but when Lady O'Gara caught up with them, Eileen was laughing and panting.

"This wretched son of yours," she said, "has run me off my feet."

"And you look the better for it," Lady O'Gara answered, her brown eyes merry and her cheeks dimpling like a girl's. "We are going for Stella, to bring her back to tea. She has not been near us for some days."

"Oh!" Eileen had gone back to the chilly voice. "She doesn't want to come. She finds us rather dull, I think."

Lady O'Gara laughed.

"I don't believe anyone could find us dull," she said merrily, "least of all Stella."

"Oh well, I suppose I'm not telling the truth," Eileen said huffily. "All I know is she asked me the last time I saw her if Terry ever brought any of his brother-officers home with him."

Terry's candid face clouded over ever so slightly; while his mother remarked that, of course, three was an awkward number for games. They wanted another man. She believed she had been talking about it.

"You might ask Major Evelyn," she said to Terry. "It is still possible to have golf when there is fine weather."

"I wonder if he would come?" Terry said ingenuously. "Think of a second-lieutenant like me asking a swell like Evelyn! Why, his decorations make a perfect breastplate when he chooses to put them on. Not that it is a matter of choice. He only does it when he can't help it. He did so splendidly in South Africa."

"I dare say he'd condescend to come," Lady O'Gara said. "Few sportsmen can resist the Castle Talbot duck-shooting."

"Do ask him," said Eileen, becoming animated. "Two's company, three's none. Everything is lop-sided without a second man."

"I'll ask him, of course," Terry said. "But I don't suppose he'll come. It is like a kid in the Lower School asking a prefect to tea. He may come, for the grub. On the other hand he may give the kid a kicking for his impudence."

After all, they had not to go as far as Inch. They met Stella exercising her dogs about half a mile from her own gates. She would like to come to tea if she might first take the dogs home and leave word as to where she had gone.

To Lady O'Gara's mind she looked small and unhappy as soon as the flush had faded which came when she saw them. She clung to Lady O'Gara, and could not be detached from her. The dogs, surrounding her, made a barrier between her and Terry, who, at first, kept as close to her as he could, leaving Eileen to walk the other side of Lady O'Gara.

But Stella did not seem to have much to say to him. She was too engrossed with the dogs and with his mother to spare him a word. The eager light which had come to his eyes when he had first caught sight of her faded. His candid face was overcast. She had been keeping him at arms-length ever since he had come back.

His mother watched him with a comprehension which was half tender amusement, half compassion. He was becoming a little sullen over Stella's persistent disregard of him. She watched the set boyish mouth, the pucker of his forehead, her baby. Terry had always had that pucker for perplexity or disappointment. Why, he had had it when the first down was on his baby head, as soft as a duckling's.

The road grew narrow. He began to lag behind, to veer towards Eileen.

"Is it worthwhile for us all to go on to Inch?" he asked in his discontented young voice. "Supposing Eileen and I go on by the river, while you and Stella take back the dogs! They wouldn't follow me or I'd offer to go home with them. It must be nearly a mile to the house from the gate."

"I've a better way than that," Lady O'Gara said on a sudden impulse. She had taken Stella's cold little hand in hers, and it made a mute appeal. She was sure Stella was unhappy, poor little motherless child. The two poor children, fretting and worrying each other about nothing at all! Her comprehending, merry, pitiful gaze went from one to the other young face.

"Suppose Eileen and I walk back. You'll overtake us before we get home. You two are such quick walkers."

Eileen's lips opened as though to protest. Her face had brightened at Terry's suggestion. She closed them again in a tight snap.

"I never can see the good of walking about wet roads," she said crossly. "It must be nice to live in a town, where there are dry pavements, and people, and shops."

A robin rained out his little song from a bough above her head, and behind the trees the sky broke up into magnificence, the sun looking from under a great dun cloud suffused with his rays, while all below him was a cool greenish bluish wash of sky, tender and delicate.

"You would not find that in a city, Eileen," Lady O'Gara said, pushing away gently Stella's cold little hand that seemed to cling to hers.

"Make her trot, Terry," she said. "Her hands are cold as little frogs, like the child's hands in Herrick's 'Grace for a Child.'

"Cold as paddocks though they be,
Still I lift them up to thee
For a benison to fall
On our meat and on us all."

She saw the sudden rush of joy to her son's face and she was a little lonely. She felt that she was no longer first with Terry.

CHAPTER XIII

THE OLD LOVE

Sir Shawn was still out when they got back, after a brisk walk. The laggard young people made no appearance for tea, though they waited a while. Eileen grumbled discontentedly over everything being cold and suggested a carelessness in Stella about other people's convenience. The tea-cakes had been kept warm over a spirit-lamp, but she was in a captious mood. Lady O'Gara wondered at the girl, who had sometimes been embarrassingly effusive in the display of her affection. Had she spoilt Eileen? or was the girl feeling sore and a little out of it?

The suggestion that Eileen might be feeling Terry's desertion of her was enough to soften his mother's heart towards the captious girl, who as soon as she had finished her tea, and a very good tea she made, went off to see how Margaret McKeon was progressing with her skirt.

At the door she turned about.

"Do you think I might have a new evening frock, Cousin Mary?" she asked. "My pink has gone out of fashion. There are such beautiful blues in some patterns I have got from Liberty's: I could make it myself, with Margaret's help. It would only need a little lace to trim it, or some of that pearl trimming Liberty's use so much."

"Certainly, my dear child. Let me know what it will cost. I have a piece of Carrickmacross lace somewhere which would make a fichu. You must remind me, Eileen. We live so quietly here that I do not remember how the fashions change."

"I've hardly noticed, either," said Eileen, with a hand on the door handle. "The pink does very well for home-wear. But if Terry is going to have friends, I should want something a little smarter."

Lady O'Gara smiled. So Eileen was interested in the coming of Major Evelyn! And she had made so good a tea that any one less ethereal-looking than Eileen might have been considered greedy! She had left very little of the abundant tea to be removed.

"We'll have a turning-out one of these days," she said. "I noticed your wardrobe was very full the other day when I was in your-room. We can send off what you don't want to Inver, and I shall add a few lengths of that Liberty silk. Brigid and Nora are so clever with that little sewing machine I gave them last Christmas that they'll turn out something very pretty for themselves."

"They've no occasion for pretty things," said Eileen. "There never was any young man there but Robin Gillespie, the doctor's son. He is in India in the R.A.M.C. Brigid liked him, I think, but he was not thinking of Brigid."

Then she closed the door on her departing footsteps, leaving Lady O'Gara to her thoughts.

She put the consideration of Eileen from her a little impatiently. She was afraid Eileen was selfish. She did not seem to have any desire to share her good things with her family, not even with her mother, yet Mrs. Creagh was a very sweet mother; Mrs. Comerford who had a cynical way sometimes had remarked one day when Eileen had been very caressing with Lady O'Gara: "If your mother is like what I remember her you need not go further for some one to love."

It was the day on which Lady O'Gara had given Eileen her necklet of amethysts and seed-pearls, a beautiful antique thing, of no great intrinsic value beyond its workmanship.

It suddenly came to her that, for a good while past, she had got into a way of propitiating Eileen with gifts. It had not occurred to her exactly as propitiation, but she had learnt that when Eileen was out of sorts the gift of some pretty thing worked wonders. Had she been spoiling the girl? Was she herself responsible for the whims and fancies which Eileen took so often nowadays? In the old days it had not been so. Eileen had been sweet-tempered and placidly selfish. There was a change in her of late. It was quite unlike the old Eileen to go away and leave her sitting alone in the drawing-room with only two watchful Poms, each with a bright eye upon her from their respective chairs, and Shot stretched at her feet, to keep her company.

She acquitted herself. Love and generosity ought not to spoil any one: they ought to lift up, to awake their like. Was Eileen in love with Terry and resenting his desertion? No; she said emphatically in her thoughts. She would have known if Eileen cared. If it had been that she could have been very tolerant.

Her thoughts went back to the first beginnings of difficulty with Eileen, and she fixed them at the date of her return from her visit home during the preceding summer. The fatted calf had been killed for the girl's return. Lady O'Gara remembered how she had anticipated it, and had thought of what Eileen liked, the special food and sweets, and so on. She had kept Margaret McKeon busy with the new chintz curtains and cushions for Miss Eileen's room, and when it was all finished had fussed about doing one little thing and another till the privileged maid had been moved to protest.

"Hasn't Miss Eileen had everything she wanted from the lucky day for her that she came here? Don't be robbin' yourself, m'lady."

Lady O'Gara had taken some of her own pretty things, a crystal clock, a silver and tortoiseshell box for the toilet table, things Eileen particularly admired, and had added them to the other pretty things, her gifts, of which the room had many. She had brought an armful of her dearest books: and she had insisted on pink roses because Eileen particularly liked pink.

After all Eileen had been cold when she came. It had been like a douch of cold water. She had not recovered her sweet placidity since that time. Lady O'Gara had commented on the change to her husband, but he had not seen it. He was fond of Eileen, in a superficial way. Indeed his devotion to and absorption in his wife were such that almost all other affection in him must be superficial by contrast. To two people his love had been given passionately, to Terence Comerford and to his wife. He never spoke of the dead friend. It was a well-understood thing in the circle that Terence Comerford was not to be spoken of carelessly, when Sir Shawn was within hearing.

Sitting alone in the firelight, except for the adoring dogs, Lady O'Gara let her thoughts wander on away from Eileen. How deep and passionate was Shawn's love when it was given. He had shrunk from that first meeting with Mrs. Comerford after all those years. He had turned pale when she had taken his hand in hers, looking at him with a long gaze that asked pardon for her past unreason and remembered that he and her dead son had been dearer than brothers. After all those years that touch with the past had opened the floodgates of grief in Shawn O'Gara. Only his wife knew the anguish, the disturbed nights and the weary days that followed. Grief in him was like a sharp physical suffering.

Dear Shawn! How glad she was that she was so strong and healthy and had such good spirits always, so as to be able to cheer and comfort him. She smiled to herself, remembering how some of her friends had pitied her because she must always be uplifting his mood. She had never wearied nor found it an irksome effort. A serious sad thought came to her; when the hour of the inevitable parting came she prayed it might be her lot to be left desolate rather than his.

She looked at her little watch, a delicate French thing, with a tiny painted picture on the back framed within pearls ending in a true-lovers'-knot, one of Shawn's many gifts. Six o'clock. It was time Shawn was home. She was very glad he had not ridden Mustapha, as he had wanted to. Patsy Kenny had dissuaded him. Terry must have stayed on at Inch for tea. It had been a cold bright day, and it must be turning to frost, for the fire was burning so redly. The cold was on the floor too, for the little dogs had left their baskets and taken to the chairs, a thing supposed to be strictly forbidden, although as a matter of fact Chloë and Cupid were always cheerfully disobedient. She wished Shawn was home. He had gone up the mountains to a shooting-lodge, where was a party of men gathered to shoot red deer. He had been out overnight and he would be very tired when he came home after a long drive on an outside car. Well, after all, it was better than Mustapha. Patsy's unwillingness to see Sir Shawn go out on Mustapha had infected her, little nervous as she was where horse-flesh was concerned.

She comforted herself. It was not like those dreadful days when there had been trouble with the tenants, and she had sat in this very room, listening in anguish for the sound of the horse's hoofs coming fast. Terry had been away at his preparatory school then. She had never told any one her terrors. Perhaps some of the servants had guessed them. She remembered the night of the Big Wind, when Shawn had been out, and the house had shaken in the first onslaught of the hurricane, before he came.

There was a butler's pantry close to the drawing-room door which had always an open window. She had often stolen in there in the dark to listen for the sound of the mare's trot. Fatima had been Shawn's favourite mount in those days, and no one could mistake the sound of her delicate feet in the distance. There, with her ear to the night, Mary O'Gara had listened and listened, her heart thumping so fast sometimes that she could not be sure if she heard the horse's hoofs. Only, as she used to say joyously afterwards, there was really no mistaking Fatima's trot when she was coming.

Once, Rafferty, the old butler, who was dead now, had opened the pantry door suddenly, and had all but let the tray of Waterford glass he was carrying fall, for the fright she had given him.

She remembered how on that night of the Big Wind, when her terror was at its worst, Patsy Kenny had asked to see her about something or other; how she had gone into the office to talk to him; how he had talked gently about Fatima, how sure-footed she was and how wise, and how little likely to be frightened as long as she was carrying her master. He had wandered off into simple homely talk, about the supply of turf, how the fair had gone, the price the people were getting for their beasts;

now and again leaving off to say, when the moan of the wind came and the house shook: "Glory be to God, it's goin' to be a wild night, so it is!" Or "That was a smart little clap o' win'. It's a great blessin' to be on dry land to-night."

Patsy's way with the dumb beasts was well known; and Lady O'Gara had said afterwards, when she had her husband warm and dry by the fire, and she too happy, being relieved of her terrors, to mind the storm which had not yet reached anything like its height, that Patsy had soothed her as though she were a nervous horse.

Shawn had been younger and stronger then. He had laughed at her fears and had insisted on making a night of it, keeping a roaring fire and lamplight all through the terrifying din, while the servants in the kitchen said their Rosary and prayed for the night to be over. Sometime in the wild late dawn, when the wind was subsiding, Shawn had made her go to bed, saying he would follow. But he had not come for a long time, and she had dropped asleep and wakened to his weary face beside her bed, and to hear him saying that, thank God, they had got out the horses, although the stables were all but in ruins.

As she thought over these things the fulness of her love for her husband swept her heart like a Springtide. It was sweet yet poignant, for she had the pity beyond all telling in her love for Shawn. Suddenly she began to be a little in dread because she had been going against what she knew were his wishes. Would he mind very much if Terry's choice were Stella and not Eileen? She hoped he would not, at first. Later on, when he knew little Stella better, with her soft appealing ways, he would be glad. Eileen would never be such a dear little daughter. Stella had not those ardent eyes for nothing.

Her disinclination to let the winds of heaven blow too roughly on the men she loved, for whom she had always the maternal pity, brought a sharp revulsion of feeling. After all, the world was for the young. They had never refused Terry anything. In a detached way the father was very fond of his boy. He was not necessary to him. No one was that except his wife: but he had been a kind, indulgent father. Why should not Terry wait a little till his father came to know Stella better? Things would be all right then. Shawn had seemed to avoid Stella, perhaps because he avoided Mrs. Comerford.

At last there was Terry's ringing step in the hall. There could be little doubt to the mother's mind of what tidings he brought. There was triumph in the step.

He burst in on his mother like a young wind.

"Darling," he said, "I'm so very sorry not to have come home for tea. I simply couldn't induce Stella to: she's so dreadfully shy, but she adores you. Congratulate me!"

He placed his two young firm hands on his mother's shoulders, and stooping, he kissed her.

"I shall never love you any less, you know," he said boyishly. "You angel, how you helped us! Not many mothers of an only boy would have done it."

To their ears came the sound of wheels, approaching the house, now near, now far, as the long avenue turned and twisted.

"It is your father," said Lady O'Gara. "He will be very tired. Don't tell him yet, Terry. He hardly knows Stella. You are very young. It will have to be something of a long engagement."

"Oh!" he said, but less disappointedly than she had feared, "You too! Mrs. Comerford said we must wait. I don't want to wait. I want to shout out to the whole world that Stella is mine, but, of course, I know. Father would rather have had Eileen. I have known Eileen since I was eight years old. Love does not come that way."

He was repeating her own words, her own thought. She was relieved that he was so amenable.

"After all," she said roguishly, "there have been moments when you seemed on the edge of falling in love with Eileen. Last June we thought it was all but settled, your father and I."

"Oh," he said shamelessly, "when the true gods come the half-gods go."

Sir Shawn came into the room. He was pale and tired and the shadows crept in the hollows of his cheeks. She was glad he was not to be disturbed by Terry's love-story to-night. She wondered if he would notice the shining radiance of the boy's face. Joy, the triumphant joy of the accepted lover, dazzled there to her eyes. She was relieved when the boy went away and left them alone. When Shawn was tired he was irresistible to her tenderness. For the moment even Terry was out of it.

CHAPTER XIV

STELLA GOES VISITING

Lady O'Gara had met Stella, had drawn her to her and kissed her warmly and softly.

"Your Granny will not have it just yet, Stella," she said, "so we need not announce it, need we? As though all the world will not read it in Terry's eyes!"

It made it easier that Mrs. Comerford was somewhat unreasonable about the engagement. There was too short an acquaintance, she said. Three months, what was three months? And they had not had three weeks of each other's society. Too slender a foundation on which to build a life's happiness. And Terry had been obviously in love, or what such children called love, with Eileen, when they came. He must be sure of himself before she gave him Stella.

She had drawn back in some curious way, Lady O'Gara felt, for she had seemed pleased when Terry openly displayed his infatuation. The most candid creature alive, although for the moment she held a secret, Lady O'Gara was puzzled by something in Grace Comerford. Once she said that she was sorry she had yielded to the ridiculous Irish passion for return: and when Mary O'Gara had looked at her with a certain pain in her expression she had railed upon the wet Irish climate. But the weather was not what she had meant. Had she not said that in Italy and Egypt she had been parched for the Atlantic rain-storms and the humid atmosphere of Western Ireland?

It was a relief that the duck-shooting had begun with the frost: that there was rough shooting in the other days to keep the men out of doors. Major Evelyn and another man, a cheerful little blonde boy named Earnshaw, had got a few days leave from the Curragh. Their presence imposed a certain restraint upon Terry in regard to his love-making, otherwise it must have been obvious even to his father, despite that growing absent-mindedness which enfolded Shawn O'Gara like a mist.

Eileen seemed happy once again. Lady O'Gara began to reproach herself; doubtless Castle Talbot in Winter was a lonesome place for the young. Young Earnshaw was obviously épris with Stella, while Major Evelyn, a big, laughing brown man, attached himself to Eileen.

Eileen, despite her dislike of the sound of a shot, she would clap her hands over her pretty ears, with their swinging hoops of turquoise, whenever a gun was fired, went out with the guns when they shot the last of the pheasants, she at least managed to accompany the lunch. In the evenings she sang to the tired happy men, her Irish songs, while Major Evelyn watched her, an admiring light in his brown eyes. He was half-Irish, and the sentiment of the songs appealed to him. Night after night Eileen went through her little repertoire, charming with her soft, veiled voice, and Sir Shawn was drawn in from his office to listen with the others. Only occasionally Stella put in an appearance, which was as well in the circumstances, Terry was so taken up attending to all possible needs of his C.O., and wondering ingenuously why Evelyn had done him the honour to come, that he bore the deprivation imposed upon him by Mrs. Comerford better than he might otherwise have done.

When she should be alone again with Shawn she would tell him, Lady O'Gara said to herself. She had surprisingly few moments alone with him these days. A few days more and the house would have settled down quietly once more. She would be passing Terry's room, with the door standing open revealing its emptiness, as she had had to do many times, always missing the boy sadly.

One of these days Eileen went out alone with the lunch while Stella came to the meal at Castle Talbot. Sir Shawn was absent. Lady O'Gara had ordered a specially dainty lunch such as a young girl would like. She loved to give Stella pleasure, and to draw out the look of adoration from her soft bright eyes, which had something of the shyness and wildness of the woodland creature. Terry had complained boyishly that Stella ran away from him, was shy of his caresses. He had had to take her by capture, he said, and his mother loved him none the less. They were going to see Mrs. Wade. Stella was already friends with Susan Horridge at the South lodge and with Georgie. She had heard much of Mrs. Wade from them, and she pitied her loneliness, as she pitied Susan's when Georgie was at school.

"Odd, isn't it, dear?" she asked in her soft deliberate voice: she had lost or nearly lost the slightly foreign way of speaking she had had at first. "Odd, isn't it, that those two natural recluses should have found each other? The other day I was talking to Susan, when someone shook the gate and there was a rattle of tins. I thought Susan would have fainted. I had to go to the gate for her. It was only a procession of tinkers, as Patsy calls them, and an impudent fellow asked me if I wanted any pots or pans mended. I asked him did I look like wanting any pots or pans mended, and he nodded his head towards the lodge. 'The good woman of the house there might,' he said. 'She keeps herself to herself. I never knew this gate locked before.' Poor Susan asked me twenty questions about what the man looked like. I think she was satisfied."

"We are going to bring Mrs. Wade a gift of a puppy," Lady O'Gara said. "You shall select one from Judy's family, with the assistance of Patsy. They are a good lot."

"I know the one she shall have," Stella said. "It is the one with a few white hairs on his breast. Patsy says they'll be a patch as big as a plate when he's older, and tells him he's a disgrace to the litter. He's a darling, much nicer than the others. May I carry him, dear?"

"Won't he be rather heavy?"

"He can walk for little bits where it is dry. But he falls over his great big puppy paws. I don't think there ever were such beautiful dogs as your setters, not even my Poms or yours."

"I did think of asking you to give Mrs. Wade a Pom, but although they are good watchdogs they would not afford such a sense of protection as a setter. I hope she'll like a setter puppy just as well. We are very proud of our setters. The old Shot strain is known everywhere. It has been in the family for at least two hundred years."

Lady O'Gara could be very eloquent about the dogs, but she refrained. This little daughter of hers was just as much a lover of the little brethren as she was. Stella simply could not endure to see anything killed, which was a reason against her going out with the guns. Once or twice when she had seen anything shot, although she had not screamed like Eileen, she had turned pale, while her dark eyes had dilated as though with fear. Lady O'Gara, noticing how close and silky the gold nut-brown hair grew, rather like feathers than hair, had said to herself that Stella had been a rabbit or a squirrel or perhaps a wild bird in one of her incarnations.

They went off after lunch to see Mrs. Wade, the waddling puppy following them, now and again tumbling over his paws. They went out by Susan's gate, where Lady O'Gara stopped to admire the garden that was growing up about the lodge.

"You have transfigured it, Susan," she said. "It used to be so damp here with the old ragged laurels. They are well away. But I would not have thought there was such good earth under them; the ground always seemed caked so hard."

"So it were, my lady," said Susan, colouring prettily. "It were Mr. Kenny. He has worked so 'ard. Him an' Georgie've been puttin' in bulbs no end these last few days, when he can spare an half-hour from his horses. It's downright pleasant to watch them do it, knowin' that the dead-lookin' things come forth in glory soon as ever this wet Winter's past."

Susan had to bring out her Michael to be presented to the puppy, who had no name as yet, but Michael only growled and disappeared into the lodge as soon as he was released, like an arrow from the bow. Jealousy, Susan pronounced it, and suggested that the puppy should be called Pansy.

"I fancied callin' Michael Pansy," she said. "But Mr. Kenny, he fair talked me out of it. His eyes do favour the brown pansies that growed in my old granny's garden in the Cotswolds."

A thousand, thousand pities, Lady O'Gara thought, as they went down the hill towards the river, that Patsy Kenny, that confirmed bachelor, should apparently have found his ideal in an unhappily married woman.

Stella was carrying the puppy, so that he should not arrive muddy at his new mistress's house. She had twined a ridiculous blue ribbon in his russet curls, which he tried to work off whenever he got a chance, desisting only to lick vigorously at her hand.

"He knew me when he was a blind puppy," Stella explained. "I had them all in my lap when they were a few hours old. Judy let me handle them. You should see Eileen's face of disgust as I sat on the horse-block in the stable-yard with my arms full of them."

"I can see it!" Lady O'Gara said, with a queer little smile.

The day had been one of heavy showers, between which a pale sun came out and gilt the dappled golds and browns of the woods, and set up a rainbow bridge on the rain cloud that had passed over. They had left the house in a fair interval. They were within sight of the Waterfall Cottage, within hearing of the water as it fell over the weir, when the heavy drops began to patter. They ran the intervening space, Lady O'Gara laughing like a girl. It was the girlishness in her that made girls love her society, while they adored her in her own proper place.

As they passed the window of Mrs. Wade's cottage, where it showed beyond the iron railing, Lady O'Gara glanced that way. The interior of the room was no longer visible to the casual passer-by. Curtains were drawn across it, but through the parting of the curtains one caught a glimpse of fire-light. It would be a pleasant rosy window in the desolate road when the lamps were lit. But probably Mrs. Wade shuttered her window against the night, although the barred opening in the wall, designed to give light to the window, was well protected by its bristling spikes atop.

The gate was padlocked. They remained shaking it long enough to make them fearful that they would have to turn back before Mrs. Wade came flying down the avenue to open to them.

"I am so sorry I kept you waiting," she said, panting: "I had just gone into the house when you came. I have been so busy getting my garden into order."

She was stooping in the act of unlocking the gate. A pale shaft of watery sunlight came and lay on her hair, showing how thick and soft it was, how closely it grew. The sun was in her eyes, dazzling, and on her cheek, making it pale. She took the hand Lady O'Gara extended to her, without looking at Stella.

"This is your little dog, Mrs. Wade," Stella said, not waiting to be introduced. "Now isn't he a darling? I think myself he's the pick of the basket, although Patsy Kenny says he's a disgrace to the place, with that old white waistcoat making a holy show of him."

Mrs. Wade looked at her, shading her eyes with her hand.

"Thank you, miss," she said humbly. "I'm sure he'll be a dear little dog and a great companion."

She had a fluttered, flustered look. Her breath came short. Lady O'Gara wondered if her heart was strong.

"I've been expecting you any day at all, m'lady," she went on. "You didn't say when you'd come, but you said you'd come and I've been expecting you, though I used to say to myself, 'She won't come yet: it's too soon to be expecting her. Maybe 'tis in a month's time or six weeks she'd be coming, with the little dog and the young lady. She wouldn't be remembering. Hasn't she her beautiful son at home?'"

Lady O'Gara was touched. She had forgotten how very lonely Mrs. Wade's lot must be. After all, Susan Horridge could not be very much of a companion to Mrs. Wade, who, despite the humility of her manner, was evidently a person of some education and refinement.

"We shall come oftener now," she said. "It has been a rather busy time. I am sure Stella will come often to see you and the dog. We must find a name for him. I once knew a man who called his dog, Dog, just that. We must find something better than that."

She was talking to set Mrs. Wade at her ease. Mrs. Wade lit the lamp; apologizing for the darkness of the firelit room. The deep pink shade flooded the room with rosy light. There was a tea-table set in the background. Lady O'Gara had a passing wonder as to whether the table had been set daily in expectation of their visit.

"Now, what do you think of your dog?" Stella asked, as soon as the lamp was lit. "See how he has made himself at home already, lying on his side on the hearthrug as though he was a big dog, and not a ridiculous tumbling-over puppy." Mrs. Wade knelt down obediently to receive the puppy's large paw, with more than a suspicion of white about the toes, which Stella laid in her hand. As the two heads met together it occurred to Lady O'Gara that the hair grew similarly on the two heads, close, silken, rippling.

She watched Mrs. Wade take the dog's paws and hold them against her breast. A very lonely woman, she said to herself. There had been something of passion in the little act and in the way she laid her cheek against the dog's head.

"I can see he's going to have a most lovely time," said Stella approvingly. "We'll call him Terry, I think, after Mr. Terry O'Gara. All my dogs are called after my friends. I haven't a Terry yet, though."

"Oh, no, not that name, please," Mrs. Wade said. "Let me call him Keep, if you don't mind, Miss. He's going to keep me and the house, and we'll keep together."

"Oh, certainly," said Stella, a little surprised at Mrs. Wade's manner. "I know some people don't like dogs called after people. There was a dear old man in Rome, Count Raimondi, Carlo Raimondi. I had a dear King Charles spaniel then. He died of distemper, poor darling! Count Raimondi did not like Carlo's being called after him. He had just the same mouth and eyes, and both were rather fond of their food. So I had to change Carlo for Golliwog, poor darling."

Mrs. Wade laughed, a sweet fresh laugh. Lady O'Gara was glad she could laugh. She asked to be excused while she made the tea, and in her absence Stella went round the room, exclaiming at the prettiness of everything.

"Only I do not like her to be so lonely," she said. "I must come very often to see her. She is a darling, is she not? Don't you feel drawn to love her? Think of her having to depend on Susan for society, nice as Susan is!"

Mrs. Wade came back with a dainty tea. She was with difficulty persuaded to share it, saying that she had had her tea earlier. But even when she yielded to persuasion she did not make much of a tea. She had picked up a fan and sat shading her eyes with it from the lamp. From the shadow her eyes doated on Stella.

CHAPTER XV

THE SHADOW

One evening some ten days later Lady O'Gara, who had been out, arrived home with the dressing-bell. Hurrying upstairs, she found her husband in his dressing-room. He had had his bath: she noticed that his hair was wet as he stood in front of the glass, knotting his white cravat. He wore hunting things in the Winter evenings, and the scarlet coat, with the little facing of blue, became his dark skin and eyes.

"Is it you, Mary?" he asked, without turning round. "What kept you so late?"

"I forgot the time. I went to see Mrs. Wade, and found Stella there. I did not know she had been there since we brought Mrs. Wade a puppy to keep her company. Stella was on her way here. She had sent on her luggage, meaning to follow."

Sir Shawn turned about completely and stared at her. She saw that his face was disturbed.

"I wonder if it was wise to take Stella there!" he said. "Poor woman! One would not deny her any happiness. But, I warn you, Grace Comerford will not like it. There is another thing, Mary. Come in and shut the door. In a few minutes we shall have to go downstairs and talk platitudes. I could wish we were alone once more."

"Why, what is the matter, Shawn!" Lady O'Gara asked, coming forward in some alarm. "You don't feel ill?"

"I feel as well as ever I feel. But I've been infernally disturbed. Evelyn, quite gaily, and showing his white teeth, as he does when he laughs, I've nothing against Evelyn, frightened me by talking about Terry and Stella. He said it was delightful to see children so thoroughly in love. I pulled him up, rather short. He turned it off with a half apology, but I could see he did not believe me when I said there was nothing. 'Oh, they haven't told him.' I could see by his eyes that he thought that. I felt infernally frightened, I can tell you!"

"Oh, but why, Shawn?" Lady O'Gara's eyes fluttered nervously in the candlelight. She was frightened at her own complicity, really frightened for the first time. "Why shouldn't the poor children be happy? I know you like Eileen better than Stella. Still it is not a question of our choice."

She had been strangely, implicitly obedient to her husband during their married life, even when she might well have departed from obedience.

"What in God's Name are you talking about, Mary?" he asked and she felt vaguely shocked. Shawn had always been reverent in using the Name of His Creator. "It is not a question of my likes or dislikes. Why, for the matter of that, I can see little Stella with the poor lad's eyes well enough. But this thing simply cannot go on. It must be killed. God knows I don't want to hurt the boy. I'd give my life to make him happy, although I don't show him affection as you do, as you can. Is it possible you did not understand? Was I stupid about explaining to you? Don't you know that Stella is Terence's daughter?"

No; she had not known. That was plain enough in her face.

"Oh, no," she said in a bewildered way. "Stella is the daughter of Gaston de St. Maur...."

"Grace Comerford said so, or she allowed people to believe it. Did she ever say so? Stella is the daughter of Terence Comerford and Bridyeen Sweeney, whom you know as Mrs. Wade. Don't you see now how impossible it is? I wish to Heaven Grace Comerford had not come back."

A sense of the piteousness, the pitilessness, of it all came overwhelmingly to Mary O'Gara. She had been learning to love Stella. The fond, ardent little creature had pushed herself into her heart. What was to happen to them all, to Terry, to Stella, to herself?

"You are sure, Shawn?" she asked, rubbing her hands together as though she were cold. But while she asked the certainty was borne in upon her. It was the starved mother-love that had burned in Mrs. Wade's eyes as they rested on the girl. It was the unconscious daughterly tenderness, the mysterious attraction which had made Stella chatter on the homeward way of Mrs. Wade and how she pitied her, she knew not for what.

She threw out her hands in a gesture of despair.

"It seems we are all going to be hurt," she said. "I would not mind if it were not for the children. Why did Grace Comerford bring Stella where she and Terry were certain to meet? The boy was bound to find her irresistible?"

She remembered suddenly that the dinner bell might ring at any moment and that the patient Margaret MacKeon was waiting to help her to dress. She sighed. It was one of the moments when one finds the social demands hard to endure.

"One of us will have to tell Terry," she said. "It is not a pretty story. Poor little Stella!"

No one would have thought from Lady O'Gara's demeanour at the dinner table that Black Care pressed hard on her white shoulders. Sir Shawn had often said that when his wife chose she could put the young girls in the shade.

She put them in the shade to-night. She had a deep, brilliant spot of colour in either cheek. Her dress of leaf brown matched her eyes and hair. She had laid aside her other jewels for a close-fitting antique collar of garnets, the deep ruby of which suggested a like colour in the gown as it did in her eyes.

Eileen was out of it with Major Evelyn and pouted. Terry was tired and happy after his day of tramping over the bogs. He seemed content to watch Stella across the bowl of growing violets which was between them. Young Earnshaw talked nonsense and Stella dimpled and smiled. She had gained the colour of the moss rose-bud since she had come back to Ireland. There was a daintiness, a delicacy in her little face with the softly moulded, yet firm features, the grey-brown eyes with dark lashes, the arched fine brows, which would have made a plain face distinguished. Her head as she moved it about in the lamplight, she had bird-like gestures, showed a sheen like a pheasant's breast. Watching her miserably Sir Shawn O'Gara said to himself that Terence Comerford's red hair had come out as golden bronze on his daughter's pretty head.

He had a girl at either hand, as Lady O'Gara had the two male visitors. Terry, the odd man, had come round and slipped in between his father and Eileen, moving her table-napkin so that she sat between him and Major Evelyn. He and his father were almost equally silent from different reasons.

Eileen at first had been crumbling her bread, sending her food away untasted or only just tasted. She was vexed about something. It was not like Eileen to be capricious over her food.

Perhaps Lady O'Gara noticed the dissatisfaction and ascribed it to the fact that Eileen was not having the attention she desired, so she drew gently out of a very interesting discussion she was having with Major Evelyn and turned to little Earnshaw, an agreeably impudent boy, with cheeks like a Winter apple and an irresistibly jolly smile. He seemed to have got over his first shyness with Stella and was conducting his veiled love-making with a rather charming audacity. Lady O'Gara had glanced a little anxiously once or twice at Terry, but there was obviously only amusement at young Earnshaw's way in Terry's face. He must be very sure of Stella.

"Don't mind him," he said across the table while she watched. "He's very young and he's apt to get excited when he stays up for dinner. Very often the Mess has to pack him off to bed."

Mary O'Gara smiled at the banter between the two boys. Now and again she inclined an ear to the conversation of Major Evelyn and Eileen. The big, handsome, jovial man of the world, whom his subalterns, while evidently deeply admiring him, called "Cecil," did not find much to interest him in Eileen, though he was too well-bred to show it.

Stella, laughing, put down her head with one of her bird-like movements. Her hair was parted in the centre and the thick masses of it, so much like plumage, went off in silken waves and curls and was looped behind her little ears where it was combed up from her white neck. She was wearing green tonight, a vivid emerald green which would have tried a less beautiful complexion.

The movement, the close fine ripple of the hair, were like Mrs. Wade's; there was no reason to doubt the relationship. Would others see it? But Mrs. Wade hardly ever walked abroad. She seemed as much afraid of her fellow-creatures as any one could wish her to be.

Lady O'Gara found herself seeking for another likeness. No; except for that slight redness in the hair there was nothing she could discover of Terence Comerford. She wondered vaguely whether Grace Comerford had looked for such a likeness and been disappointed.

She let her thoughts slip away from things around her. She asked herself whether in the circumstance Mrs. Wade was a fit companion for her daughter, and answered herself, with a little scorn, that there was nothing to fear from the mother's influence. She remembered something she had caught sight of at the end of a little cross-passage in Waterfall Cottage. There was a statue, a throbbing rosy lamp in the darkness. Mrs. Wade was at 7 o'clock Mass at the Convent every morning despite her recluse habits. She was a good woman, whatever there was in her past.

Lady O'Gara recalled herself with a start to the things about her. How long had her thoughts been straying? Not very long, for the plates were being taken away that had been full when last she was aware of them.

Her eyes rested on Eileen's face. A name caught her ear, Robin Gillespie. Oh, that was the doctor's son of whom Eileen had spoken with a certain consciousness. Eileen's manner had suggested that Robin Gillespie was in love with her, while she said: "Of course he has not a penny and never will have."

Eileen was listening now, absorbed in what Major Evelyn was saying. Her lips were parted, her eyes and colour bright. The air of slackness which so often dulled her beauty had disappeared. For once she was animated.

Major Evelyn perceived that his hostess was listening and turned to her with a courteous intention to include her in the conversation. He was charming to all women, this big man, with the irresistible gaiety. Poor Eileen, she had been playing off all her little charms upon him, and in vain. He showed openly his preference for an old woman, as Mary O'Gara called herself in her thoughts, wincing a little.

"I've discovered that Miss Creagh knows Gillespie, the young doctor who has defied all the Army Regulations. It was quite an excitement in India. The Rajah of Bundelpore had a very bad attack of Indian cholera one night. His own doctors could do nothing for him. Some one, the Rajah's heir who had been at Harrow, probably, sent over for the regimental doctor, who happened to be Gillespie. He found all sorts of devilry going on while the Rajah writhed and turned black and green. Gillespie took him in hand, I heard his treatment was nearly as weird as that of the native doctors. There was something about blackberry jam stirred in boiling water for an astringent drink. Anyhow the Rajah pulled through. He's got a constitution like a horse. And as soon as he was well he presented Gillespie with a horse that was the very Kohinoor of horses, Gillespie sold him, for a preposterous sum I believe, to Lord Nutwood, magnificent jewels and a lakh of rupees."

"How much is a lakh of rupees?" Eileen asked with breathless interest.

"Oh, a big sum, somewhere about fifty thousand pounds. The jewels are worth as much. Then came in the Indian Government and the Army Regulations. They ordered Gillespie to return the Rajah's gifts. Gillespie, who hadn't a penny to bless himself with, it was understood that all he could squeeze out of his pay went home to his people in Ireland, snapped his fingers at them. They bid him choose between leaving the Service and giving up the Rajah's gifts. Gillespie quite unhesitatingly, I believe they really thought there could be a question of choice, gave up the Service. I hear he's come home and means to set up as a specialist in Cavendish Square. They said there was a girl in the case, some girl who wouldn't have him, and that took the savour even out of the lakh of rupees. I don't suppose it's true. Do you happen to know him, Miss Creagh? He is from your part of the world, Donegal way."

"My people know him quite well," said Eileen, her breath coming and going fast. "Just fancy, I never heard of it. You'd have thought someone would have written to me."

She frowned, looking down at her plate.

At bed-time when Lady O'Gara, putting her own preoccupations aside, went to say good-night to Eileen she found her in tears.

"My dear, what is it?" she asked in dismay.

"Oh, Cousin Mary, you know that story Major Evelyn told us about Robin Gillespie. Well, isn't it awful?" she broke into sobbing. "I wouldn't listen to him when he asked me to be engaged to him. He said he knew he was a poor ... poor ... beggar, but ... with that to spur him on ... he could do anything. I was ... horrid. I told him to ask ... Brigid. He said it wasn't Brigid he wanted ... it was me. He got ... angry at last ... and now... I know I loved him ... all the time."

Lady O'Gara troubled as she was, could not refrain from smiling, but as Eileen's tears apparently had overtaken her during the process of brushing her hair, and the long mantle of greenish grey, silver-gold hair hung about her face, Lady O'Gara's smile passed unnoticed.

"Do you think ... it would seem ... very forward of me to write to him?" asked Eileen; and then looked from the curtain of her hair with wet eyes but a new hopefulness.

"I should ask Brigid. He may have acted on your advice."

"Oh, but he hadn't time," said Eileen, whose strong point was not humour. "He went away at once, broken-hearted. Besides, I should have known if he had made any advance to Brigid. Cousin Mary, would you mind very much if I went home for a little visit? I know that I have only just come back, but still..."

"Certainly not, Eileen." Lady O'Gara had a feeling that just at present Eileen might be a jarring element. "Make your own arrangements, my dear. I am very glad if it will make you happier."

"Oh, thank you," said Eileen, with effusion. "You are always so sympathetic and understanding, darling Cousin Mary. You see, if Robin has come back as Major Evelyn says, he might be with his people just at this moment."

CHAPTER XVI

THE DEAD HAND

Terry came to his mother a week later with a look in his face which made her want to take his young head in her arms and weep over it. A shadow had fallen on his comely youth. He looked "grumpy," as he had been accustomed to look in his darling childhood when he was about to have a croupy attack, at which times the sense of injury against all the world had been part humorous, whole poignant, to his mother's mind.

"What is it, darling?" she asked, although she knew before he spoke what was the matter.

"I have been talking to Father," he broke out. "Mother, it is intolerable. He says he will not consent to my engagement to Stella. As though he or anybody could prevent it."

"You have not quarrelled?" she asked in quick alarm, anxious for both her men.

He laughed angrily.

"Oh, we didn't shout at each other, if that is what you mean. He told me he would never consent to my engagement. Why? In the name of Heaven why? I asked him that and he wouldn't answer me. He told me to come to you. What bee has he got in his bonnet? I should have thought, Stella is a sort of little sister of Terence Comerford, from whom I am called, whose death I have always understood shadowed Father's life. Oh, I know you've been throwing cold water on me, leading me up to this. I knew when you would not let me shout it out that first night, as I wanted to, before all the world. Father said something about Eileen. Ridiculous! We have never thought of each other. As a matter of fact she has a young man of her own. I always knew he wanted me to marry Eileen. As though I ever could have married anyone but Stella!"

She did not at all resent her husband's laying the burden of comfort upon her. He had always left Terry to her.

She looked at his young angry face. He was ramping up and down the little boudoir like an animal in a cage. He was adorably young and she loved him. What was she to say?

"I'm not a child," Terry went on. "Things can't stand like this, as Father expects them to, apparently. One doesn't throw over a girl one loves better than life for no reason at all, and Father will give none except that the marriage is unsuitable. How can it be unsuitable except that I am so unworthy of her? Mother", he stopped suddenly in his pacing to and fro, "you can do anything with Father. Make him see sense. You know my whole happiness depends on this, and hers. It has gone deep with me."

Suddenly he turned away, and putting his two arms on the mantelpiece he laid down his face upon them.

She went to him and stroked his hair softly. He looked up at her and his eyes were miserable, and so young.

"Darling," he said, "you have always been good to me. Can't you talk Father over? I am going away to-morrow. If he persists in this insanity I shall chuck my commission, go off to Canada and try to make a home there for Stella."

"Terry!" The name was wrung from her like a cry.

"You see I couldn't stay, darling, hanging round in the hope that Father might change his mind. I couldn't stick being engaged and not engaged. I should hate to leave you, of course, darling, but then you wouldn't come. You'd never leave Father. He says his decision is final, but he gives me no reason for it. It is the maddest way of treating a man I ever heard. What does he mean by it?"

"He was always a very indulgent father, Terry. If he refuses you a thing you desire so much he must have a good reason."

She felt the feebleness of her plea even before he turned and looked at her.

"That is really foolish, Mother," he said. "I beg your pardon if I am rude. I'm not a child, to be kept in the dark and told that my elders know what is best for me. Do you know his reasons?"

She had been dreading the question, yet she was unprepared with an answer.

"I see you do," he went on grimly. "But of course you won't tell me, if Father will not, though he sent me to you."

The poor lady was profoundly wretched. Tears were not far off. She would not for the world have wept before the boy. He had enough to bear without her tears.

"Where is your father?" she asked.

"He is in his office. You will speak to him? You angel! Tell him how impossible it is that Stella and I could give up each other. You love her, Mother, don't you? The bird-like thing! I remember you said at first that she was like a bird. She has flown into my heart and I cannot turn her out. Say..."

"I will say all I Can, Terry. Do you feel fit to go back to the others?"

"They don't want me. They are quite happy knocking about the billiard-balls. Evelyn would know, and I don't think I could stand little Earnshaw's chaffing ways."

Boyishly he looked at himself in the glass. He had rumpled his hair out of its usual order. There was a bright colour in his cheeks. He looked brilliantly handsome. What he said was:

"Lord, what an outsider I look!"

She left him there and went off to look for her husband. Her heart was very heavy. Already she knew that the compromise she had to suggest would be received with scorn. It was a weak womanly compromise, just the kind of thing a man will put his foot on and squelch utterly.

He turned round as she came in.

"Well, Mary," he said. "I've been having a very unpleasant discussion with Terry. It ended where it began. He would not listen to me."

She came and stood behind his chair. The fire was low in the grate. There was the intolerable smell of a smoking lamp in the room. The reading-lamp on the table was flaring. She turned it down and replenished the fire. The discomfort of it all, the room felt cold and dismal, depressed her further.

"The poor boy!" she said. "What are we to do, Shawn? You can't expect him to give up Stella without any explanation. He would be a poor creature if he could, not your son or mine. Shawn, you will have to tell him. How could you leave it to me?"

"And if I do, what then?"

She shook her head. She did not know what then: or rather she did not wish to answer the question.

She was sitting on the arm of his chair. He leant his head against her wearily. In the glass above the chimney-piece, tilted towards them, she saw his face and was frightened. Were the purple shadows really there, or did she only imagine them?

"If such a story had been told to me about you, Mary," he asked, "do you suppose it would have made any difference? I would have said like an ancestor of mine:

"Has the pearl less whiteness
Because of its birth?
Has the violet less brightness
For growing near earth?

That is what any lover worth his salt would say: yet when one is older and very proud of one's family the bar sinister is not a thing to be thought of."

"You said yourself that Bridyeen was an innocent creature. You forgave Terence, who was her tempter. You love his memory and you have called your one son after him. Is it fair, is it just?"

She was frightened at her own temerity. The subject of Terence Comerford had always been like an open wound to her husband.

"Did I forgive Terence?" he asked with a wonder that had something child-like about it; "I was very angry with Terence, dreadfully angry. Do you remember that passage, Mary?

"Alas they had been friends in youth;

you know how it goes on:

"And to be wroth with one we love
Doth work like madness in the brain."

She had slipped an arm about his neck, and her hand went on softly caressing his cheek.

"I think we shall have to tell Terry," she said, "if we persist in our refusal. We could not take up such an untenable position. Unless...", she hesitated.

"Go on, Mary," he said.

"Unless we were to accept Grace's story of Stella's birth. Why should it not be true?" She asked the question piteously. "Are you sure, Shawn, about the other thing?"

But while she said it she remembered Stella's likeness to Mrs. Wade. Why, any one might see it, any one. A new fear sprang up in her heart, troubled by many fears. This time it was for Stella. Any day, any hour, someone besides herself might discover that likeness. Why, for all she knew the place buzzed with it already. Sooner or later someone would recognize Mrs. Wade as Bridyeen Sweeney. Then it would be easy to piece the old story together. Already people had noticed that Stella had the Comerford colour, which had been, in her own case, the Creagh colour. Grace Comerford ought not to have come back. Shawn was quite right. She ought not to have come back.

"You are a very clever woman, Mary. But it seems to me a cheap novel kind of suggestion. I think we must face the thing as it is. I shall tell Terry to-night."

Terry was told. He came to his mother's room after hearing the story. She had been expecting him. In the end her men always brought her their troubles. So she had piled up a bright fire, had set a couple of softly cushioned chairs side by side, as though the physical comfort would reach the wounded spirit. She smiled to herself rather piteously at the thought. Men were susceptible to comfort, to being petted, no matter at what age one loved them, or in what grief one would comfort them.

She was in her silk dressing gown, her hair in two long plaits before Terry came. Despite his miserable preoccupation his face lightened at sight of her.

"How sweet you look, Mother!" he said. "And so young with your hair like that."

"Come and sit down, my darling boy."

He came and sat by her, and presently he laid his face on her shoulder to conceal, she divined, set eyes.

"What am I to do, Mothereen, at all, at all?" he asked, going back to the phraseology of his nursery days.

"Your father has told you?"

"Yes, he has told me."

"It is pretty bad," she said compassionately.

"Mother," he lifted his face and his eyes were bloodshot. "Why did you call me after that villain? Why does my father love him still? I have never heard you say one word against him."

She flinched before the accusation.

"Dear," she said. "I have only just been told of this. Your father kept it from me all those years."

"And you were engaged to him at the time! Good Lord!" he broke out with young passion. "Don't tell me, Mother, that there is any excuse for him. I could not bear that from you. One law for the man, another for the woman: it is the easy way of the world. My poor little darling!"

Suddenly he choked and got up and went away from her. She found nothing to say.

He was back again in a second, while she watched him helplessly.

"I don't want her to know," he said. "She must not know. What am I to do? She ought to enter this family as its loved and honoured daughter. Mother, I do not intend to give her up."

She had been waiting for it. If he had said otherwise she would have been bitterly disappointed, however much she might have tried to deceive herself. It was a pity, a thousand pities, the child could not have come to them without that smirch. But it had not touched her: there was no stain on her. Thinking upon Stella's mother she said to herself that no levity in the girl she had been had led to her downfall. Why, Shawn had said she was the simplest, whitest of creatures. It made Terence's sin all the blacker.

She drew her boy's head down to her and kissed it.

"I did not ask you to give her up," she said. "I do not take the world's view of such things."

He looked at her with an incredible incredulous relief.

"You angel mother!" he said with a deep sigh. "I might have trusted you. There is one thing. Stella must never know."

"She must never know," she repeated after him.

Her husband's foot sounded in the adjoining room and Terry went away comforted. Shawn did not come in to say good-night to her as usual, by which omission she conjectured the trouble of his mind. She prayed for light, almost in despair of finding it, and slept, although she had expected to lie awake, seeking unhappily a way out of this threatening sorrow for all dear to her.

She awoke somewhere in the small hours. The moon was on her bed and the air was very cold. She came awake suddenly, with a thought in her mind so concrete that it was as though someone had spoken it aloud.

"Is it quite certain that Terence did not marry Bridyeen Sweeney?"

She caught at it as a drowning man catches at a straw. Her heart gave a wild bound towards it. It was so thin, so frail a hope, that while her fingers closed upon it she knew the futility. Again she slept, and the thought was with her when she awoke in the grey morning.

CHAPTER XVII

MISS BRENNAN

She was grateful to the exigencies of the Service which made it absolutely necessary for Terry to be back in barracks next day. He had gone off after breakfast with Major Evelyn and Mr. Earnshaw, forbidding her to come to see him off. Sir Shawn, who was High Sheriff for the year and had to be in the county town for the opening of the Assizes, took the party to the station on his way. She was left with the morning on her hands.

How to use it? Oh, she had been impatient for them to be gone! The hope which had seemed so frail in the night had strengthened and failed, strengthened and failed many times since. This morning it was strong within her. It was founded on so little. Terry had called Terence Comerford hard names last night. A villain. She did not think Terence was a villain. He had been a kindly, affectionate fellow, very quick to be angry about a cruelty to any helpless thing. A good heart: oh, yes, Terence had had a good heart: but, even to her had come the dreary knowledge that good-hearted people can be very cruel in their sins.

She had looked at it from many points of view. Supposing Terence had meant to marry the girl and been prevented by his sudden death! Something came into her mind, dreary and terrible. "The way to Hell is paved with good intentions." Poor Terence, who had laid this coil for their feet, tangling their lives and happiness in the meshes of his passion, had he been paving Hell, just paving Hell, with good intentions never to be realized?

Early as they had started she had found time to speak to her husband about the possibility of there having been a marriage. He had found her beside his bed full-dressed when he opened his eyes on the grey morning.

"Shawn," she had said, "Could Terence have married Bridyeen Sweeney?"

The maze of sleep was still in his eyes. For a moment he stared at her as though she had given him a new idea. Then he turned away fretfully.

"No," he said, "no. Put that out of your head. If it was so would he have let me go on suffering as I did? It was the whiskey was at the root of the trouble. He would never have spoken to me as he did if it had not been for the whiskey."

She passed over the irrelevancy. Shawn was not yet all awake.

"Would he have righted her if he had lived, do you think, Shawn?"

"My God, Mary, how can I tell? Why do you torture me with such senseless questions? You know how that old tragedy has power to upset me.

"I'm sorry, Shawn," she said humbly. "It was for the boy's sake."

She left him, his face turned to the wall, her heart heavy because the hope had failed. But a little later she had the house to herself, and the hope came back again and asked the insistent question.

She was going to see Mrs. Wade for herself and discover if there was hope for Terry and Stella. Common sense whispered at her ear, that it was not likely Mrs. Wade would choose to be Mrs. Wade all those years if she might have been Mrs. Terence Comerford, living at Inch, honoured and with the love of her child. She would not listen to that chilling whisper. She had known many strange things in life, quite contrary to common sense. It would not be common sense now for Terry to want to marry a girl born out of wedlock. It would not be common sense that the girl should be kept in ignorance of the stain on her birth. But these things happened. A wryness came to Mary O'Gara's sweet mouth with the thought that if Terry married Stella his children would be born of a nameless mother. So the world was so strong in her! Scornfully in her own mind she defied the world.

She took a roundabout way to Waterfall Cottage, because she did not want the slight interruption of speaking to Susan Horridge if she went out by the South lodge, the nearest way. By a détour through her own park she entered O'Hart property, which had been in Chancery since she remembered it, the house going to rack and ruin. Her way led her round by the Mount in which was the tomb of old Hercules.

The earth was warmly beautiful, covered with the rust-coloured Autumn leaves.

Under the trees overlooking the river there were many strangely coloured fungi pushing in rows and ranks from the damp earth on which the foot slid, for it was covered thickly by a moss that exuded slimy stuff when trodden upon as though it was seaweed.

She was just by the vault where the Admiral's coffin stood on its shelf, plain to be seen by anyone who had the temerity to peep through the barred grating in the iron door. Suddenly a little figure dipped in front of her and she recognized Miss Brennan, who had once been a lady's maid to a Mrs. O'Hart and had survived the provision made for her before the O'Harts were off the face of the earth. She had come to live in one of the dilapidated lodges on the place, with very little between her and starvation beyond the old-age pension, supplemented by contributions from charity. The old woman was nearer ninety than eighty, but was still lively and intelligent, despite her eccentricity. The big apron she was wearing was full of sticks and she had a bundle in her arms as well.

"Good morning, my Lady," she said, with her little dip. She always prided herself on her superior manners and her traditions, and the neighbours good-naturedly acknowledged her pretensions by addressing her always as Miss Brennan.

"Good morning, Lizzie," returned Lady O'Gara, who was one of the privileged ones to call the old woman by her name. "How are you keeping? It is very rheumatic weather, I'm afraid."

"I'm as well as can be since your Ladyship gave me the beautiful boarded floor to my little place, may the Lord reward you! Squealin' and scurryin' I do hear the rats under the floor, but I'm not afraid now that they'll bite my nose off when I fall asleep."

"I wish I could make it more comfortable for you. Lizzie. I'll see that you get a couple of cribs of turf. Your lodge is damp under the trees."

"Thank your Ladyship," said the old woman with another dip. "I'm wonderful souple in my limbs, considerin' everythin'; for the same house would give a snipe a cowld. The blankets are a great comfort. They're as warm as Injia."

"Oh, I'm glad of that."

She was about to go on her way when Miss Brennan jerked her thumb backward in the direction of Waterfall Cottage.

"She's gone," she said.

"Who is gone?"

"Mrs. Wade, she calls herself. I knew as soon as ever I laid eyes on her she was little Bride Sweeney, old Judy Dowd's granddaughter. She kep' out of the way o' the people that might ha' known her. She stopped to spake to me one day I was pickin' sticks an' brought me in an' made me a lovely cup o' tay. She thought I was too old to remember. The little lady that's at Inch now would be her little girl. I've seen them together when they didn't know any wan was lookin'. Them beautiful pink curtains don't meet well. I've seen little Missie on a footstool before the fire an' the mother adorin' her."

Lady O'Gara was overwhelmed. What had been happening during the days, there were not twenty of them, since she had first taken Stella to see Mrs. Wade.

"When little Missie wasn't there Bridyeen would be huggin' the dog the same as if he was a babby. Some people make too much o' dogs. I kep' my old Shep tied up till he died. He was wicked and I wasn't afraid o' tinkers with him about. I saw her once when she didn't think any wan was peepin' in. She was cryin' on the dog's head an' him standin' patient, lickin' her now and again with his tongue. I never could bear the lick of a dog."

Lizzie looked at Lady O'Gara with the most cunning eyes. Apparently she expected contradiction, but she met with none. Lady O'Gara was in fact too dumbfounded to answer.

"Many's the time I took notice of Bridyeen," the old woman went on. "She was well brought up. She respected ould people. When she wint away out of the place I said nothin', whatever I guessed. I said nothin' all those years. It was to me she kem when Mr. Terence Comerford was kilt. 'Tisn't likely I wouldn't know her when I seen her agin. What's twinty years when you're my age? She didn't say I'd made a mistake when I called her Bridyeen. She's gone now, an' I'll miss her. 'Tis a lonesome road without a friend on it, for I'm too ould to take to an Englishwoman, though yon's a quiet crathur at the lodge."

Lady O'Gara was recovering her power of speech. Still she did not feel able to contradict this terrible old woman of the bright piercing eyes, with whom it seemed useless to have any subterfuges.

"You don't be afeard I'll tell, me Lady. I keep meself to meself, away from the commonality round about here. She needn't have gone for me. I'd have held my tongue. 'Twasn't likely I'd want to set tongues clackin' about her that was good to me. As I sez to the little lady...."

Terror seized upon Lady O'Gara. What had the old woman said to Stella?

"You didn't tell the young lady anything?" she said, very gently, remembering not to frighten the frail old creature before her.

"Not me. I said no more than 'Your Mamma's left.'" She looked with a peering anxiety into Lady O'Gara's face, as though she had just begun to doubt her own wisdom. "I didn't do any harm sayin' them words, did I? Didn't I know they was that to each other, seein' them through the chink in the curtain lovin' an' kissin'?"

Was it possible that Stella knew? Anyhow it was no use frightening old Lizzie.

"No, no," Lady O'Gara said. "You did nothing wrong. Only remember, I depend on you for silence. The people are so fond of gossip about here like all country-people."

"I let them go their own ways an' I go mine," Miss Brennan said, and looked down at the sticks which she had dropped. "I don't know who's goin' to pick them up," she said plaintively. "I've picked them up wance an' me ould knees are goin' under me. I don't consider I could do it twicet."

"I'll pick them up and carry them for you," Lady O'Gara said. "It is not far to your lodge. Indeed you ought not to be picking up sticks or carrying them. I'll speak to Patsy Kenny. He'll see that some dry wood is sent down to you, as much as you want. You have only to ask for it to have it any time. That is, if I forget."

"Thank your Ladyship kindly," Miss Brennan said with one of the dips which perhaps kept her limbs "souple" as she said. "I'll be glad o' the dry sticks. The green do be makin' me cry. All the same I like to pick up sticks. Isn't it what the Lord sends us, what matter if they're green itself. 'Tis the chancey things I love havin', the musharoons and the blackberries, straight from God, I call them. But I couldn't let your Ladyship carry sticks for the like o' me. I hope I know me place better. If your Ladyship was to give me a hoosh up wid them? My back's not too bent if only they was to be tied in a bundle."

She performed a series of little dips which would have made Lady O'Gara smile at another time.

"The sticks are very light," she said. "Supposing we share the burden? Then we can talk as we go along. I suppose there never will be any news of Mr. Florence O'Hart, who went to Australia and was lost sight of?"

It was enough for Miss Brennan, who forgot even to protest when Lady O'Gara took the big bundle of sticks and gave her a few light ones to carry. She could always be set off chattering on the topic of the O'Hart who might have survived the family debâcle and might come home one day to restore the fallen splendours of the place. Lady O'Gara walked as far as the lodge with the old woman, and laid the sticks away in the corner by the fireplace. It was a very short distance, though it counted as long to Miss Brennan.

As she went back along the road, the old woman, watching her disappear through the arch of orange and scarlet and pale fluttering gold, for the trees were not yet bare, talked to herself.

"There she goes!" she said, "an' she's proud to the proud an' humble to the humble. 'Tis the great day for you, Lizzie Brennan, to have the likes o' Lady O'Gara carryin' home your bits o' sticks. I hope I wasn't wrong sayin' what I did to the little lady. It seemed to get on her mind, for she wasn't listenin' to what I was sayin' for all she kep' her head towards me. Still an' all little Missie couldn't be without knowin' the light in a mother's eyes whin she seen it."

CHAPTER XVIII

THE DAUGHTER

Lady O'Gara went away quickly from the rusty gate overhung by ivy, not looking back to see how Miss Brennan watched her out of sight. She had not indeed heard one word of what the old woman had been saying about the O'Harts. She was dreadfully perturbed. The fair placidity of her face was broken up. In either cheek two spots of vivid colour pulsed. Seeing them one would have said she was in pain.

She hastened back along the tree-overhung road, over the dead leaves where the fine silver veining of last night's frost was yielding to a sodden dampness, to the gate of Waterfall Cottage.

She had half-expected to find it locked, but it was open. There was a thick carpet of dead leaves on the gravel sweep. Between the boughs sparsely clothed with leaves and the slender tree-trunks she caught a glimpse of the bronze and amber river running over its stones, or winding about the big dripping boulders that were in the bed of the stream. A damp, rheumatic place, she said to herself, although she loved the river; and its backwaters, full of wild duck and dabchick and the moorhens, were enchanting places.

The grounds which she remembered as neglected and overgrown had become orderly. The little beds cut in the turf were neat in their Winter bareness, despite a few dead leaves which had fluttered on to them. Her eyes fell on a pair of gardening gloves and a trowel lying on the grass by one of the beds. From the open mouth of a brown paper bag a bulb had partly rolled before it became stationary. There was a hole dug in the turf. Someone had been planting bulbs and had gone away leaving the task unfinished.

From the house-wall hung a branch of clematis torn down by the rough wind. A ladder stood close by. Someone had had the intention of nailing up the branch, and had not carried it into effect.

She lifted her hand to the knocker and found that the door yielded to her slight touch. It was open. For a second she had a wild thought that Miss Brennan might have been wandering in her wits, that Mrs. Wade, or Bridyeen Sweeney, she had come to calling her that in her mind, was still in the house.

She looked into the little hall. It was bright with a long ray from the white sun that peered below a cloud, seeming to her dazzled eyes surrounded by a coruscation of coloured rays. The white sun portended rain to come, probably in the afternoon.

Shot had pushed his way before her into the hall. She had almost forgotten that Shot had come with her when she had left the Poms at home because of the muddy roads. He had disappeared into Mrs. Wade's little parlour. The plume of his fine tail caught a flash from the sun's rays on its burnished bronze. She heard the dog whine.

No one answered her knock nor did Shot return, so, after a second's hesitation, she followed the dog.

She was not prepared for what she saw. The only occupant of the room beside the dog, who had dropped on to the hearthrug, and lay with his nose between his paws and his melancholy eyes watching, was Stella, Stella kneeling by a chair in an abandonment of grief, her face hidden.

The little figure kept its grace even in the huddled-up attitude. The face hidden in the chair, childishly, as though a child suffered pain, was lifted as Lady O'Gara touched the bronze-brown head. The misery of Stella's wide eyes shocked her. Stella's face was stained and disfigured by tears. The soft close hair, which she had taken to wearing plaited about her head, was ruffled and disordered.

"Stella, darling child!" Lady O'Gara said, with a gasp of consternation. She had never seen Stella before without brightness, the brightness of a bird. Now the small ivory pale face had lost the golden tints of its underlying brownness. The child was wan under the disfigurement of her tears.

She got up with a groping motion as though tears obscured her sight. She came to meet Lady O'Gara and held out her hands with a piteous gesture of grief.

"She has gone away," she said.

Her hands were chill in Mary O'Gara's warm clasp. The woman drew the girl to her, holding the cold hands against her breast with a soft motherliness.

"Now, tell me what is the matter?" she said, while her voice shook in the effort to be composed. "Where has Mrs. Wade gone to?"

"That is what I do not know, Lady O'Gara," Stella answered, with a catch of the breath. "I came to her as I have come every day of late. She was gone. I thought she would come back at first; but she has not come. While I stood looking out of the gate watching for her an old woman came by picking up sticks for her fire. She said", something like a spasm shook the slender body and her face quivered, "that she, Mrs. Wade, was gone away. Do you know what she called her, Lady O'Gara? She called her my mother, my mother."

The suffering eyes were full upon her. Lady O'Gara found nothing to say that could serve any useful purpose.

"Yes, I know," she said aimlessly. "It was old Lizzie Brennan. She lives at that gate-lodge a little way down the road."

"She said my mother."

The eyes, grey in one light, brown in another; made a piteous appeal.

"How could Mrs. Wade be my mother?" Stella asked, with a quiver of the lip, clasping and unclasping her hands. "My mother died long ago. I am Stella de St. Maur, although Granny will have me called by her name. But I love Mrs. Wade; I love her. I have never loved anyone in the same way."

Lady O'Gara took the bewildered head into her arms and stroked it with tender touches as though it was the head of a frightened bird, one of those birds that sometimes came in at her windows, and nearly killed themselves trying to escape before she could give them their liberty. She sought in a frightened way for something to say to the girl and could find nothing.

"Granny is so angry with me," Stella went on. "She has found out that I came here. She said she would not have me keep low company, that she was shocked to find I could slip away from her to a person not in my own class of life. She had noticed that I was always slipping away. She talked about throwbacks. What did she mean by that? She was very angry when she said it."

"Oh, I am sorry you made her angry, Stella." Mary O'Gara had found her tongue at last. She had no idea of the inadequacy of what she said. Her thoughts had gone swiftly back to the days when she had trembled before Grace Comerford's cold rages. Her thoughts, as though they were too tired to consider the situation of the moment, went on to Terence. Poor Terence! She remembered him red and white before his mother's anger, her tongue that stung like a whip, the more bitter where she roved.

"I ran away from her," Stella went on. "She told me to go to my room, as though I was a child. I went, but I got out of the window: it is not far from the ground. I came here only to find her gone. I had been running all the way thinking of how she would comfort me. She has taken nothing with her but Keep. I expect Keep followed her. I would not have minded anything if she had been here. The old woman called her my mother. Is she mad, Cousin Mary? How could Mrs. Wade be my mother?"

Her eyes asked an insistent question. Lady O'Gara was a truthful woman. The candour of her face did not belie her. She tried to avoid the eyes, lest they should drag the truth from her.

"She is only very old," she answered, haltingly. "Not mad, but perhaps..."

"The odd thing is," Stella put by what she had been about to say as a trivial thing, "that I wish what the old woman said was true. I wish it with all my heart. She was like what I think a mother must be to me. I have always been running away to her, ever since you brought me first. She comforted me. I have always felt there was something I did not know. Granny would never tell me about my father and mother. If she is not my mother why should I feel all that about her? She made up to me for everything. And Sir Shawn was cold. He used to like me, but now he does not. He is afraid," a little colour came to her cheek, "that I will marry Terry. He need not be afraid. If Mrs. Wade is my mother I shall not marry Terry. He can marry Eileen Creagh and please his father! Do not tell me she is not my mother."

Was the mother, the nameless mother, worth all that to her child? It seemed so.

"Oh, the poor boy!" Lady O'Gara said, with sudden tears, clasping her hands together. "Is he to have no word in it?"

"Not if I am Mrs. Wade's daughter. She told me how she lived with her grandmother who kept a shop in the village long ago. Of course Sir Shawn would not like it. I see that quite well, and I am not thinking of marrying Terry or any one. I am only thinking that Mrs. Wade may be my mother. I've always wanted a mother. How I used to envy the Italian children when I was little. They had such soft warm, dark-eyed mothers. And I had only Granny, and Miss Searle. Miss Searle was fond of me but she was often cross with me. Granny never loved me as a mother would have. I was sometimes afraid of her though she was good to me", her cheeks were scarlet by this time, "I am going to stay here and wait for Mrs. Wade to return. If she does not come I must go to look for her. Terry need not trouble about me, nor Sir Shawn...."

"Oh, the poor boy!" said Lady O'Gara again, with the soft illogicality that her lovers loved in her. "But, Stella, love, you cannot stay here. Think how people would talk. Come home with me. You can wait just as well at Castle Talbot. Every day you shall come and see if she has returned. It would be better, of course, for you to go back to Inch..."

"But Granny will lock me in my room. I cannot go to Castle Talbot, for Sir Shawn would look coldly at me and I should not like that."

Lady O'Gara was suddenly decided. "You cannot stay here, Stella," she said. "It is quite out of the question."

In her own mind was a whirl of doubt and fear. Who was going to tell Stella? Who was going to tell her? Apparently Stella suspected no worse than that she was peasant-born. She had not yet arrived at the point of asking for her father. At any moment she might ask. What was any one to answer?

"Come with me, dear child," she said. "My husband comes home dead-tired these hunting days, has some food and stumbles off to bed. I am all alone. We can have the days together. I will write to your Granny that you are paying me a visit. Let us lock up here."

Someone paused in the road outside the window to look in, leaning impudently on the green paling. It was a ragged tramp bearded like the pard.

As he shuffled on his way Lady O'Gara said with a rather nervous laugh.

"There, Stella! You see the impossibility of your being here alone. I wonder where that creature came from! We don't get many of his sort here. Think of the night in this place! We could not possibly allow it. Mrs. Wade is sure to come back. She would not have gone away leaving all her things here. Was the door open when you came to it?"

"It was locked. I found the key where she used to put it if she went out. She sometimes walked over there across the Mount, where the people do not walk because they are afraid of the O'Hart ghosts. I thought I would wait for her till she came back."

"Let us lock up and put the key where she left it. She is sure to return. The place does not look as if she were not coming back."

"Everything is in order," said Stella, a light of hope coming to her face. "I have been in her bedroom. The lamp is burning on her altar. There is a purse lying on her bed with money in it."

"She will come back," said Lady O'Gara.

There was a sound of carriage wheels which made two pairs of eyes turn towards the window.

"It is Granny," said Stella, drawing back into the shade of the window curtains. "And she is very angry. She is sitting up so straight and tall. When she is like that I am afraid of her. Is she coming here?"

"Do not be afraid; I will stay with you," said Lady O'Gara.

The carriage re-passed the window, going slowly and without its occupant. Almost immediately came the sound of the knocker on the little hall-door.

CHAPTER XIX

ANGER CRUEL AS DEATH

Lady O'Gara met Mrs. Comerford in the hall. Despite the shadows of all the greenery outside flung through the fanlight across the White Horse of Hanover, which stands in so many Irish fanlights, she could see that the lady was in one of the towering rages she remembered and had dreaded in her youth. Looking at her, with a stammering apology on her lips, she had a wandering memory of the day at Inch long ago when Terry had broken a reproduction of the Portland Vase. He had been a big boy of sixteen then and he had flatly refused to meet his mother, going away and laying perdu in a stable loft for two or three days till she had forgotten her anger in her fear for him.

"Stella is here, I suppose," said the icy voice. That suggestion of holding herself in check, which accompanied Mrs. Comerford's worst anger, had been a terrifying thing in Mary Creagh's experience of her.

"I believe it is you I have to thank for introducing her to her mother. What a fool I was to have come back. I thought that shame was covered up long ago. What a mother for Stella!"

She spoke with a fierce scorn. She had not troubled to lower her voice.

Lady O'Gara lifted her hand in a warning gesture, glancing fearfully back over her shoulder. But the angry woman did not heed her.

"Have you told her what her mother is, what she is?" she demanded furiously. "Did you understand what you were doing, Mary O'Gara? It was your husband who told me Bride Sweeney had come back, who urged me to get Stella away. I was mad ever to have come home."

"Hush, hush!" said Lady O'Gara, wringing her hands and whispering. "Stella is in there; she will hear you..."

"Perhaps I mean her to hear me. She shall know what sort of woman it is who has crept back here to disgrace her and me and to ruin her life."

There came out into the hall a little figure gliding like a ghost, Stella, her eyes wide and piteous, her pretty colour blanched.

"My mother is a good woman," she said, facing Mrs. Comerford. "You must never say a word against her. I would follow her through the world. I have had more happiness with her in those stolen meetings than you could ever give me."

A pale shaft of Winter sunshine stole through the low hall window, filtered through red dead leaves that gave it the colour of a dying sunset. It fell on Stella's hair, bringing out its bronzes. She had the warm bronze hair of her father's people. It came to Lady O'Gara suddenly that she and Stella had much the same colouring. In Terence Comerford it had been ruddier. Why, any one might have known that Stella was a Comerford by that colour; not the child of some dark Frenchman.

"You stand up to me better than your father ever did," said Mrs. Comerford in white and gasping fury. Had she no pity, Mary O'Gara asked herself; and remembered that Grace Comerford's anger was sheer madness while it lasted. She had always known it. She had a memory of how she and Terence had tried to screen each other when they were children together.

"You dare to tell me that your shameful mother is more to you than I am!" the enraged woman went on. "It shows the class you have sprung from. I took you out of the gutter. I should have left you there."

"Oh, hush! hush!" cried Lady O'Gara in deep distress. "You do not know what you are saying, Grace. For Heaven's sake, be silent."

Mrs. Comerford pushed her away with a force that hurt. A terrible thing about her anger was that while she said appalling things her voice had hardly lifted.

Stella looked at her in a bewildered way. "I do not understand," she said. "You always told me my father was a gentleman. You said little about my mother. What have you against my mother except that she was a poor governess?"

"All that was fiction," said Grace Comerford, with a terrible laugh. "Very poor fiction. I often wondered that any one believed it. Your father was my son, Terence Comerford. He disgraced himself." She was as white as a sheet by this time. "Your mother was the granddaughter of the woman who kept the public-house in Killesky."

"Then I am your granddaughter?"

"In nature, not in law. My son did not marry your mother."

Stella groped in the air with her hands. They were taken and pressed against Mary O'Gara's heart. Mary O'Gara's arms drew the stricken child close to her.

"Go," she said to the pale, evil-looking woman, in whom she hardly recognized Mrs. Comerford. "Go! and ask God to forgive you and deliver you from your wicked temper. It has blighted your own life as well as your son's and your granddaughter's. Go!"

Mrs. Comerford put her hand to her throat. Her face darkened. She seemed as if she were going to fall. Then she controlled herself as by a mighty effort, turned and went out of the house. The bang of the hall-door as she went shook the little house. A second or two later her carriage passed the window, she sitting upright in it, her curious stateliness of demeanour unaltered.

Mary O'Gara did not look through the window to see her go. Her eyes were blind with tears as she bent over the child who was the innocent victim of others.

All her life afterwards she could never forget the anguish of poor Stella, who was like a thing demented. She could remember the objects that met her eyes as she held the two hot trembling hands to her with one hand while the other stroked Stella's ruffled hair. She felt as though she were holding the girl back by main force from the borderland beyond which lay total darkness. She could remember afterwards just the look of things, the Autumn leaves and berries in the blue jars on the chimney-piece; the convex glass leaning forward with its outspread eagle, mirroring her and Stella; Shot lying on his side on the hearthrug, now and again heaving a deep sigh. How pretty the room was, she kept thinking! What a quiet background for this human tragedy.

She knew that her heart was gabbling prayers for help, eagerly, insistently, while her lips only said over and over: "Hush, Stella! Be still, darling child!" and such tender foolish phrases.

At last the heart-broken crying was over. The girl was exhausted. Now and again a quiver passed through her where she sat with her face turned away from Lady O'Gara, but the terrible weeping was done.

"Come," Lady O'Gara said, at last. "We must find some water to bathe your face, you poor child. You are coming back with me to Castle Talbot. You are mine now. I shall not give you up again."

Stella shook her head; she stooped and kissed Lady O'Gara's hand as though she asked pardon. The swift dipping gesture like a bird's was too painful, recalling as it did the bright Stella of yesterday. Her hair was roughened like the feathers of a sick bird. Lady O'Gara, her hand passing softly over it, had felt the roughness with a pang.

"I am not yours, dear Lady O'Gara," she said. "I am no one's but my mother's. I am not going to Castle Talbot. I shall stay here for the present. If she does not come back I will go to look for her. All that other life is done with."

With a gesture of her little hands she put away all that had been hers till to-day, including Terry. His mother's heart began to ache anew with the thought of Terry. What would he say when he knew that Stella knew? Poor boy, he had a very gentle and faithful heart. Oh, what a tangle it all was, what a coil of things!

"But you can't stay here, darling child," she said tenderly. "How can you stay in this lonely little house by yourself? I will take you away somewhere where you do not know people, if you think that would be better. There are griefs that are more easily borne under the eyes of strangers. Let me see! There is a convent I know where you could be quiet for a little time, and I could trust the Reverend Mother, Mary Benedicta is her name; she is a cousin of mine and a dear friend, to be as loving to you as myself."

"She would be my ... father's cousin," said Stella; and a shudder ran through her. Then she said piteously:

"I never thought of my father as wicked."

Oh, poor Terence! How was she going to explain to the child to whom he had done this hideous wrong? Was it any use saying that Terence had always been good-natured? She remembered oddly after many years a day when he had turned away from the glazing eyes of a wood-pigeon he had shot. What use to tell such things to his daughter, whose life was laid in ruins by that sin of his youth? Those tragical eyes would confute her in the midst of her excuses. She could not yet make any plea for forgiveness for the dead man.

"Mother Mary Benedicta would be gentle with you," she said, "if you will not come to Castle Talbot. But, dear, no one need know. You shall take Eileen's place with me. You shall be my little daughter."

Her loving heart was running away with her. Shawn would never forgive her if she brought Stella to Castle Talbot, to which Terry might return at any time. Mary Benedicta would know how to tend the wounded spirit, if poor little Stella would but consent.

"It is getting late," said Stella, breaking in on the confusion of her thoughts. Her voice, which seemed drained of tears, was suddenly composed. "You will be late for lunch."

"And you, Stella, what about your lunch?"

She could have cried out on the futility of this talk of lunches.

Stella shook her head.

"There is food here if I want it. My mother had taken to storing dainty food for me, since I have been so much with her, as though her food was not good enough for me. I shall not starve, Lady O'Gara."

"Stella, I tell you it is impossible for you to stay here alone."

Lady O'Gara spoke almost sharply. She had a foreboding that Stella's will would be too strong for her.

"She will come back. She has left everything behind; even her purse with money in it. She must find me here when she comes home. We can go away together."

Lady O'Gara looked at the little face in despair. It was so set that it was not easy to recognize the soft Stella who had crept into all their hearts. Even Shawn had felt her charm though he had locked the door of his heart against her. A thought came to Lady O'Gara's mind. Stella's remaining at the cottage for the present would at least give time. Prudence whispered to her that she must not bring Stella to Castle Talbot. She might have felt equal to opposing Shawn, but, perhaps, she was relieved by the chance of escape. Shawn was not well, those dark shadows were more and more noticeable in his face. Other people had begun to see them and to ask her if Sir Shawn was not well. Presently Stella might be more amenable to reason, and go to Mother Mary Benedicta at St. Scholastua's Abbey. Benedicta was like her name. She, if any one, could salve the poor child's wound. She was as tolerant as she was tender, and she had been fond of Terence Comerford in the old days. No fear that she would be shocked at the story, as some women, cloistered or otherwise, might have been! Benedicta was perfect, Mary O'Gara said to herself and heaved a sigh of relief because there was Benedicta to turn to.

She felt tired out with her emotions, almost too tired to think. Suddenly she had a happy inspiration. She and Stella should eat together. The girl looked worn out. If she left her she was tolerably sure Stella would not think of food.

"No one will be alarmed if I do not come back for lunch," she said. "I often do not trouble about lunch when I am alone. They will expect me in for tea. Sir Shawn will not be home till late. Do you think you could give me some food, Stella?"

"Oh, yes, it will be a pleasure," Stella said, getting up with an air of anxious politeness. "I am sure there are eggs. You will not mind eggs for lunch, with tea and bread and butter. I am afraid the kitchen fire may be out, but the turf keeps a spark so long. It is alight when you think it is out."

She took the poker and stirred the grey fire to a blaze, then put on turf, building it as she had seen others do in the narrow grate.

"There are hearths in Connaught on which the fire has not gone out for fifty years," said Lady O'Gara, watching the shower of sparks that rose and fell as Stella struck the black sods with the poker.

Neither of them ate very much when the meal was prepared, though Stella drank the tea almost greedily. She had begun to look a little furtively at Lady O'Gara before the meal was finished as though she wished her to be gone. It hurt Mary O'Gara's kind heart; though she understood that the girl was aching for solitude. But how was she going to leave her in this haunted place alone, a child like her, in such terrible trouble?

Suddenly she found a solution of her difficulties. It would serve for the moment, if Stella would but consent.

"Would you have Mrs. Horridge to stay with you?" she asked. "You know you cannot stay here quite alone. She is a gentle creature, and very unobtrusive. I shall feel happy about you if she is here."

To her immense relief Stella consented readily.

"She has been very good to my mother," she said; "and they are both victims of men's cruelty."

Lady O'Gara, who was looking at Stella at the moment, noticed that her eyes fell on something outside the window and a quick shudder passed through the slight body. She went to Stella's side and saw only a heap of stones for road-mending. They must have been newly flung down there, for she did not remember to have seen them when last she passed this way.

Was it possible that Stella knew? That her eyes saw another heap of stones, and upon them a dead man lying, his blood turning the sharp stones red?

CHAPTER XX

SIR SHAWN HAS A VISITOR

The sun was low, almost out of sight, as Lady O'Gara climbed up the hill from Waterfall Cottage to her own South lodge. Through the bars of the gate she caught a glimpse of a red ball going low, criss-crossed with the bare branches of the trees. The air nipped. There was going to be frost. Before she left she had seen the lamps lit at Waterfall Cottage and bidden Stella lock herself in and only open to a voice she knew.

She had delayed, washing up the tea-cups with Stella, trying to distract the girl from her grief to the natural simple things of life: and all the time she had felt that Stella longed for her to be gone.

She had narrowly escaped being caught in the dusk, without the flashlight Terry had given her, which she usually carried when she went out these short afternoons. Was she growing as stupid as the villagers? She had glanced nervously at the heap of stones as she passed them by where the water made a loud roaring noise hurrying over the weir. She had to remind herself that it was not really dark but only dusk, and that she had never been afraid of the dark. Rather she had loved the kind night, the mantle with which God covers His restless earth that she may sleep. As she went up the hill she thought uneasily of the tramp who had passed the window of Waterfall Cottage a few hours earlier. The shambling figure had a menace for her. She could not keep from glancing over her shoulder and was glad to come to her own gate.

She called through the bars and Patsy Kenny came to open for her. Seeing him she sighed. More complications. Her mind was too weary to tackle the matter of Patsy's unfortunate attachment to Susan Horridge. Not that she doubted Patsy. She had a queer confidence that Patsy would not hurt the woman he loved. People would talk, were talking in all probability. What a world it was! What a world!

Of late Patsy had refrained from visiting the South lodge so far as she knew. Sir Shawn had said to her only a day or two before that Patsy had taken up the fiddle again, Patsy was a great fiddler, that he could hear him playing his old tunes night after night. There had been an interval during which the fiddle had been silent. She thought that, with the simple craft of his class, Patsy might have played the fiddle to let possible gossips know that he was at home in the solitude which in the old times before Susan came he had never seemed to find solitary.

"Is that you, m'lady?" said Patsy. "The dark was near comin' up wid ye. I'd like if you'd the time you'd come in and see Susan. She's frightened like in herself an' she won't listen to rayson."

"Why, what's the matter?" asked Lady O'Gara, turning towards the lodge, while Patsy re-padlocked the gate. She did not wait for his answer, which was slow of coming. Patsy was always deliberate.

In the quiet and cheerful interior of the lodge she found a terrified Susan. Michael lay on the hearth-rug before a bright fire, Georgie sat by the white, well-scrubbed table, his cheek on his hand, the lamplight on his pale fine hair, watching his mother anxiously; the lesson book on top of a pile of others, was plainly forgotten.

Susan seemed desperately frightened. She got out the reason why at last, with some help from Patsy Kenny. She shook as she told the tale. She had been washing, outside the lodge, earlier in the day, fortunately out of view of the gate, when someone had shaken it and cursed at finding it locked. Susan had seen his hand, a coarse hairy hand, thrust through the gate in an attempt to force the lock. The man, whoever he was, had gone on his way, seeing the futility of trying to enter by the strongly padlocked gate. Susan had locked herself in the lodge till Georgie had come home from school, when the two of them had fled to Patsy Kenny for protection.

"The poor girl will have it that Baker has come back," said Patsy, scratching his head. "She says she knew his voice an' the wicked-looking hand of him. If it was to be him itself, but I had the Master's word for it he had gone to America, he wouldn't know she was here. I keep on tellin' her that, but she won't listen."

Lady O'Gara had a passing wonder about Shawn's having known that Susan's husband was gone to America, she had not associated the person who had saved Shawn from accident at Ashbridge Park with Susan's graceless husband.

"He might find out by asking questions," said Susan. "He's only got to ask. There's many a one to tell him."

"I was goin' to your Ladyship," said Patsy. "The two frightened things can't be left their lone in this little place. The heart would jump out of her. Can't I see it flutterin' there in her side like a bird caught in your hand."

"I came to ask Susan if she would go down to Waterfall Cottage to look after Miss Stella Comerford, who is there alone."

Lady O'Gara's eyes fluttered nervously. She was aware of the strangeness of the thing she said, and she felt shy about the effect of it on her listeners. She hastened to make some kind of explanation.

"Miss Stella has had a disagreement with Mrs. Comerford and will not return to her, for the present. She wishes to stay at Waterfall Cottage, but, of course, she cannot stay alone."

"The poor young lady," said Susan, looking up; she added hopefully: "Baker would never look for me there. The people would think I was gone away out of this place. Few pass Waterfall Cottage, and we could keep the gate locked."

"Where at all is Mrs. Wade gone to?" asked Patsy; not seeming to find it strange that Miss Stella should be at Waterfall Cottage.

"Could Georgie be very wise and silent?" asked Lady O'Gara.

Georgie flushed under her look and sent her a worshipping glance.

"Georgie would be silent enough if it was likely his father would find us," said Susan. "Not but what he's quiet by nature. Baker used to say that Georgie would run into a mouse-hole from him. Not that I let him knock my Georgie about. I told him if he laid a hand on Georgie I'd do him a mischief, and he believed me. He knocked me about after that."

"God help the two o' ye," said Patsy with sharp anguish in his voice. "If I was to see the rascal I couldn't keep my hands off him."

"He might do you a harm. The hands of him are dangerous strong. He used to say he'd choked a man once. It isn't likely I wouldn't know the wicked hands of him when I saw them."

"I'd take my chance," said Patsy with a baleful light in his eyes. "The one time I seen him I was mad to kill him. I never felt the like before for any man. 'Twas like a dog I seen when the Master an' me was in South Africay. He'd found a nest of vipers, and I never seen anything like the rage o' that dog whin he wint tearin' them to tatters. I felt the same way with that blackguard that owns you, Susan, my girl."

Patsy was pale, and in the lamplight little drops of perspiration showed on his forehead and about his lips.

"Very probably the man who frightened Susan was not her husband at all," Lady O'Gara put in. "But in the remote case of its being Baker, Susan will be better away for the present. She can have Georgie with her, or perhaps he could stay with you, Patsy?"

"I'd like to have Georgie with me, if he didn't mind keepin' to the house in the daytime," said Patsy with a fatherly look at the boy. "He'd have the run o' the books, what he's always cravin' for."

"Georgie can go to Mr. Penny's," said Susan. "He'll be safe there an' my mind'll be easy about him."

"I'll leave you then, Susan, to put out the fire here and lock the door," Lady O'Gara said. "Be as quick as you can. I don't like to think of Miss Stella in that lonely place. Here is the key of the gate. I locked it when I came through. Miss Stella will let you in when you knock. Patsy will take you down there. You won't be afraid with him?"

"Not with Mr. Kenny, m'lady," said Susan with a flattering fervour.

Lady O'Gara went on her way, refusing the offer of Georgie as an escort. She was quite safe with Shot, she said; adding that she was not at all a nervous person. She was a bit puzzled now about her panic coming up the dark road, under the trees, from Waterfall Cottage to the South lodge.

She stepped out briskly. It was nearly a mile from the South lodge to the house. The darkness increased as she went. She was quite pleased to see the light shining from the window of the room Sir Shawn called his office, through the bay trees and laurestinus and Portugal laurels which lay between her and it. She was glad Shawn was at home. She had forgotten for once to ask Patsy if the Master was at home. After all the years of their life together her heart always lifted for Shawn's coming home before the dark night settled down upon the world.

She had only to tap on the French window and he would open it and let her in, as he had done so many times before.

She took the path by the side of the house, between the ivied wall and the shrubbery.

As she approached the window Shot uttered a low growl. At the same moment she became aware that her husband was not alone. Someone had crossed between the light and the window. For a second a huge shadow was flung across the gravel path almost at her feet.

With a sigh she went back again, entering by the hall-door way. She was sorry Shawn had one of his troublesome visitors. She wanted so much to talk to him, to tell him of all the trouble about Stella. She felt chilled that he was not ready to listen to her when she needed to talk to him so much.

"Sir Shawn has returned, m'lady," said Reilly, the new butler, the possessor of a flat large face with side whiskers which always made her want to laugh. Reilly's manners, she had said, would befit a ducal household, and it had been no surprise to her to learn that he had lived with an old gentleman who had a Duke for a grandfather, and that a part of his duties had been to recite family prayers, understudying his master.

"Yes," she said, "has he had tea, Reilly?"

"No, m'lady. He did not wish for tea."

"He has a visitor? Has this person been long with him?"

"I don't know, m'lady. No one came in this way. I went a while ago to see if the fire was burning, and I found the door locked, m'lady, I concluded Sir Shawn did not wish to be disturbed."

"Sir Shawn's visitors on business come in by the window that opens on the lawn. The handle of the office door is rather stiff. I don't think it could have been locked."

She went on down the passage to the office door. She heard voices the other side of the door. Sir Shawn was speaking in a fatigued voice. She had hardly ever known him to speak angrily. She listened for a second or two. The other voice answered; it was thick and coarse: she could not hear what was said. She went back to the drawing-room, where a little later Sir Shawn joined her.

Even when they were alone she always dressed in her most beautiful garments for her husband's eyes. To-night she had chosen a pink satin dress, close-fitting and trailing heavily, with her garnets.

She was sitting by the fire when Sir Shawn came in and his eyes lighted as they fell upon her.

"You look like your own daughter, Mary," he said, "only so much more beautiful than the girl I married. What a wonderful colour your gown is! It makes you like a beautiful open rose."

She laughed. His compliments were never stale to her.

"Where were you when I came in?" he asked. "'I looked in your chamber, 'twas lonely?'"

She evaded the question for a moment. "I made an attempt to enter by your window as I came back, but you had a visitor."

He was standing with his back to the fire, looking down at her, and she saw the ominous shadows come in the hollows of his cheeks.

"A troublesome visitor, Mary," he said. "When I come to you you exorcise all my troubles. You are the angel before whom the blue devils flee away."

She did not ask him further about his visitor. So many of them were troublesome. She often wondered at Shawn's patience with the people. The family quarrels over land were apt to be the worst of all: but there were other things hardly less disagreeable.

"Poor Shawn!" she said tenderly. "Sit down by me and let me smoothe that line out of your forehead! It threatens to become permanent."

She stooped, half playfully, to him as he sat down beside her leaning his head back against a cushion, and touched his forehead with her finger-tips gently.

"Go on doing that, Mary," he said. "It seems to smoothe a tangle out of my brain. I cannot tell you how restful it is. I saw Terry off, and the others. The boy looked rather down in the mouth. What have you been doing all day?"

It was a quiet hour. She had dressed early on purpose to have this hour. No one had business in the room till the dressing bell rang. She had learnt by long use to watch his moods. She knew her own power over him, to soothe, to assuage. The moment was propitious. So she told him the tale of the day's happenings, in a quiet easy flow, now and again patting his hand or stroking his forehead with her delicate finger-tips.

"Good Lord, what a kettle of fish!" he groaned when she had finished. "And you take it so easily, Mary! I wish to the Lord, Grace Comerford had never come back. It was an ill day."

She almost echoed the wish. Then she found herself, to her amazement, setting Stella against all the trouble, putting her in the balance against all that had happened and might happen. To her amazement Stella counted against all the rest. She was just the little daughter she had wanted all her days, to stay with her when the insistent world snatched her boy from her. She acknowledged to herself that she was jealous of the woman who was Stella's real mother, whom the girl had chosen before everything, everyone else.

She sought in her own mind, with what her husband called her incurable optimism, for a bright side to this dark trouble and could find none. She must leave it where she left everything, at the foot of the altar. God could unpick the black knot of Stella's fate. He could smooth out the tangle. She must only pray and hope.

She had meant to talk the matter out thoroughly with Shawn. She had so often found that light and comfort came that way. But Shawn would not discuss things thoroughly. He would only say that it was a pretty kettle of fish; that he wished Grace Comerford had never come back, that he wished they could send Terry somewhere out of harm's way. And presently he fell asleep with his head against her shoulder. He had had a hard day and a tiring one. Of late he had taken to dropping asleep in the evenings.

She let him sleep, remaining as motionless as she could so as not to disturb him. When he awoke he was full of repentance. She had not even had a book to solace her watch. That which she had been reading was out of reach.

"You are the perfect woman, Mary," he said gratefully, "and I am an unworthy fellow. I don't know how I came to be so sleepy. You make me too comfortable."

Her face lit up. Shawn was often unreasonable in these latter days. Indeed he had not been the easiest of men to live with since Terence Comerford's tragic death. But when he was like this his wife thought that all was worthwhile.

CHAPTER XXI

STELLA IS SICK

A few days passed by and Mrs. Wade had not returned. Mrs. Comerford had written an icy message to Mary O'Gara.

"When Stella comes to her right mind this house is open to her. I have said to my servants that she is with you. I was once a truthful woman."

Reading this brief epistle Mary O'Gara had said to herself that it was lucky there was distance enough between Inch and Castle Talbot; also that though she considered herself a truthful woman there was nothing she would not say in order to shield Stella from gossiping tongues. She was bitterly angry with Grace Comerford for the cruel and evil temper which had done so much hurt to an innocent thing.

"Does she think," she asked herself hotly, "that so easily Stella will forget her cruelty? I do not believe the child will ever go back to her."

She had written to Mary Benedicta about the case, giving her a cautious account of poor Stella's plight, abstaining from mentioning Terence Comerford's part in the story. She could have told that: she could not write it. Mary Benedicta would think that Stella's trouble came from the fictitious French father. There was little or no communication between the nun and Mrs. Comerford, who had quarrelled with her over her choice of a conventual life long ago.

Mary Benedicta had answered the letter with another full of the milk and honey of a compassionate tenderness.

The best solution of the problem Lady O'Gara could find was that Stella should go for a time at least to the Convent. Terry had not written. Terry would have his say in the matter presently. He had gone off chilled for the time by Stella's disinclination towards him: but he would come back. If he only knew Stella's plight at this moment he would surely break all the barriers to get back to her.

Poor Stella's plight was indeed a sad one. Susan Horridge, watching her like a faithful dog, reported that she ate little, that she walked up and down her room at night when she ought to have been sleeping, that she started when spoken to, that she spent long hours staring before her piteously, doing nothing.

"If Mrs. Wade don't come back soon the young lady will either go after her or she'll have a breakdown," Susan said.

Sometimes Lady O'Gara wondered how much Susan knew or suspected, but there was in her manner an entire absence of curiosity, of a sense that anything out of the way was happening, that was invaluable in a crisis like this. Lady O'Gara thought more highly of Susan every day. The weather had turned very wet, but Waterfall Cottage glowed with brightness and roaring fires of turf and wood. The rain and darkness were shut out. Stella could not have been in better hands.

About the fifth day came a hunting morning. The meet was fixed for a distant part of the country. Lady O'Gara got up in the dark of the morning to superintend her husband's cup of tea, to see that his flask was filled and his sandwiches to his liking.

"I wish you had been coming out too, Mary," he said wistfully as he stood on the steps drawing on his gloves. "You are growing lazy, old lady."

"I'll come out with you on Saturday," she said, and patted his shoulder.

Patsy was late in bringing round Black Prince, the beautiful spirited horse which was Sir Shawn's favourite hunter that season. It was unlike Patsy to be late. The first grey dawn was coming lividly over the sky. Standing in the lamplit hall Mary O'Gara looked out and caught the shiver of the little wind which brings the day.

"I'll be late at the Wood of the Hare," Sir Shawn said, fuming a little. "I don't want to press the Prince with a hard day before him."

Still Patsy did not come.

"Good-bye, darling," Sir Shawn said at last. "Go back to bed and have a good sleep before breakfast. I'll see what's up with Patsy."

She had gone upstairs before she heard her husband ride out of the stable yard. So Patsy had been late. Was it possible he had overslept? It would be so unlike Patsy, who, especially of a hunting morning, had always slept the fox's sleep.

She had a long day before her, with many things to do. She ought to write to Terry, but she knew the things Terry expected to hear. There had been a letter from him, asking roundly for news of Stella.

"Why don't you write?" it asked. "Are you going to treat me like a child as Father does? I've made up my mind about Stella. I will marry her, if she will have me; and she shall never know anything from me. Are you looking after her, keeping her happy? For Heaven's sake don't take Father's view of it! That would be ruin to everything, but I warn you, that if you do, it will not alter me. Tell me what she says, how she looks. Has her colour come back? Does she speak of me? There are a thousand things I want to know."

There had been a postscript to the letter.

"By the way, Evelyn has discovered that the man who got the lakh of rupees, you remember? had been rather badly treated by Eileen, or so Evelyn's informant said. It is a she, a cousin of Evelyn's who is married to somebody up there. Evelyn says he will come again to Castle Talbot if you ask him. He says the duck-shooting was splendid, and he congratulated me on you, darling. I did myself proud. Just imagine, Evelyn!"

She did not know how to answer his letter. It was not in her to put off the boy with a letter which should disappoint him. She imagined him running through it with a blank face, looking for what she had not written. No: she could not write without telling him the truth: and the truth would make the boy miserable. She supposed it would have to be told, presently, but she would wait till then. She was not one to deal in half-truths and subterfuges.

She went forth after breakfast with an intention of seeing Stella, and afterwards going on to old Lizzie Brennan, who required some looking after, in cold weather especially. She had rather mad fits of wandering over the country, from which she would return soaked through with rain, hungry and exhausted. More than once Lady O'Gara had discovered her after these expeditions, choking with bronchitis, in a fireless room, too weak to light a fire or prepare food for herself. Lady Conyers, a neighbour of Castle Talbot at Mount Esker, had tried to induce Lizzie to go into the workhouse, with many arguments as to the comfort which awaited her there. But Lizzie was about as much inclined for the workhouse as the free bird for the cage, and, rather to Lady Conyers' indignation, Lady O'Gara had abetted the culprit, saying that she would look after her.

There was not much to be done with Stella, who had begun to look sharpened in the face and her eyes very bright. Susan repeated that her charge did not sleep. She had gone in to her half a dozen times during the night and found her wide-eyed on the pillow, staring at the ceiling.

"I never see any one take on so," Susan said. "Seems to me if Missie don't get what she wants she won't be long wantin' anything."

Stella had shown no inclination to get up and Susan had left her in bed.

"Seems like as if gettin' up was more than she could a-bear," said Susan. "I did try to coax her out when the day were sunny, but 'twas no use. That poor old fly-away Miss Brennan came to the door this mornin' with a bunch of leaves and berries. I asked her into my kitchen, and gave her a cup o' cocoa. There, she were grateful, poor soul!"

"You must have the four-leaved shamrock, Susan," Lady O'Gara said. "Lizzie is so very stand-off with most people."

"So Mr. Kenny was tellin' me. He used your Ladyship's words. I never 'eard of the four-leaved shamrock before. She has a kind heart. There, I'd never have thought it. She was fair put out over the poor young lady. She talked about a decline in a way that giv me a turn. But people don't go into a decline sudding like that. It's something on Miss Stella's mind. Take that away and she'll be as bright as bright. So I said to the old person, an' she took a fit o' bobbin' to me, and then she ran off a-talkin' to herself."

Lady O'Gara went up to the pretty bedroom which had been Mrs. Wade's. It was in the gable and was lit from the roof and by a tiny slit of a window high up in the wall through which one saw the bare boughs across the road, with a few fluttering leaves still on them. A similar window on the other side had a picture of the wet country, the distant woods of Mount Esker, and the sapphire sky just above the sapphire line of hills.

The little windows were open and a soft wet wind blew into the room. When Lady O'Gara had climbed up the corkscrewy staircase and stepped into the room she was horrified to find the ravages one more day's suspense had wrought in Stella's looks. Her eyes were heavy and there were dark red spots in her cheeks.

"Is that you, Lady O'Gara?" she asked in a low voice, "I've been asleep, and I've only just wakened up. You are very good to come to see me, but now you need not trouble about me any more. I am going away from here. I do not think she will come back. She must have got a long way on her road in these endless seven days of time. I should have followed her at first and not wasted time waiting for her here."

"But, my poor child, where would you have gone?" Lady O'Gara asked, sitting down beside the bed and capturing one of the restless hands.

"I think that old woman, Lizzie Brennan, knows something about where she is. She was here yesterday, and she looked in at me and seemed frightened. 'God help you, child,' she said. 'Don't you be wearin' your heart out. She'll come back fast enough as soon as she knows you want her. You see, mavourneen, it's a long time since she was anything but a trouble to people.' I thought she was only talking in her mad way. But since I've wakened up I've been thinking that maybe she knows something."

"Oh, I wouldn't build on it, child. Lizzie often talks nonsense, though she's not as mad as people think."

"I was just going to get up when I heard your foot on the stairs. I feel stronger this morning, and I want to get out-of-doors. The house is stifling me. I have been listening so hard for the sound of her foot or her voice that when I try to listen I can't hear for the thumping of my heart in my ears. I want to be with her. I too am only a trouble to people. She and I will not be a trouble to each other."

Lady O'Gara had a thought.

"If you will get up and dress and eat your breakfast to my satisfaction I shall go with you to Lizzie Brennan's lodge. It is only about half a mile down the road. You have been too much in the house."

She went away downstairs, leaving Stella to get up and dress. There was a dainty little breakfast ready for her when she came down, but she did it little justice. Lady O'Gara had to be content with her trying to eat. She seemed tired even after the slight exertion of dressing, but she was very eager to go to Lizzie Brennan.

"If only I knew I should find my mother I should not be so troublesome to you kind people," she said with a quivering smile, which Lady O'Gara found terribly pathetic.

She said to herself that Grace Comerford must have lacked a good deal in her relation towards Stella to have left the child so hungry for mother-love. Again there was something that puzzled her. Stella seemed to have forgotten everything except the fact of her mother's disappearance. Did she understand the facts of her birth, all that they meant to her and how the world regarded them? Or was it that these things were swallowed up in the girl's passion of love and loss?

Stella started out at a great pace, but lagged after a little while, and turned with an apology to Lady O'Gara.

"I feel as though I had had influenza," she said. "I suppose it's being in the house so much and not eating or sleeping well. Oh, I must not get ill, Lady O'Gara; for I cannot stay here unless my mother comes back..."

"I thought you liked us all, Stella," Lady O'Gara said, rather sadly. "You seemed very happy with us always."

"That was before my mother came, before I knew that she and I belonged to each other and were only a trouble to people."

She harped on old Lizzie's phrase.

"My poor little mother!" she said. "All that time I was living in luxury my mother was working. Her poor hands are the hands of a working woman. I cannot bear to look at them."

"She was in America, was she not?" Lady O'Gara asked, by way of saying something.

"She never spoke of America. I do not think she was there. She was housekeeper somewhere, to a priest. She said he was such a good old man, innocent and simple. He had a garden with bee-hives, and a poodle dog she was very fond of. She said it had been a refuge to her for many years; and she did not like leaving the good old man, but something drew her back. She was hungry for news of me."

The child was not ashamed of her mother. Perhaps she did not understand. Lady O'Gara was glad. She remembered how Shawn had always said that Bridyeen was innocent and simple.

They had arrived at the gate, one half of it swinging loose from the hinges; the stone balls, once a-top of the gate-posts, were down on the ground, having brought a portion of the gate-post with them.

Lady O'Gara glanced at the lodge. It had been a pretty place once, with diamond-paned windows and a small green trellised porch, over which woodbine and roses had trailed. There were still one or two golden spikes of the woodbine, and a pale monthly rose climbed to the top of the porch to the roof; but the creepers which grew round the windows had been torn down and were lying on the grass-green gravel path.

"Lizzie is out," Lady O'Gara said, glancing at the door hasped and padlocked. "We shall have to come another time."

CHAPTER XXII

A SUDDEN BLOW

There was always a good deal of interest for Lady O'Gara in the affairs of Castle Talbot. She went out after her solitary lunch to look for Patsy Kenny. She wanted to talk to him about the turf and wood to be given away to the poor people for Christmas. Little by little Patsy had slid from being stud-groom into being general overlooker of the business of the place.

Having found him she went with him into the stables where the light was just failing, going from one to the other of the horses, talking to them, fondling them, discussing them with Patsy in the knowledgable way of a person accustomed to horses and loving them all her days.

Suddenly she caught sight of Black Prince, wrapped up in a horse-cloth, hanging his long intelligent nose over his stall and looking at her wistfully.

"Why," she said, "I thought Sir Shawn was riding the Prince!" She put out her hand to fondle the delicate nose and Black Prince whinnied.

"No, m'lady. The Prince was coughin' this mornin': and Tartar was a bit lame. You might notice I was late comin' round. I didn't want the master to ride Mustapha. Not but what he's come on finely and the master has a beautiful pair of hands. You'll remember Vixen that broke her back at the double ditch at Punchestown, how she was a lamb with the master though a greater divil than Mustapha to the rest of the world?"

She knew that way Patsy had of talking a lot about a subject when he was really keeping something essential back. It was quite true that Mustapha had been coming to his senses of late, and Shawn had a beautiful pair of hands, gentle yet as strong as steel. She had thought Patsy's anxiety about Mustapha's being ridden by anyone but himself unnecessary, perhaps even with an unconscious spice of vanity underlying it. Patsy had conquered Mustapha. Perhaps he would not be altogether pleased that the horse should be amenable to someone else, yet Mustapha had taken a lump of sugar from her hand, only yesterday, as daintily as her own Chloë, his muzzle moving over her hands afterwards with silken softness.

"I hope Mustapha will repay all the time and care you have spent on him, Patsy," she said, and would not acknowledge that her heart had turned cold for a second.

She hoped Shawn would be home early, before she had time to feel alarmed. Of course there was no cause for alarm. Patsy himself said that Mustapha had come to be that kind that a lamb or a child could play with him. It was absurd of Patsy not to be satisfied about Shawn's riding the horse.

There were some things Patsy needed, a bandage for Tartar, some cough-balls for Black Prince, which could be procured at the general shop in Killesky.

She went into Sir Shawn's office to write the order. Patsy would come for it presently.

After she had written it she went out by the open French window and climbed the rising ground at the back of the house. Very often she went up there of afternoons to look at the sunset. She had always loved sunsets.

The afternoon had been grey, but at the top of the hill she was rewarded for her climb. On one side the sloping valley was filled with a dun-coloured mist. Over it leant the dun-coloured cloud which was a part of the grey heavens. To the other side were the hills, coloured the deep blue which is only seen in the West of Ireland. Behind them were long washes of light, silver and pale gold. The dun cloud above had caught the sapphire as though in a mirror. Round the Southern and Western horizon ran the broad belt of light under the sapphire cloud, while to North and East the dun sky met the dun-coloured mist.

She went back after a while, her sense of beauty satisfied. From that hill one could hear anything, horse or vehicle, coming from a long way off. The sound ascended and was not lost in the winding and twisting roads. But she would not acknowledge disappointment to herself. She had gone up to look at the evening sky and it had been beautiful with one of the strange kaleidoscopic effects which makes those Western skies for ever new and beautiful.

The tea had been brought in and the lamps lit when a visitor was announced, Sir Felix Conyers. She was glad she had not heard the noise of his arrival and mistaken it for Shawn's.

Sir Felix was an old soldier who had held an important command in India. He was a rather fussy but very kind-hearted person whom Mary O'Gara liked better than his handsome cold wife with her organized system of charities.

"This is kind, Sir Felix," she said. "Shawn is not home yet. They met at the Wood of the Hare this morning. The scent must have lain well. We were a little anxious about the frost before the wind went to the South-West."

Then she discovered that Sir Felix, a transparently simple person, was labouring under some curious form of excitement. He stammered as he tried to answer, and looked at her furtively. He dropped his riding whip, which he was carrying in his hands, stooped to look for it and came up rather apologetic and more nervous than before.

"The fact is ... I came over, Lady O'Gara ... to ... to ..."

"Is anything the matter, Sir Felix?"

Down went her heart like a plummet of lead. Shawn! Had anything happened to Shawn? Had this stammering, purple-faced gentleman come to prepare her? Her heart gave a cry of anguish, while her eyes rested with apparent calmness on Sir Felix's unhappy face. Of course it was Mustapha. Would he never speak? Why could they not have found a better messenger than this unready inarticulate gentleman?

At last the cry was wrung from her: "Has anything happened to my husband?"

"No! God bless my soul, no!"

Her heart lifted slightly with the relief and fell again. She had been frightened and had not got over the shock.

"It is a perfectly absurd business, Lady O'Gara. Your husband will, I have no doubt", he emitted a perfectly unnatural chuckle, "be immensely amused. I should not have mentioned it ... I should have shown the ruffian the door, only that new District Inspector ... Fury ... a very good name for him ... mad as a hatter, I should say ... brought the fellow to me."

"What is it all about, Sir Felix?" asked Lady O'Gara, in a voice of despair.

"My dear lady, have I been trying you? I'm sorry." Sir Felix pulled himself together by a manifest effort.

"I apologize for even telling you such a thing, though I don't believe one word of it. The fellow was obviously drunk and so I told D.I. Fury. I absolutely refused to swear him, but I had to issue a summons. Yes, yes, I'm coming to it now! Don't be impatient, my dear lady. A low drunken tramp went to the police with a ridiculous story that your husband was privy to the death of young Terence Comerford, poor fellow! Ridiculous! when everyone knows there was the love of brothers between them. The ruffian maintains that he was on the spot, that your husband and Comerford were quarrelling, that your husband struck him repeatedly, he not being in a way to defend himself, finally that he lashed the horse, a young and very spirited horse who would not take the whip, saying:

'You'll never reach home alive, Terence Comerford! You've forced me to do it.' My dear lady, don't look so terrified. Of course there's nothing in it. Your husband will have to answer the charge at Petty Sessions. It won't go any further. If it were true itself they couldn't bring it in more than manslaughter. Indeed, I doubt if any charge would lie after so many years."

He stopped, panting after the long speech.

"It was very kind of you to ride over this dark night to tell us. Of course it is a ridiculous tale. But the mere suggestion will upset my husband. As you say, they were so devoted, dearer than brothers. Why should this person come with such a tale at this time of day?"

"That is exactly what I asked, my dear lady. Trumped up, every bit of it, I haven't the smallest doubt. Only for Fury it would end where it began. The fellow says, I beg your pardon, Lady O'Gara, that Sir Shawn paid him to keep silence, that he has grown tired of being bled and told him to do his worst. As I said to Fury, you had only to look at the fellow to see that the truth wasn't in him."

Lady O'Gara was very pale.

"Would you mind waiting a second, Sir Felix?" she said gently. "You were not here at the time of the dreadful accident. The one who really all but witnessed it is here, close at hand. You might like to hear his version of what happened."

She rang the bell and asked the servant who came in answer if Mr. Kenny was waiting. Patsy was Mr. Kenny even to the new butler.

Patsy came in, small, neat, in his gaiters and riding breeches, his cap in his hand. He stood blinking in the lamplight, looking from Lady O'Gara to Sir Felix Conyers.

"Sir Felix would like to hear from your lips, Patsy, the story of what you saw the night Mr. Terence Comerford was killed."

There was a wild surmise in Patsy's eyes. Not for many a year had that tragedy been spoken of in his hearing.

"I would not recall it," Lady O'Gara went on in her gentle voice, "only that Sir Felix tells me some man has been saying that Sir Shawn flogged Mr. Comerford's horse, using words as he did so which proved that he knew the horse would not take the whip and that he had it in his mind to kill Mr. Comerford."

"Who was the man said the likes of that?" asked Patsy, his eyes suddenly red.

"It was a sort of ... tramping person," said Sir Felix, putting on his pince-nez the better to see Patsy. "He has been in these parts before. A most unprepossessing person. Quite a bad lot, I should say."

"A foxy man with a hanging jowl," said Patsy. "Not Irish by his speech. Seems like as if he'd curse you if you come his way. No whiskers, a bare-faced man."

"That would be his description."

"It's a quare thing," said Patsy in a slow ruminating voice, "that for all the rage I felt agin him, so that I wanted to throttle him wid me two hands, I never thought of him with the man that was there the night Mr. Terence Comerford was killed. Did you notice the big hairy hands of him? They all but choked me that night. I thought I'd cause enough to hate him when he came my way again because o' the poor girl and the child. I could scarce keep my hands off him. The villain! I'd rather kill him than a rat in the stable yard."

"You seem to have a very accurate idea about the person who has made this grotesque charge against your master," Sir Felix said in his pompous way. "Your feelings do you credit, but still ... I should not proceed to violence."

"Please tell Sir Felix what happened that night, Patsy," Lady O'Gara said. She had stood up and gone a little way towards the window. She spoke in a quiet voice. Only one who was devoted to her, as Patsy was, could have guessed the control she was exercising over herself. Patsy's eyes, in the shadow of the lamp, sent her a look of mute protecting pity and tenderness.

"'Tis, sir, that I was in the ditch that night." Patsy turned his cap about in his hands. "I was lookin' for the goat an' she draggin' her chain an' the life frightened out of me betwixt the black night and the ghosts and the terrible cross ould patch I had of a grandfather, that said he'd flog me alive if I was to come home without the goat. I was blowin' on me hands for the cowld an' shakin' wid fright o' bein' me lone there; an' not a hundred yards between me an' that place where the ould Admiral's ghost walks. When I heard the horses' feet comin' my heart lifted up, once I was sure it wasn't ghosts they was. They passed me whin I was sittin' in the ditch. No sooner was they gone by than I let a bawl out o' me, an' I ran after them for company, for it come over me how I was me lone in that dark place. You see, your Honour, I was only a bit of a lad, an' th' ould grandfather had made me nervous-like. Just then I caught the bleat of the goat an' I was overjoyed, for I thought I'd ketch her an' creep home behind Sir Shawn an' the walkin' horse. They parted company where the roads met, an' I heard Sir Shawn trottin' his horse up the road in front o' me, an' Spitfire, that was Mr. Comerford's horse, was unaisy an' refusin' the dark road under the trees. You couldn't tell what the crathur saw, God help us all! No horse liked that road. Thin I heard Spitfire clatterin' away in the dark an' I ran, draggin' the little goat after me to get past the place where the unchancy ould road dips down. Somewan cannoned into me runnin' out o' the dark road. I couldn't see his face, but he cursed me, an' I felt his hairy hands round me neck and me scratchin' and tearin' at them. It was that villain that's comin' here to annoy the master, or I think it was. Mind you, I never seen him. But he took me up be me little coat an' he dashed me down on the road an' nigh knocked the life out o' me. The next thing I knew I was lying in the bed at home an' me sore from head to foot, an' able to see only out o' wan eye be rayson of a bandage across the other: an' me grandfather an' the neighbours wor sayin' that Mr. Terence Comerford was kilt, and that Sir Shawn O'Gara was distracted with grief. But the quarest thing at all was hearin' the ould man sayin' that I was a good little boy, after all the divils and villains he'd called me, as long as I could remember."

Patsy stopped, still turning his hat about in his hands, his velvety eyes fixed on Lady O'Gara, where she stood leaning by the mantelpiece, her face turned away, one slender foot resting on the marble kerb. If Sir Felix had been aware of the expression of the eyes he might have been startled, but even the pince-nez were not equal to that.

"Thank you very much," he said. "That story should knock the bottom out of our friend's statement. Merely vexatious; I said so to D.I. Fury. Sir Shawn and Mr. Comerford parted in perfect amity?"

"Like brothers," said Patsy with emphasis, "as they wor ever an' always. Sure the master was never the same man since. I often heard the people sayin' how it was the love of brothers was betwixt them, an' more, for many a blood brother doesn't fret for his brother as the master fretted for Master Terence. He was never the same man since."

CHAPTER XXIII

THE HOME-COMING

After Sir Felix had gone off, profuse in his apologies, and anathematizing Mr. Fury's zeal, Lady O'Gara went to a desk in the corner of the drawing-room, a Sheraton desk which she did not often use. She found a tiny key and unlocked a little cupboard door between the pigeon-holes. She felt about the back of one of the three little drawers it contained and brought out a sliding well, one of the innocent secret receptacles which are so easily discovered by anyone who has the clue. She drew out a little bundle of yellow papers from it, newspaper cuttings. These she took to the lamp and proceeded to read with great care.

Once or twice she knitted her fair brows over something as she read; but, on the whole, she seemed satisfied as she put the papers back into their secret place, locked the little door and put away the key.

Then she remembered that she had not given Patsy his orders.

She went to Sir Shawn's office-room and wrote them out. While she put the second one in its envelope Patsy tapped at the door and came in, closing it carefully behind him.

"No wan 'ud be expectin' the master home from the Wood o' the Hare yet," he said. "'Tis a good step an' Sir John Fitzgerald would be very sorry to part with him after he'd carried him in for his lunch. Maybe 'tis staying to dinner he'd be."

Lady O'Gara looked at her watch.

"It's quite early," she said; "not much after six."

"'Tis a dark night," said Patsy. "Maybe 'tis the way they'll be persuadin' him to wait till the moon rises. Sorra a bit she'll show her face till nine to-night."

Mary O'Gara's heart sank. She knew that Patsy was nervous.

"He may come at any moment," she said. "I don't think he'll wait for the rising of the moon."

"It isn't like the troubled times," said Patsy, "an' you listenin' here, an' me listenin' by the corner o' the stable-yard where the wind brings the sounds from the bog-road whin 'tis in that quarter. Your Ladyship had great courage. An' look at all you must ha' went through whin we was at the War!"

He looked compassionately at her as he went towards the door.

"I'll be sendin' a boy wid this message," he said. "Or maybe Georgie an' me would be steppin' down there. It's lonesome for the child to be sittin' over his books all day whin I'm busy."

He opened the door, looked into the empty hall and came back.

"I wouldn't be troublin' the master wid them ould stories," he said. "Didn't I tell my story fair!"

"You did, Patsy. There were some things in it were not in the evidence you gave at the time."

"See that now! T'ould mimiry of me's goin'. Still, there wasn't much differ?"

There was some anxiety in his voice as he asked the question.

"Nothing much. You said nothing long ago of running towards the upper road after Sir Shawn."

"Sure where else would I be runnin' to? It isn't the lower road I'd be takin', now is it your Ladyship! It wouldn't be likely."

"I suppose it wouldn't," she said, slightly smiling.

"I remember it like as if it was yesterday, the sound of the horse's hoofs climbin' and then the clatter that broke out on the lower road whin Spitfire took the bit between his teeth an' bolted. I'll put the stopper on that villain's lies. I'd like to think the master wouldn't be troubled wid them."

"I'm afraid he'll have to hear them, Patsy. Sir Felix was obliged to issue a summons. It might have been worse if Sir Felix had not been a friend."

"The divil shweep that man, Fury," said Patsy with ferocity. "If he hadn't been a busy-body an' stirrer-up of trouble, he'd have drowned that villain in a bog-hole."

He went off, treading delicately on his toes, which was his way of showing sympathetic respect, and Lady O'Gara returned to the drawing-room.

She was very uneasy. She tried reading, but her thoughts came between her and the page. Writing was no more helpful. She went to the piano. Music at least, if it did not soothe her, would prevent her straining her ears in listening for sounds outside.

The butler came and took away the tea-things, made up the fire and departed in the noiseless way of the trained servant. Her hands on the keys broke unconsciously into the solemn music of Chopin's Funeral March. She took her hands off the piano with a shiver as she realized her choice and began something else, a mad, merry reel to which the feet could scarcely refrain from dancing. But her heart did not dance. The music fretted her, keeping her from listening. After a while she gave up the pretence of it and went back to the fireside, to the sofa on which she and Shawn had sat side by side while she comforted him. She could have thought she felt the weight of his head on her shoulder, that she smelt the peaty smell of his home-spuns. He would be disturbed, poor Shawn, by what she had to tell him. It would be an intolerable ordeal if he should be dragged to the Petty Sessions Court to refute the preposterous charge of being concerned in the death of the man he had loved more than a brother.. Poor Shawn! She listened. Was that the sound of a horse coming? He would be so disturbed!

It was only the wind that was getting up. She drew her work-table to her and took out a pair of Shawn's stockings that needed darning. Margaret McKeon's eyes had been failing of late, and Lady O'Gara had taken on joyfully the mending of her husband's things. Her darning was a thing of beauty. She had said it soothed her when Sir Shawn would have taken the stocking from her because it tired her dear eyes.

Nothing could have seemed quieter than the figure of the lady sitting mending stockings by rosy lamplight. She had put on her spectacles. Terry had cried out in dismay when he had first seen her wear them, and she had laughed and put them away; her beautiful eyes were really rather short-sighted and she had never spared them.

But while she sat so quietly she was gripped by more terrors than one. She was trying to keep down the thought, the question, that would return no matter how she strove to push it away, had she been told all the truth about Terence Comerford's death?

There had always been things that puzzled her, things Shawn had said under the stress of emotion, and when he talked in sleep. There had been a night when he had cried out:

"My God, he should not have laughed. If he had wanted to live he should not have laughed. When he laughed I felt I must kill him."

She had wakened him up, telling him he had had a nightmare and had thought no more about it. There were other things he had said in the stress of mental sufferings. She began to piece them together, to make a whole of them, in the light of this horrible accusation. And Patsy had been lying, had been ready to lie more if necessary. Patsy was a truthful person. Conceivably he would not have lied unless there was a reason for it, unless there was something to conceal.

She got up at last, weary with her thoughts, and went upstairs to dress. Before doing anything else she opened her window and leant out. It had come on to rain. She had known the beautiful strange sky was ominous of wet weather, although for a little time in the afternoon it had seemed inclined to freeze. The heavy raindrops were falling like the pattering of feet. A wind got up and shook the trees. She said to herself that she would not fancy she heard the horse's hoofs in the distance. When they were coming she would have no doubt.

She dressed herself finely, or she permitted Margaret McKeon to dress her, in a golden brown dress which her husband had admired. Through the transparent stuff that draped the corsage modestly her warm white shoulders gleamed. Her arms were very beautiful. She remembered as she sat in front of the glass, while the maid dressed her hair, that her husband had said she was more beautiful than the girl he had married.

She went back to the drawing-room where Shot lay, stretched on the skin-rug before the fire, now and again lifting his head to look at her. The Poms were in their baskets either side of the fireplace. It was very quiet. Not a sound disturbed the silence of the room beyond the ticking of the clock over the mantelpiece and the purring and murmuring of the fire.

She had a book in her hand, but she did not read it. She was too concerned about real actual happenings for the book to keep her attention. She held it indeed so that she might seem to be reading if a servant came into the room. She wondered if the story of the tramp's charge against Sir Shawn had reached the kitchen. Very probably it had. The police would know of it and from them it would spread to the village and the countryside. The people were insatiable of gossip, especially where their "betters" were involved. Probably the tramp, Baker, was it? poor Susan's husband and Georgie's father, had made the statement at every place where he had satisfied his thirst. What a horrid thing to have happened! How would Shawn take the accusation? Of course it was absurd, nevertheless it was intolerable.

Reilly came in presently and asked if her Ladyship would have dinner at the usual hour. It still wanted a quarter of the hour, eight o'clock.

She answered in the affirmative. Shawn was always vexed if she waited for him when he was late, wishing she would remember that he might be detained by twenty things. It would be something to do and would suspend for a while the listening which made her head ache. She hated these hours of listening. Of late years she had forgotten to be nervous when Sir Shawn was not in good time. He had said that he would not give her the habit of his punctual return lest a chance unpunctuality should terrify her. To-night she had only gone back to the listening because Shawn was riding Mustapha. Besides, the news she had to give him had upset her nerves out of their usual tranquil course.

The rain beat hard against the windows. She hoped Shawn was not crossing the bog in that rainstorm. Some horses hated the wind and the rain and would not face them. It would be so terribly easy for Mustapha if he swung round or reared to topple over where the bog-pools lay dark and silent below the road, on either side.

A thought came to her with some sense of companionship that Patsy Kenny was doubtless listening round the corner of the stables for the sound of Mustapha's hoofs, coming closer and closer. She had thought she heard them so often without hearing them. Before she came down the stairs to dinner, she had turned into the private chapel to say her night-prayers, praying for her beloved ones, and for all the world; and as she knelt there in the dimness she had been almost certain she heard Mustapha come. Now, sitting by the drawing-room fire, the river of prayer went flowing through her heart, half articulate, broken into by the effort of listening that might become something tense and aching.

The dinner gong began, rising to a roar and falling away again. She smiled as she stood up, saying to herself that Reilly sounded the gong with a sense of the climax.

As she stood up the Poms bristled and Shot suddenly barked and listened. He sat up on his haunches and threw back his head and howled. The dogs knew the master was out and that something vexed the mistress, and were uneasy.

As she passed across the hall, her golden-brown dress catching the light of the lamps, suddenly the hall door opened. There came in the wind and the rain. The lamps flared. Patsy Kenny stood in the doorway. He was very wet. As he took off his hat mechanically the rain dripped from it. His hair was plastered down on his face and the rain was in his eyes. He was panting as though he had run very hard.

"The master's comin'," he said with a sound like a sob. "He's not kilt, though he's hurted. I'm telling you the truth, jewel. It was well there was a pig-fair in Meelick to-morrow or he might have lain out all night. An' wasn't it the Mercy o' God the cart didn't drive over him?"

"Where is he?" she asked, going to the door and peering out into the darkness. "Where is he?"

"He's comin'. They're carryin' him on the tail-board o' the cart. He's not kilt. Did ye ever know your poor Patsy to decave you yet? I ran ahead lest ye'd die wid the fright. Here, hould a light, you."

He spoke to Reilly, who had never been spoken to so unceremoniously in the whole course of his professional career. The hall was full of the servants by this time, peering and pushing from the inner hall with curious or disturbed faces.

Reilly brought a lamp, more quickly than might have been expected of him. There was the measured tramp of men's feet and something came in sight as the lamplight streamed out on the wet ground.

"Stand back!" Lady O'Gara said, pushing away the crowding servants with a gesture. "Can they see, Patsy?"

"They can see," said Patsy. "God help you! But mind ye he's not kilt. I'm goin' for the doctor. I won't be many minutes."

Into the hall came Tim Murphy, the road-contractor and small farmer, who lived up a boreen from the bog. He was under the tailboard of the cart. Behind was his son Larry. There was a crowd of wet faces and tousled heads crowding in the dark looking into the hall.

The men were carrying the silent figure of Sir Shawn O'Gara, hatless, his scarlet coat sodden and mud-stained, his eyes closed and his head fallen to one side.

CHAPTER XXIV

THE SICK WATCHERS

Patsy had told the truth. Sir Shawn was not dead. Whether he was going to live was another matter.

Patsy had brought back Dr. Costello with unhoped for speed. The doctor had just come in from a case and had only to get what he thought he might need and come as fast as his motor-bicycle would carry him. He was a kind, competent doctor who might have had a wider field for his ambition than this lonely bog country. One of the big Dublin doctors had said to a patient: "Haven't you got Costello at Killesky? I don't know why he wastes himself there. It is very lucky for you since you need not trouble to be coming up to me."

It was a comfort to the poor woman's desolation to see the pitying capable face.

"Patsy has told me all about it as we came along," he said in the slow even voice that had quieted many a terrified heart. "I got him to leave his bicycle at my place and come back with me in the side car. The horse broke his back in the bog, I believe. Better the horse than the man. Is there any one here who will help me to undress him?"

"The butler valets my husband," Lady O'Gara replied. "He was with an invalid before he came to us, and he was highly recommended for his skill and gentleness in nursing. I did not think then that we should have need of these qualifications."

"The very man I want. Can you send him?"

As she turned away he put his hand on her arm. The pale smile with which she had spoken touched the man who was accustomed to but not hardened by human suffering.

"It is not as bad as it seems," he said. "I think he will recover consciousness presently. He must have been thrown rather violently."

She went away somewhat comforted. Outside the door she found Patsy seated on a chair, his head fallen in his hands. Shot was sitting by him, his nose on Patsy's knee. They looked companions in suffering.

"The doctor is hopeful," she said, with a hand on Patsy's shoulder. "Go down and tell Reilly to come. The doctor wants him."

The flat-faced, soft-footed Reilly was to prove indeed in those sad days and nights an untold help and comfort. Patsy watched him curiously and enviously, going and coming, as he would, in and out the sick-room.

Absorbed as she was Lady O'Gara noticed that sick look of jealousy on Patsy's face. She herself was content to sit by her husband's bed and let others do the useful serviceable things, unless when by the doctor's orders she went out of doors for a while.

"We don't want him to open his eyes on a white face he doesn't know. The better you look, my Lady, the better it will be for him," said Dr. Costello.

The afternoon after the accident a watery sun had come out in fitful gleams. It had been raining and blowing for some hours. There was still no sign of returning consciousness in the sick man. Sir Shawn's face looked heavy and dull on the pillow, where he lay as motionless as though he were already dead.

"Concussion, not fracture," said the doctor, lifting an eyelid to look at the unseeing eye. "He will come to himself presently."

And so saying he had sent her out to walk, bidding her exercise the dog as well as herself, for Shot was a heartbreak in these days, lying about and sighing, a creature ill at ease.

"So long as he does not howl," she said piteously, "I do not mind. I could not bear him to howl."

"Dogs howl for the discomfort of themselves or their human friends," said the doctor. "You are not superstitious, Lady O'Gara?"

"Oh, no," she said, huddling in her fur cloak with a little shiver.

"You must believe in God or the Devil. If in God you can't admit the Devil, who is the father of superstition as well as of lies."

"Oh, I know, I know," she said. "But, just now, I cannot bear to hear a dog howl."

On the hall table she found a telegram from Terry. He hoped to be with her by eleven o'clock.

The news from Terry turned her thoughts to Stella. For twenty-four hours she had not remembered Stella. Terry would ask first for his father and next for Stella.

She would go and ask for Stella. She turned back from the path that led to the South lodge, remembering that the gate was locked.

Patsy would have the key. She went in search of him, accompanied by the melancholy Shot and the two Poms, rescued from the kitchen regions, to which they had been banished because of their inane habit of barking with or without reason. She was grateful to the Poms, now that she was out of hearing of the sick-room, for the manner in which they leaped upon her and filled the air with their clamorous joy. There was nothing ominous about their yapping.

Patsy came to meet her as she entered the stableyard. The small neat figure had a disconsolate air. Patsy's eyes were red, his hair rumpled.

"How is he?" he asked.

"There is no change. The doctor is not alarmed."

"Ah, well, that's good so far. Master Terry'll be comin'; that's better. I'll be meetin' him at the late train?"

"How did you know?" she asked surprised; "the telegram has only just come."

"The gorsoon that brought it spread the news along the road. We was the last to hear it."

"Oh, of course," she said listlessly.

He looked at her anxiously.

"There'll be no use to trouble the master about that blackguard's lies?"

"No fear of that," she answered. "Nothing to hurt or harm him shall enter that room."

"Sure God's good always!" Patsy said reverently.

She went on to ask him for the key of the South lodge.

"Wait a minit, m'lady," he said, "I'll come wid you."

She waited while he fetched the key. He came back swinging it on his finger.

"I never seen a quieter little lad thin that Georgie," he said. "He's very fond o' the books. I don't know how I'll give him back to his mother at all. He's great company for me."

They went on, past the house and into the path that led to the South lodge.

Out of sight of the house Patsy suddenly stopped, and nodded his head towards where the boundary wall of Castle Talbot ran down to the O'Hart property.

"It never rains but it teems," he said. "I was waitin' about to see you. There's trouble down there."

His pointing finger indicated the direction of the Waterfall Cottage.

"What's the matter?" she asked in quick alarm.

"It's little Miss Stella. She strayed away last night. Susan didn't miss her till the mornin'. She found her just inside the gates of the demesne, by old Lizzie's lodge. She was soaked wid rain an' in a dead faint. I wonder Susan ventured with that blackguard about. She brought Miss Stella to and helped or carried her back. She's wanderin' like in her mind ever since, the poor little lady."

"Give me the key," Lady O'Gara said. "Go back and bring Dr. Costello."

"It was what I was venturin' to recommend," said Patsy, giving her the key.

She went on quickly, a new cause for trouble oppressing her. She had not waited to ask questions of Patsy.... Was Stella very ill? What had happened to the poor child? How was she going to tell Terry? These were some of the questions that hammered at her ears as she hurried on as fast as her feet could carry her.

She was at the South lodge before she remembered the dogs. Shot might be trusted to be quiet, but the Poms, in a strange house, would bark incessantly. She shut the gate between them and her, leaving it unlocked for the doctor. Their shrill protests followed her as she went down the road.

She stood by the gable-end of the house and called up to the window, open at the top, which she knew to be that of Stella's room. While she waited expectantly, she became aware of a low voice talking very quickly in a queer monotonous way. Susan came to the window and looked out above the lace blind. She made a signal that she would open the gate and disappeared.

Lady O'Gara went on to the gate and saw Susan coming down the little avenue. Susan, dropping the curtsey which had doubtless been the meed of the Squire's lady, opened the gate for her.

"I'm troubled about the poor young lady, m'lady," she said, jerking her thumb backwards towards the cottage. "I wish her mother'd come back. She do keep callin' for her, somethink pitiful."

"Leave the gate open, Susan; I expect the doctor immediately."

"I'm sorry for your own trouble, m'lady," Susan said. "I hope Sir Shawn's doin' nicely now?"

"There is no change yet. But the doctor seems confident."

"There: I am pleased," said Susan.

They went back to the little house, Susan explaining and apologizing. She did not know how she had come to sleep so soundly. She supposed it must have been because she'd been sleeping the fox's sleep, keeping one eye open on Miss Stella, for several nights past, till she was fair worn out. Still, she didn't ought to have done it.

As they stood by the end of the little brass bed on which Stella lay, tossing in fever, she told the rest of the tale, how she had awakened with the first glimmer of dawn and realized that she had slept the night through; how, going to Stella's room she had missed her; how she had searched house and garden in a frenzy without finding any traces of her; finally she had discovered that the gate stood open.

"I declare to goodness, m'lady," said Susan. "I never even thought of Baker when I went out to look for her. After all, if Georgie was safe, there isn't much more he could do to me than he's done. I don't know why it was I turned in at old Lizzie's cottage, an' there I found the poor lamb up against the door, for all the world as though she'd tried to get in and dropped where she was. She've been talking ever since of some one follerin' her. And then she calls out for her mother to come. Once or twice I thought I heard her callin' Master Terry to come and save her. I can't tell whether she was frightened or whether she fancied it. But she do cry out, poor little soul, in mortal terror of some one or something."

Standing there by the foot of the bed Lady O'Gara's heart went out in tenderness to the sick girl as though she was her own little daughter. What maze of terror had she passed through, whether in dreams or reality, that had brought that look to her face? While they watched Stella got up on her elbow and peered into the corners of the room with a terrible expression. She struggled violently for a moment as though held in a monstrous grip. Then she fell back on her pillow, exhausted.

There came a knocking at the door. The doctor. In a few seconds Dr. Costello was in the room with his invaluable air of never being flurried, of there being no need for flurry. He did not even express surprise, though he must have felt it, at seeing Stella there, nor at the state in which he found her.

"I shall explain to you presently," Lady O'Gara said, "why she is here instead of at Inch. Mrs. Comerford has quarrelled with her."

"Ah," said the doctor, getting out his clinical thermometer. "It has been her bane, poor lady, that difficult temper. Years have not softened it apparently."

"But for all that she has a noble nature," Lady O'Gara said. "This will be a terrible grief to her."

"If they have fallen out I should not recommend her presence here when Miss Stella returns to herself," the doctor said quietly. "She must be kept very quiet. Evidently she has had a bad shock of some kind, following on a strained condition of the nerves."

After his examination Lady O'Gara told him something of Stella's case. He did not ask for more than he was told. He did not even show surprise at hearing that Stella had a mother living.

"Ah," he said, "if her mother's face could be the first thing for her eyes to rest upon when she comes out of that bad dream, it would do a good deal to restore her sanity."

"Unfortunately we do not know where the mother is," Lady O'Gara said sorrowfully.

"I will give the patient something to keep her quiet to-night," the doctor went on. "Perhaps you could send some one over to my house for the medicine."

"Patsy Kenny will go."

"Now let me take you back to the house. It is growing dusk. Is there any one you could send to stay with Mrs. ... Mrs. ...?"

"Susan Horridge. Oh, yes. I can send Margaret McKeon, my maid. She never talks."

The doctor gave no indication of any curiosity as to why no talking made Margaret McKeon a suitable person for this emergency. The world was full of odd things, even such a remote bit of it as lay about Killesky. The place buzzed with gossip. Everyone in it knew already the story of the charge made by the drunken tramp against Sir Shawn O'Gara. It had reached Dr. Costello at an early stage in its progress. He remembered the death of Terence Comerford and the gossip of that time. In his own mind he was piecing the story together: but he was discretion itself. No one should be the wiser for him.

He was on his way home, having left Lady O'Gara safely at her own door, when he did something that very nearly ran the bicycle with the side-car into the bog. Patsy, his passenger, merely remarked calmly: "A horse 'ud have more sinse than this hijeous thing."

The doctor, piecing together the details of the old tragedy to explain the new, had had an illumination as blinding as the flash of lightning widen reveals a whole countryside for a moment before it falls again to impenetrable blackness.

"By Jove," he had said to himself, "Stella is Terry's daughter. And the woman at Waterfall Cottage, they will talk even though I don't encourage them, is Bridyeen Sweeney that was. I wonder some of them didn't chance on that."

He murmured excuses to Patsy for the peril he had narrowly escaped.

"She answers to my hand like a horse," he said. "That time I was dreaming and I pulled her a bit too suddenly."

As he got out at his own door he said something half aloud; being a solitary bachelor man he had got into a trick of talking to himself.

"I did hear that boy of the O'Garas' was sweet on her," he said. "My word, what a pretty kettle of fish!"

"I beg your pardon, doctor?" said Patsy.

"Oh nothing, nothing. I was wool-gathering. Come in and wait; I'll have the medicine ready in less than no time."

CHAPTER XXV

IN WHICH TERRY FINDS A DEAD MAN

Terry arrived a little before midnight, having made the difficult cross-country journey from the Curragh, looking so troubled and unhappy that his mother's heart was soft over him as when he was the little boy she remembered.

He bent his six foot of height to kiss her, and his voice was husky as he asked how his father was.

"He is asleep, thank God," she answered. "He came to himself for a little time while I was out this afternoon. Reilly, who is invaluable, a real staff, tells me it is healthy sleep now, not unconsciousness."

"Imagine Reilly!" said Terry, with a sigh of immense relief. "You poor darling! to think of your having to bear it alone! The Colonel was so decent about leave. He told me not to come back till you could do without me. A son's not as good as a daughter. Still, I'm better than nothing, aren't I, darling?"

"You are better than anyone," his mother said, caressing his smooth young cheeks.

"You should have wired for Eileen. What's that selfish minx doing? Making up with the lakh of rupees, I suppose?"

"Do you know I never remembered Eileen," she said, and laughed for the first time since the accident. Her heart had lifted suddenly with an irrational, joyful hope.

She wanted to get Terry to bed and a night's sleep before he knew anything about Stella's illness. In the morning the girl might be better. Terry looked very weary. He explained to her with a half-shy laugh what terrible imaginings had been his companions on the railway journey.

"By Jove, darling," he said, "I never want an experience like it again. And how the train dragged! I felt like trying to push it along with something inside me all the time till I was as tired as though I had been really pushing it. At one place the train stopped in the middle of a bog, someone had pulled the communication cord, and the guard and the fireman ran along the carriages, using frightful language, only to pull out seven drunken men going home from a fair, in charge of one small boy who was sober. He was explaining that he couldn't wake them up at the last station, and that as soon as they came awake they pulled the cord. 'Go on out o' that now, ye ould divil!' said the guard giving a kick to the last of them. I assure you I didn't feel inclined to laugh, even then, darling, though it was so ridiculous!"

She pressed him to eat, but he was too weary to eat much; and she vetoed his seeing his father before morning, being afraid that the strange pallor on the face of the sick man would frighten the boy.

She got him off at last, unwillingly, but out of consideration for her weariness. She was going to bed, she said; Reilly was taking the night watch. She had not slept all the preceding night. He had not asked about Stella, although several times she had thought he was about to ask. She hoped he would not ask. How was she to answer him if he did?

She said good-night to him in his warm fire-lit room, feeling the sweetness and comfort of having him there again despite all the trouble: and, half-way to the door, she was stopped by the question she had dreaded.

"Mother, have you seen Stella?"

"You shall see her to-morrow," she answered, and hurried away, feeling dreadfully guilty because she imagined the light of joy in his young face.

Despite all her troubles she slept soundly, the sleep of dead-tiredness: and when she awoke it was half-past seven. She could hear the maid in the drawing-room below her lighting the fire. It was still grey, but there were indications of a beautiful sunrise in the long golden-yellow light that was breaking in the sky: and a robin was singing.

She did not feel inclined to lie on. She was refreshed and strengthened for the many difficulties of the day before her. She got up, dressed and went down to the sick-room. Reilly was just coming out with a scuttle-full of ashes: he had been "doing" the grate and lighting the fire. He had expressed a wish that there might be as few intruders in the sick-room as possible.

"The thing is to keep him quiet, m'lady," he had said. "They are well-meaning girls", referring to the maids, "but as like as not they'd drop the fire-irons just when he was in a beautiful sleep."

Reilly looked quite cheerful; and Lady O'Gara began to think that the flat side-whiskered face had something very pleasant about it after all. He did not wait for her to make inquiries.

"He's doing nicely, m'lady," he said. "He's been awake and asked for your ladyship."

"Oh!" she said with a catch of the breath, "you should have called me."

"He'd have been asleep before your ladyship could have come. Sleep's the best of all medicine."

She had her breakfast and relieved Reilly. Somewhere about ten o'clock Terry opened the door and peeped in.

"Come!" she beckoned to him.

He came and stood beside her looking down at the bandaged head and pale unconscious face. The deadly pallor of yesterday had passed. A slight colour had come to the cheeks, driving away the blue shadows.

Tears filled the boy's eyes as he looked, and his mother loved him for the sensibility.

She went out with him into the corridor to speak. There was so much she had to tell him that could not be told in a moment or two.

"I shall be off duty by three o'clock," she said. "Can you wait till then?"

"I suppose I couldn't ... they wouldn't want me at Inch? I have written to Stella and she has not answered."

"She has not been very well. I will tell you about it. Only be patient, dear boy. I must not stay away from your father too long."

"Very well," he said resignedly. "I'll take out Shot and we'll pot at rabbits, a long way from the house, darling. It's good to be here, anyhow."

"It's good to have you," she said gratefully.

He had not taken up what she said about Stella's not being well, and she was glad of that. Stella had not been at her best when he left. She might have alarmed him and set him to asking questions which she would have found it difficult to parry.

Twice during the morning hours, while she sat in the clean well-ordered room, with its bright fire and its sudden transformation to a sick-room, she was called to the door. Once it was to interview Patsy Kenny. He had brought word that Susan had spoken to him from the window of Waterfall Cottage and had said that Miss Stella was no worse. Patsy was to watch by Sir Shawn for the afternoon and evening: so much had been conceded to him.

She was expecting the doctor when another summons came, this time it was Sir Felix Conyers, who came tip-toeing along the corridor since she could not go downstairs to him.

"I'm terribly sorry for this dreadful accident, Lady O'Gara," he said. She noticed with a wondering gratitude that Sir Felix was quite pale. "I've only just heard it. The whole countryside will be shocked. Such a popular man as Sir Shawn, such a good landlord and fine specimen of a country gentleman. Upon my word, I'm sorry."

She saw that he was, and she put out her fair be-ringed hand and took his, pressing it softly.

"Thank you, Sir Felix," she said. "I know you feel for us and I am very grateful. Thank God, it is not as bad as it might have been. My husband is sleeping quietly. The doctor is quite pleased."

"Thank God for that," said Sir Felix, echoing her. "He'll be back amongst us again in no time. I came to tell you as soon as I could that the ruffian Fury brought to me the other night has disappeared. The effects of the drink worn off, I said to Fury, and gave him a sharp touch-up about too much zeal. The fellow walks like a dancing-master, and talks picking his words to conceal want of education. I pity the men under him, I do indeed. I'm really sorry, Lady O'Gara, that I troubled you with that cock and bull story the other night. I don't anticipate that we'll hear any more about it."

"I'm glad my husband was not troubled with it," she said, and left her hand in the kind gentleman's: he was wringing it hard, so that the rings hurt her, but she would not have betrayed it for worlds.

A few more expressions of sympathy and of a desire to help and Sir Felix was gone. She was left to her watch once more.

The house seemed extraordinarily quiet. The clock in the corridor ticked away, marking the flight of time. Now and again a coal fell from the fire on to the hearth, or someone came to know if anything was wanted. Mary O'Gara, usually so full of energy, was content to sit watching her husband's face on the pillow. Sir Felix's visit had brought her a certain relief. She could put that worry away from her, for the time. If the man had disappeared he had probably good reasons for disappearing. Perhaps he would not come back. He might be frightened of the thing he had done. Anyhow, she was grateful for so much relief; and if Shawn was going to live she felt that she could endure all other troubles.

After a time she remembered something, something that must be done. Mrs. Comerford must be told about Stella. Perhaps the anger had died down in her by this time, leaving her chilled and miserable, as Mary O'Gara remembered her in the old days after some violent scene with Terence.

She went to the writing-table in the room and wrote a note. She had just placed it in its envelope when the doctor came and she gave it to the servant who showed him up; bidding her give it to Patsy Kenny to be sent to Inch by a special messenger.

The doctor was well satisfied with Sir Shawn's condition. While he examined him the patient opened his eyes. How dark they looked in the white face! They rested on the doctor with recognition, then passed on to his wife, and he smiled.

"Have I ... been very troublesome?" he asked. "I remember ... now ... that brute, Spitfire ... always was a brute...."

The eyes grew vague again and closed, but the lips kept their faint smile.

"He'll sleep a lot," said the doctor. "Much the best thing for him too. He had run himself down even before the accident. He'll be able to talk more presently."

He had taken her out to the corridor before he told the latest, most sensational news.

"I found a new nurse by the little girl's bedside this morning," he said. "Apparently she is the lady who occupied the Cottage, Mrs. Wade. The patient seems wonderfully improved. Hardly any fever; she kept watching her new nurse as though she dreaded letting her out of her sight."

"Ah, that is good!"

There was another lightening of the heaviness of Lady O'Gara's heart. Some mothers in her place might have had an unacknowledged feeling that Stella's death would not be altogether the worst solution of a difficult situation. It would have been easy to think with a kindly pity of how much better it would be for the poor child without a name to drift quietly out on the great sea. Not so Lady O'Gara. Her whole being had been in suffering for the suffering of this young thing who had crept into her heart. Now she was lifted up with the thought of Stella coming back to life and health. For the rest it was in the future. With God be the future!

Terry was late for lunch. Patsy Kenny had begged and prayed to be allowed to help in "lookin' after the master," so he took the afternoon watch, setting Lady O'Gara free to be with her son. It was not like Terry to be late for lunch. He was a very good trencherman and had always been the first to laugh at his own appetite. But to-day he did not come. His mother waited, turning over the newspapers which came late to Castle Talbot. He must have gone farther afield than he had intended. She was not nervous. What was there to be nervous about? Terry had forgotten in the joy of rabbiting that the luncheon hour was gone by: that was all.

At last he came, almost simultaneously with a wild idea in his mother's head that he might have wandered towards Waterfall Cottage and somehow discovered that Stella was there.

She got up quite cheerfully when she saw him.

"You are late, dear boy," she said. Her heart had gone up because so many good things had happened this morning. Shawn was better and had recognized her. The wretch who would have hurt him in the secret places of his heart had gone on farther. Stella was doing well. It was always the way with her to be irrationally hopeful. Many and many a time she had had to ask herself why, on some particular day, she was feeling particularly happy, and had had to trace back the cause to something so small that even she had forgotten it. The founts of happiness in her were very quick to flow.

"There is a cold game pie here," she said, "and there is some curry which I have sent down to keep warm. Also there is pressed beef and a cold pheasant on the sideboard. I suggest that you begin with the curry and go on to the other things."

He did not answer her, but sat down with a weary air. She looked at him in quick alarm. He was not looking well.

"What is the matter, Terry?" she asked anxiously.

"Oh, nothing, darling, to make you look so frightened. Only I have had a rather gruesome experience. I found a dead man, and such an ugly one!"

"A dead man!"

"Yes, just by old Hercules O'Hart's tomb. The place will have twice as bad a name now."

"What sort of a man?"

"Oh, a tramp, apparently. He appeared to have fallen from the Mount. He might have been running in the dark and shot out violently over the edge. From the look of him I should say he had broken his neck. You know how thick the moss is there under the trees. You would not think the fall could have hurt him, but he is stone-dead. I didn't want him brought here so I ran off and got some men who are building a Congested Districts Board house on the Tubber road to lift him. The body is in the stable belonging to the pub. There will have to be an inquest, I suppose, and I shall have to give evidence. A beastly bore." He began to cut himself a slab out of the game pie absent-mindedly.

"Terry," she said, "I think I know the man. He has been about here lately. Patsy would know. If he is the man I think, he is the husband of Susan Horridge, the little woman at the South lodge."

"Oh, that Patsy's so sweet on! He was a bad lot, wasn't he? A brute to that poor little woman and the delicate child. He didn't look a nice person."

He gave a fastidious little shudder.

"We're too squeamish," he said. "It comes of the long Peace. I've sent word to Costello. I suppose I'll have to appear at the inquest. They say a wise man never found a dead man. No one would accuse me of being wise."

A queer thought came to her. If Shawn had not been lying as he was, helpless, might not he have been suspected of a hand in the death of the man who had made such charges against him?

CHAPTER XXVI

MOTHER AND DAUGHTER

Lady O'Gara left Terry eating his curry, the Castle Talbot cook made a particularly good and hot curry, with a quickly recovered appetite, and went upstairs to where Patsy Kenny was sitting by the fire in the sick-room.

"He woke up an' took his milk," said Patsy in an ecstatic whisper, "an' he knew me! 'Is that you, Patsy, ye ould divil?' says he. Sorra a word o' lie in it! An' Shot had twisted himself in unbeknownst to me, an' when he heard the master spakin' he up an' licked his hand."

"I've asked Reilly to come on duty now, Patsy. I shall be up to-night, so he has taken a short sleep."

"You think I'm not fit to be wid him," said Patsy mournfully. "Maybe there's the smell o' the stables about me, though I put on me Sunday clothes and claned me boots."

"No, no; Sir Shawn wouldn't mind the stable smell. Nor should I. I want you to do something for me. I'll tell you in the office. Here's Reilly now."

Reilly came in, cat-footed. Lady O'Gara delayed to tell him what had happened during her watch. Then she followed Patsy downstairs, Shot going with her.

In the office where Patsy stood, turning about his unprofessional bowler in his hands, and looking quite unlike the smart Patsy she knew in his slop-suit of tweeds, she told him how Terry had found a dead man.

"Murdered?" asked Patsy. "Sure it was no sight for a little young boy like him!"

"No; not murdered, fortunately. He was lying huddled up by the Admiral's tomb. Just as though in the dark he had stepped out over the edge of the Mount, not knowing there was a sharp drop below. Mr. Terry thought his neck was broken by the way he was lying."

She had a thought that but for Terry's rabbiting, which had led him anywhere without thought of trespass, the body might have lain there a long time undiscovered. Very few people cared, even in daylight, to go close up to the tomb.

"What sort of a man?" asked Patsy, beetling his brows at her.

"A tramp, Mr. Terry thought."

"It wouldn't be that villain."

"That is just what I thought of. The police have the key of the stable where the body is. They would let you see it if you asked."

"It would be a pity if it was some harmless poor man," said Patsy, with fire in his brown eyes.

He went towards the door and came back.

"It might be the hand of God," he said. "I had a word with Susan this mornin'. She was tellin' me Miss Stella does be cryin' out not to let someone ketch her, an' screamin' like a mad thing that she's ketched. Supposin' that villain was to have put the heart across in the poor child, an' she out wanderin' in the night! Wouldn't it be a quare thing for him to tumble down there an' break his dirty neck before he was let lay hold on her?"

It gave Lady O'Gara fresh food for thought, this hypothesis of Patsy's. She put away the thoughts with a shudder. To what danger had poor fevered Stella been exposed, wandering in the night? And what vengeful Angel had interposed to save her?

She went back to Terry. He had made a very good lunch, she was glad to see, and was just lighting a cigarette.

He looked up expectantly as she came in.

"You said I should see Stella if she would see me. It did not seem like it last time."

A shade fell over his face as he concluded.

She sat down by him and told him of Stella's illness, of the disappearance of her mother and her return. Of Patsy's suggestion she did not speak. It would be too much for the poor boy, who sat, knitting his brows over her tale, his face changing as he looked down at the cigarette between his fingers. He had interjected one breathless question. Was Stella better? Was she in any danger? And his mother had answered that Dr. Costello was satisfied that the girl would mend now.

"I suppose I must wait till she is better before seeing her," he said, when his mother paused. "Poor little darling! I may tell you, Mother, my mind is not shaken. I shall marry Stella if she will have me."

"You can walk with me if you like to the Waterfall Cottage," she said, "and wait for me. There is something about the place that makes a coward of me. It will be worse than ever now after your discovery."

She laughed nervously.

"Poor mother, you have too many troubles to bear!" he said with loving compassion. "You carry all our burdens."

"I have sent Patsy to identify your dead man. I think he can do it."

She was saying to herself that never, never must Terry know the charges that had been brought against his father. They might become a country tale, but the whole countryside might ring with the story without any one having the cruelty to repeat it to Terry.

The night was closing down, Christmas was close at hand, and it was already the first day of the Shortest Days, when they started. A few dry flakes of snow came in the wind as they crossed the park to the South lodge, silent now and empty. Under the trees as they went down the road it was already dark.

The window of the little sitting-room of the Waterfall Cottage threw its cheerful rosy light out over the road. The bedroom window above showed a dimmer light.

"Perhaps, after all," she said, "you might come in and wait for me. I see Susan has lit the fire downstairs. She has not been lighting it since Stella's illness, I have got a second key for the padlock, so we shall not have to wait, rattling at the gate."

"You think I may come in?" he asked eagerly.

"We shall consult Mrs. Wade."

Susan received them with a great unbolting and unlocking of the door. She apologized for her slowness.

"It isn't that lonesome now Mrs. Wade's come," she said. "Yet I've had a fear on me this while back. Maybe it's the poor child upstairs and her thinkin' somethink's after her. It fair gave me the creeps to hear her. She's stopped that since Mrs. Wade's come back. She takes her for her Ma. Now she's got her she doesn't seem scared anymore."

Susan had curtseyed to Terry.

"I've that poor old soul, Miss Brennan, a-sittin' in my kitching, as warm as warm," she went on. "Didn't you know, m'lady? 'Twas 'er as went to look for Mrs. Wade. How she knew as Mrs. Wade would content a child callin' for 'er Ma, passes me."

"Oh, I am glad you have poor Lizzie. I never liked to think of her alone in that wretched place. Yet when we talked of her leaving it she always seemed so afraid her liberty would be interfered with.

She is really too old to be running all over the country as she does, coming back cold and wet to that wretched place, where she might die any night all alone."

"She do seem to have taken a fancy to me," Mrs. Horridge said placidly. "I might take her for a lodger, maybe. Georgie's not one to annoy an old lady like some boys might. I'd love humourin' her little fancies; I could always do anythink for an old person or a child."

"I am going up to see Miss Stella," Lady O'Gara said. "Do you think Mr. Terry may wait by the fire? I shall tell Mrs. Wade."

"He'll be as welcome as the flowers in May, as the sayin' is," Mrs. Horridge said, briskly pushing a chair for Terry nearer the fire and lamplight. "An' plenty o' books to amuse you, sir, while your Ma's upstairs."

Lady O'Gara left Terry in the cheerful room and went up the winding staircase. As she entered Stella's room she had an idea that the place had become more home-like with Mrs. Wade's presence. Mrs. Wade was wearing the white dress of a nurse and a nurse's cap, the white strings tied under her chin. The room was cosy in fire and lamplight and yet very fresh. Stella was awake. She turned her head weakly on the pillow and smiled at Lady O'Gara.

"My darling child, this is an improvement," Lady O'Gara said, quite joyfully.

"My mother has come back," Stella whispered, and put out a thin little hand to Mrs. Wade, who had stood up at the other side of the bed and was still standing as though she waited for Lady O'Gara to bid her be seated.

"I am very glad," Lady O'Gara said, and bent to kiss Stella's forehead. It was cool and a little moist. The fever had quite departed.

"You should not have gone away and left her," she said reproachfully to Mrs. Wade. "You see she cannot do without you."

"I shall not leave her again," Mrs. Wade said. "She chooses me before all the world."

Oh, poor Terry! There was something of a definite choice in the words. They meant that Stella had chosen her mother before all the world might give her. And the poor boy was sitting just below them, bearing the time of waiting with as much patience as possible, listening to the sounds upstairs, his mother divined, with a beating heart.

"Won't you sit down?" said Lady O'Gara. "I cannot sit till you do."

"Thank you," replied Mrs. Wade, and sat down the other side of Stella. Her profile in the nurse's cap showed against the lamplight. It was a beautiful soft, composed profile, like Stella's own. And her manner was perfect in its quiet dignity. A Nature's lady, Lady O'Gara said to herself.

Lady O'Gara could not have told what inspired her next speech. It was certainly not premeditated.

"My son is waiting for me downstairs in your pretty room."

Mrs. Wade bowed her head without comment on Terry's waiting. "We were sorry to hear of the accident to Sir Shawn. I hope he is better," she said.

How quietly they were talking! It might have been just conventional drawing-room talk. No one looking on could have guessed at the web of difficulties they were snared in, at the tragedy that menaced so many harmless joys. Again Lady O'Gara felt surprise at her own attitude towards Mrs. Wade, at Mrs. Wade's towards her. She had no feeling of inequality, nothing of the attitude of the woman who has always been securely placed within reverence and affections, to the woman who has gone off the rails, even though she be more sinned against than sinning. Mrs. Wade met her so to speak on equal grounds. There was no indication in her manner of the woman who had stepped down from her place among honoured women.

And yet, the mere saying that Terry was in the house had somehow affected Mrs. Wade. There was agitation under the calm exterior. In the atmosphere there was something disturbed, electrical.

She hardly seemed to hear Lady O'Gara's answer to her inquiry about Sir Shawn. She got up after a few minutes, and, saying that she would get some tea, went out of the room; to recover her self-possession, Lady O'Gara thought.

When she had gone Stella turned her eyes on Lady O'Gara's face.

"When I get well," she said, "I am going away with my mother. It will be best for everybody. I shall begin a new life with her."

"Oh, Stella, child! You can't give us up like that! You have made your place in our hearts."

There were tears in Mary O'Gara's kind eyes and in her voice.

Stella reached out and patted her hand as though she were the older woman.

"You needn't think I shan't feel it," she said. "You have been dear to me, sweet to me; and I shall always love you. And poor Granny -" A little shiver ran through her and for a second she closed her eyes. "I am sorry for her, too, poor woman! but it will be kinder to you all for me to go away. I did think that I was going to die and that would have made it so much easier for everyone. Only, now that my mother has come back and needs me, I must go on living, but at a distance from this place. Terry will forget me and marry Eileen and be very happy."

The tired voice trailed off into silence. Evidently the long speech had been an effort.

"Terry is obstinately faithful," said Lady O'Gara, with a sound like a sob in her voice. "But now, I think you have talked enough. Go to sleep, child. We shall have plenty of time for talk, even if you do keep to your resolve to leave us all."

Stella opened her eyes again to say:

"No one is ever to say a word against my mother. She never did anything wrong, my poor little mother, even if she was deceived. I honour her more than anyone in the world."

"Don't talk about it, child. No one will dare to say anything," Lady O'Gara assured her, eager to stop something which she felt too poignant, too intolerable to be said or heard.

Almost at once Stella was asleep. There came a little knock at the door. It was Susan to say that, please would Lady O'Gara come down to tea, while she sat with Miss Stella.

Again Lady O'Gara felt the strangeness of it all. There was Mrs. Wade pouring out the tea, handing cakes and toast, doing the honours like any assured woman in her drawing-room, except that she would not take tea herself and could not be prevailed upon to sit down with them.

Once or twice Lady O'Gara thought she intercepted a soft, motherly glance, with something of beaming approval in it, directed from Mrs. Wade's eyes upon Terry. There was light upon Terry's dark head from Mrs. Wade's eyes. The boy was shy, ill at ease. He was dying to ask questions, but he felt that the situation craved wary walking. He fidgeted and grew red: looked this way and that; was manifestly uncomfortable.

None of them had heard the hall-door open nor any one enter, but Keep, stretched on the hearthrug, growled. Shot lying under the table answered him. From Michael, in the kitchen, came a sharp hysterical barking. Michael was not so composed, not so entirely well-mannered as his brothers of the famous Shot breed.

The door opened. In came Mrs. Comerford, tall, in her trailing blacks, magnificent, the long veil of her bonnet floating about her. She looked from one to the other of the group with amazement.

"I am surprised to find you here, Mary O'Gara," she said. "But perhaps you come to see my child. Where is Stella? I have brought the carriage to take her back to Inch."

"Oh, the poor child is too ill to be moved," said Lady O'Gara tremblingly.

"You should be by your husband's side," Mrs. Comerford said, as though Mary O'Gara was still the child she had loved and oppressed.

She had not looked at Mrs. Wade since the first bitter contemptuous glance. Suddenly Mrs. Wade spoke with an air as though she swept the others aside. She faced Mrs. Comerford with eyes as steady as her own.

"Stella will not go with you, she said. She stays with me."

"You! her nurse. I did not know the child was so ill as to need a hospital nurse."

"Her mother, Mrs. Comerford. You did not satisfy her in all those years since you took her from my breast. I take her back again."

CHAPTER XXVII

THE STORY IS TOLD

Lady O'Gara's first terror was of a scene which should waken Stella and alarm her in her weak state. She made as if to stand between the two women: she looked fearfully for the signs of the rising storm as she remembered them in Mrs. Comerford, the heaving breast, the working hands, the dilated nostrils. But there were none of these signs. Instead Mrs. Comerford was curiously quiet.

For a moment the quietness seemed to possess the little house. In the silence you might have heard a pin drop. Shot sighed windily under the table and Keep laid his nose along his paws and turned eyes of worship on his mistress. Long afterwards Mary O'Gara remembered these things and how the wind sprang up and drove a few dead leaves against the window with a faint tinkling sound.

Then the momentary tense silence was broken.

"You are Stella's mother, Terence's..."

What she would have said was forever unsaid.

"Your son's wife, Mrs. Comerford," said Mrs. Wade proudly. She held out her hand with a gesture which had a strange dignity. On the wedding finger was a thin gold ring.

There was a silence, a gasp. Mrs. Comerford leant across the table and stared at the ring.

"Terence's wife!" she repeated slowly. "You don't expect me to believe that! Why, my God, if it were true", her voice rose to a sudden anguish, "if it were true, if it could be true, why didn't you tell me long ago? Why did you let me go on thinking such things of my boy? I won't believe it. I tell you I won't believe it. You would have been quick enough to step into my place, old Judy Dowd's granddaughter! Is it likely you'd have gone all these years without your child, in disgrace, the mother of a child born out of wedlock? It's a lie, Bride Sweeney, it's a lie!"

"It is not a lie," Mrs. Wade said wearily. "I know it seems incredible. There is no difficulty about proof. We were married in Dublin, when Terence was at the Royal Barracks and I was staying with Maeve McCarthy, a school-friend. She was my bridesmaid."

Mrs. Comerford put a bewildered hand to her head. Her other hand clutched the rail of a chair as though her head reeled. Lady O'Gara and Terence looked on as spectators, out of it, though passionately interested. Lady O'Gara gave a quick glance at her son. There was a strange light on his face. He put out his hand and steadied Mrs. Comerford, helping her to a chair. As she sat down, the long black draperies floating about her, she looked more than ever a tragedy queen.

"You have your marriage certificate?" she asked with an effort.

"I have never parted with it."

"If you are not mad, will you tell me why you masqueraded as my son's mistress when you were his wife?"

"Because your son was so afraid of you, you may believe it or not as you will, that he made me swear never to tell it to any one till he gave me leave. Poor Terence! He did not live to give me leave. He had made up his mind to tell you. He said our child should be born in his old home. Then he was killed, and my baby was born, and the world was at an end for me. I only wanted to go away and die somewhere. My grandmother had been terrible; and then you came and you were terrible too: and you took away my baby. I don't think I knew or thought how it was going to affect the baby. You said that she would be brought up to inherit Inch if I never claimed her. I was very innocent, very ignorant. I kept the oath I had sworn to Terence. I have kept it all these years."

"He need not have been afraid of me," Mrs. Comerford said in a heart-broken voice. "I loved him so much that I could have forgiven him his marriage. Do you think that I would have kept your place from you all these years? That I would have lied and lied to keep the world from knowing what I thought the shameful secret of Stella's birth?"

"I think nothing. I only know that he who was afraid of nothing else was afraid of your anger."

The two women stared at each other. Something of pity came into Mrs. Wade's face.

"It might be that he loved you so well he couldn't bear to bring you trouble," she said. "I was only a poor girl from the village, Judy Dowd's grand-daughter, who served in the bar of the little public-house. It would have been a bitter story for you to hear, and you so proud."

"Terence would have raised his wife to his own station. What insanity! I was always hot-tempered but I soon cooled and forgave. What was there in my anger for my six-foot son to be afraid of?"

Mary O'Gara remembered how Terence shook with terror of his mother's anger after some boyish escapade. Grace Comerford deceived herself! Apparently she had no idea of how terrible her fits of temper could be, how the fear of them overclouded the lives of children, defenceless before her.

"You wanted her," Mrs. Wade indicated Lady O'Gara, "for Terence's wife. It was not likely you could have put up with me instead."

"She preferred Shawn O'Gara," said Mrs. Comerford, with a queer bitterness. "I might have turned to you who loved Terence. I had nothing against Shawn O'Gara. He loved Terence better than a brother. I meant not to lose sight of you though I forbade you ever to claim the child. You disappeared from the place where I had sent you. I did not mean you to want for anything. After all you were Terence's."

Her voice ended on a queer note of tenderness.

Suddenly Terry O'Gara spoke, coming out of his corner, the bright light on his glowing eager young face.

"Stella will not refuse to listen to me, now," he said. "You will not refuse me Stella, Mrs. Comerford?"

He addressed Mrs. Wade. The name sounded most strangely in the ears of those who heard it. The woman addressed coloured and looked at him with softly parted lips. Her eyes were suddenly dewy.

"If it had been as ... as ... the poor darling thought," the boy blushed vividly, averting his gaze from the face that was so like Stella's in its softness and wonder and shyness, "it would have made no difference. My mother knows. It would have made no difference. The only barrier would have been Stella herself. I was afraid of Stella's will."

"Stella must decide for herself. Thank God, she did not turn from her mother. I thought I would go away and that this tale need never be told. I knew I had been wrong to come back. I never thought any one would have had the heart to tell my child that story."

She turned suddenly accusing eyes on Mrs. Comerford.

"Even yet she does not know that I was married to her father," she went on. "But she does not shrink from me. My little daughter! That such an anguish as that should ever have come to her! She has chosen me even so before all the world!"

She lifted her head proudly as she said it. Then her expression softened as she saw the shadow on Terry O'Gara's candid face.

"Give her time," she said. "If your father and mother will not mind her being my daughter, why, I think you should ask her."

"Where have you been hiding yourself all this time?" Mrs. Comerford asked, with a certain roughness. "If I had known where you were I might have extracted this story from you earlier. I suppose it is true. How I have suffered by your folly! Do you know that I have had hard thoughts of my dead son, that he disgraced me?"

"He thought you would call his marriage disgrace."

"He wronged me there. It would have been a bitter pill, but I'd have got over it. To think of all those years during which I believed that my one son had betrayed a girl and left her to suffer the shame."

"You should not have thought it; you were his mother," Mrs. Wade, or Mrs. Comerford, said simply. Then she settled down as to a story-telling.

"My grandmother kept her word to you, Mrs. Comerford," she said. "You told her I was not to come back. She did not live very long after we left Killesky. We had reached Liverpool on our way to America, and she became ill there. She was very old and she had gipsy blood. She thought I had disgraced her. Even then I kept my oath to Terence, till almost the very end when she was dying, I thought he would forgive, I whispered in her ear that I was married. She died happy because of that word."

"What folly it was! What cruel folly!" the other woman said, as though she were in pain.

"I came back again," Mrs. Wade went on, "after some years. I did go to America, but the homesickness was terrible. It was bad enough wanting the child, but wanting the country was a separate pain. It was like a wolf in my heart. I used to look at an Irish face in the street and wonder if the man or woman suffered as I did. I believe that if I had had Stella I should have still suffered as much, or nearly as much."

"I know," Mrs. Comerford said. "It was not as bad with me, but I had to come back."

"I did not dare come near Killesky, though I knew that trouble had altered me. I came to Drumlisk on the other side of the mountain. You had been generous, Mrs. Comerford, and my grandmother had saved money and I wanted for nothing. I lived in a little cottage there and I nursed the poor. Father Anthony O'Connell, the priest there, was very good to me. He is a dear old saint. He had a terrible woman for housekeeper. She had a wicked tongue, and she persecuted him with her tantrums, and half-starved him because she was too lazy to cook for him or get up in the morning to keep his house. He used to say, 'Ah well, she doesn't drink!' He'd find some good in the worst. He wouldn't get rid of her, but at last she got rid of herself. She went off to look after a distant cousin, who was old and dying and had a little money to leave. I hope she didn't hasten the creature's death. I was with him three months, I loved to work for him: he was such an old saint and so grateful, when she came back and wanted to take up the place again. She hadn't got the money, I believe, after all. But by that time I knew more about her than the saintly old man did, and I threatened to tell, and so got rid of her. I was very happy there at Drumlisk, there was a light upon the house. Why wouldn't there be with a Saint in it? and the least thing you did for him he was so grateful. I told him about my marriage and the oath I'd taken. He absolved me from that oath. He said it wasn't binding, and that I was in the wrong to let people think me something I was not, much less the wrong to the child deprived of her father as well as her mother."

"He was quite right there," Mrs. Comerford said. "I never had Stella's heart. She wanted you if she could not have her father."

"I had too low an opinion of myself. I said to myself that Stella would grow up a lady and I was a poor woman. I had done better for her by not claiming her, no matter what sorrow it had meant to me. I had my spies out all the time. Lizzie Brennan recognized me one day she wandered into the church at Drumlisk when I was cleaning the sanctuary lamp. It was no use denying it. She knew me. I made her promise she'd never tell. The creature was grateful for the little I could do for her. She told me Inch was empty all those years. Then, when Father O'Connell died, and I was in grief for him, she came and told me Mrs. Comerford had come back with the little lady. The longing grew on me, I was very lonely and so I came to Waterfall Cottage, that I might see the child I'd been longing for all my days."

"You should have walked into Inch and said out that you were my son's lawful wife. I am not the woman to turn my back on his wife, even though you were Judy Dowd's grandchild," Mrs. Comerford said fiercely.

"I never thought of doing that. I only wanted to get a glimpse of the child now and again. Then you, Lady O'Gara, brought her to me, and the love leapt up alive between us the minute we met. I gave myself up to it for a while, feeling as though I was committing a sin all the time. Then I was frightened by old Lizzie. She discovered somehow that Stella was my daughter. She was getting less reliable, being so old. I did not want to stand between Stella and her happiness." She looked at Terry. "So I ran away, meaning to send for my things. I never meant to come back. I returned to my old cottage at Drumlisk till I could make up my mind where I was to go to. Lizzie found me there. It is a long way over the mountains. She walked it in the wind and rain to tell me Stella was here and pining for me, so I came."

"Go up and tell the child, if she can listen to you, that we are friends," Mrs. Comerford said. "Tell her you are Terence's wife and my daughter. Tell her I am not such an ogre as she thinks and you think. Tell her that you and she are to come to Inch as soon as she can be moved. Tell her all that, Mrs. Terence Comerford. Perhaps then she will consent to see me."

She pointed a long finger at Stella's mother, looking more than ever like a priestess, and Mrs. Wade, as she had called herself, obeyed meekly.

When the door closed behind her Mrs. Comerford turned to Terry.

"Good-bye," she said. "The future will be yours. You are like your mother, and she never had any worldly wisdom. I love you for it, but now you had better go."

So Terry and his mother went away, passing in the dark road Mrs. Comerford's carriage with its bright lights and champing and impatient horses.

CHAPTER XXVIII

THE VIGIL

Some time in the night when Lady O'Gara had nodded in the chair beside her husband's bed, she came awake sharply to the knowledge that he had called her name.

"Mary! Mary!"

She could not have dozed for long, since the fire which she had made up was burning brightly.

"Yes, Shawn, I am here," she answered.

"Move your chair so that I may see your face. I want to talk to you."

His voice was quite strong. There was something in the sound of it that spoke of recovering strength.

"I've been lying awake some little time," he said. "I didn't like to wake you, you poor sweet woman. I liked to hear your breathing so softly there close to me, as you have been all these years."

"You are better, Shawn, wonderfully better," she said, leaning down to see his face, for firelight and the shaded lamp did not much assist her short-sighted eyes.

"I am free of pain," he answered. "I don't know when it may return. Give me something to keep me going while I talk."

She gave him a few spoonfuls of a strong meat extract mixed with brandy, supporting his head on her arm while he took the nourishment.

"How young you look, Mary," he said, when she had laid down his head again on the pillow. "Sit there, just where you are. What a burthen I have been to you all these years, holding me up from the abyss. And yet your eyes and your skin are like a child's. I suppose it is prayer and quiet and honest thoughts."

"You really feel able to talk, Shawn?" she asked anxiously.

"I feel as strong as a horse at this moment. That stuff is potent. But I had better talk while I am able. There is much I want to tell you, Mary, and there may be no great time."

Her eyes looked at him in dumb protest, but she said not a word.

"To go back to the beginning, Mary. I have not told you all the truth about myself and Terence. It was not the loss of my friend that darkened my life. That would have been unnatural when I had you beside me. It was, Mary, it was I who sent Terence Comerford to his death."

"You, Shawn! You are dreaming! There was more than the love of brothers between you!"

"My mind is perfectly clear. You won't turn away from me when I tell you? My need of you is bitter."

She dropped on her knees by the bed and laid her face against his hand. She did not want him to see her eyes while he told his story.

"Nothing could make me turn away from you," she answered. "Nothing, nothing. We are everything to each other."

"You are everything to me. But you have Terry. I am fond of Terry, but I have only need of you. I will tell you what happened the night Terence was killed. I had been praying and pleading with him to right Bridyeen, for I knew that there was a baby coming. Never had I so pleaded with any one. I remember that I sweated for sheer anguish, although the night was cold. I don't know what possessed Terence, unless it was the whisky. He told me to go and marry you and leave his affairs alone. And then he laughed. A laugh can be the most terrible and intolerable thing in the world. It maddened me. It was not only poor Bride; but there was you. I thought he would leave Bride and her baby and go back to you. I believed you loved him. I begged and prayed him not to laugh, and he but laughed the louder. He said hateful things; but it was not what he said; it was the way he laughed. It mocked as a devil might have mocked, or I thought it did. It drove me mad. I knew Spitfire would not take the whip and that Terence was in no state to control her. I leant out and I lashed her with all my strength. I can remember shouting something while I did it. Then Spitfire was off, clattering down the road, and suddenly the madness died in me. I would have given my life for his, but I had killed him. I had killed myself. I have never since been the man I was when Terence and I were closer than brothers."

He ended with a sob.

"You can't forgive me, Mary?" he asked, in a terrified whisper, as she did not speak. "For God's sake say something."

She got up and put her arms about his head. Whatever grief or horror there was in her face he should not see it. She laid her face against his, embracing him closely and softly.

"The only thing I find it hard to forgive," she whispered, "is your not telling me. It would not have been so bad if you had told me, Shawn. I could have helped you to bear it. I could have carried at least half your burden."

"You understand, Mary," he asked in a wondering voice, "that when I struck Spitfire, I meant to kill Terence."

"It was madness," she said. "I would almost say it was justifiable madness. No one could believe it was deliberate."

"A jury might have brought it in manslaughter," he said. "Only for you and Terence I would have tested it long ago. You cannot imagine what a weight I have carried. Even telling it has eased me as though a stone had been rolled from off my heart."

"You should have shared it," she said. "That is all I have to forgive, that you carried it alone all those years."

"Oh, incomparable woman!" he said. "Indeed I have felt the wrong I did you in marrying you, in chaining your brightness and sweetness to a doomed man like me."

"You have made me perfectly happy," she said. "I would not have changed my lot for anything else in the world. Why do you talk of doom? It is going to be happiness for both of us now that you have spoken at last."

"I have made you happy?" he asked wonderingly. "Why, if I have, it is not so bad after all."

"Did Patsy know?" she asked on a sudden thought.

"Patsy knew, though he has tried to keep the fact of his knowledge from me. He must have heard what I said. One other knew and has blackmailed me ever since. No matter how much money I gave him he came back again. I was so weary of it and so weary of the burthen I was carrying that the last time I refused him. He went away cursing and swearing that he would have me brought to justice. I felt I didn't care. I told him to do his worst. He is the husband of that poor thing you sheltered at the South lodge, one of the many your goodness has comforted. A bad fellow through and through."

"He will not harm us, Shawn. He is dead. He was found with a broken neck just by the doorway of the Admiral's tomb. He must have stepped over the edge of the Mount not knowing there was a steep fall."

"I am glad for your sake and Terry's. For my own sake I should welcome any atonement."

He went on in a low voice.

"A strange thing happened to me, when was it, the day I went hunting?"

"It is the third day since that day."

"I did not know it was so long. You remember that Black Prince was lame. That was why Patsy was late. He wanted me not to ride Mustapha, but I was determined. The horse went all right during the day, a bit difficult and sulky at some of the jumps, but I kept coaxing him and got him along. It was a long day. We put up three foxes. The last gave us a smart run before we lost him the other side of Altnabrocky. It was late by then and it was raining. You'd think Mustapha would have come home quietly. There was the devil in him, poor brute; and Patsy could not exorcise it. I suppose he is dead?"

"He broke his back."

"Ah, well, he meant to break mine, I think. You know what wild country there is about Altnabrocky. The dusk came fast and I lost my way. I knew it was going to be very dark before the moon rose; the rain was beating in my face and Mustapha kept jibbing and trying to turn round, for he hated the rain and the wind on his eyes. I was considering whether I ought to lead him, and wondering where on earth we were, when a low white light came under the rim of an immense cloud. It was like daylight come back for a little while. By the light I saw a little farmhouse up a boreen off the road. I was dreading to lose the road in the darkness, for it was not much more than a track. Mustapha had been dancing about a bit, but suddenly he whinnied and made a rush for the boreen. It was all right, as I wanted to go there, but he'd have gone whether I wanted to or not.

"An extraordinary thing happened. The door of the cottage opened and out stepped a little old man. I could see his figure against the light within: and Mustapha, who was such a devil with all of us, started whinnying and nuzzling the old fellow, who seemed just as delighted to see him.

"'How far am I from the main road to Galway?' I asked; for I knew I'd be all right once I got on to that. I had quite lost my bearings.

"'A matter of a couple of miles, your honour,' said he. I saw then that he was a little innocent-looking old man like a child, and I remembered Patsy's description of the one he'd bought Mustapha from in the fair of Keele.

"'The horse seems to know you,' said I.

"'It's a foal of me own rarin',' said he, 'an' more betoken he was out of a mare that kilt a man, an' a fine man, poor Mr. Terence Comerford, Lord rest him! She was a beauty, an' I could do anything with her. She was sent to the fair to be sold and no one 'ud touch her. I got her for a twenty-pound note. Only for her foals the roof wouldn't be over me head. This wan was the last o' them.'"

Sir Shawn's voice failed and died away.

"Give me a little more of that stuff, Mary," he said weakly. "I want to finish, and then I can sleep. You don't know how it has oppressed me."

She obeyed him, and, after an interval, he went on again.

"So that was where Spitfire went. I never could make out. And there was I riding a colt of hers, and a worse one than Spitfire to manage. I had great difficulty in getting Mustapha away from his old master, but at last I succeeded, and we jogged along: as he covered the long road he seemed to become quieter. I think I dozed in the saddle. I know I thought it was Spitfire I was riding and not Mustapha. I remember calling him Spitfire as I woke up and encouraged him.

"The night was as dark as I expected, but there was some glimmer from overhead and I could see the bog-pools either side of us as we crossed the bog. It wasn't much guidance to keep us to the road, but we'd crossed the railway bridge, and I could see the lights of Castle Talbot; I was lifting my heart towards you, Mary, as I've always done at that point when, something ran across the road, it might have been only a rabbit, just under Mustapha's feet. Then he was out of control. He reared backwards towards the bog, trying to throw me. I had a struggle with him. It could hardly have lasted a minute, but it seemed a long time. There did not seem any chance for either of us; all I could think of was that I was riding Spitfire's son and that he was going to kill me, and that, maybe, it was a sort of reparation I had to make. Besides, I should be free of Baker and his threats, and he could never harm you through me. But all the time the instinct to live was strong, and I'd got my feet clear of the stirrups, for I didn't want to go with him into the bog. Then he threw me and I heard his hoofs tearing at the stones of the road as he went over, and he squealed. It's horrible to hear a horse squeal, Mary."

He ended with a long sigh of exhaustion.

"Now you are not to talk any more," she said. "The doctor would be angry with me if he knew I had let you talk so much."

"I had to get it off," he said. "I am going to sleep till morning now. Dear Terence! He would have forgiven me if he knew how I suffered."

"He has forgiven you," she said steadily. "I want to tell you, before you sleep, that Terence had married Bride Sweeney secretly. He swore her to silence, because he dreaded his mother's anger; and, poor girl, she bore all that unmerited shame and the loss of her child to keep faith with him."

"He had married her after all!"

Sir Shawn, by an immense effort lifted his head from the pillows. There was a strange light on his face.

"I thought I had cut Terence off in his sins, I who loved him. I said he would wake up in Hell. Terence has been in Heaven all these years. It has been Hell to me that I had sent Terence to Hell. Now I can sleep."

He slept quietly all through the morning hours, till Reilly came to relieve her.

"He looks a deal better, m'lady," said Reilly, looking at him curiously. "I thought yesterday, if you'll excuse me, m'lady, that you were going to lose him. He has taken a new lease of life."

Later on Dr. Costello corroborated Reilly's verdict.

"Something has worked a miracle," he said, patting Lady O'Gara's hand kindly. "I should have said yesterday that we could not keep him very long. There is a marked change for the better. I've been watching Sir Shawn these many years back and I was never satisfied with him."

"There! there!" he said as the joy broke out over her face. "Don't be too glad, my dear lady. I was afraid the spine might have been injured, or something internal. I have made a thorough examination this morning. He is not seriously injured in any way. His thinness and lightness must have saved him when he was thrown. He is very thin. We must fatten him. But, my dear lady, he is going to be more or less of an invalid. There is heart-trouble. No more strenuous days for him! He will have to live with great care. You will be tied to him, Lady O'Gara. I can see he depends on you for everything. He will be more dependent than ever."

He said to himself, looking at her wonderfully fresh beauty, the beauty of a clear soul, that it would be hard on her to be tied up to a sick man. But her face, which had been changing during his speech, was now uplifted.

"If I can only keep him," she said, "all the rest will be nothing. He is going to be so happy with me."

She said it as though she made a vow.

CHAPTER XXIX, AND LAST

THE LAKH OF RUPEES

Mrs. Comerford acted with characteristic thoroughness. Perhaps she felt that she had much to atone for.

It was Christmas Day by the time Stella could be moved to Inch, where amazement reigned. Mrs. Comerford had given her orders. Miss Stella's room was to be prepared. She was coming back again, with her mother. The Bride's Room, which was the finest bedroom at Inch, was to be prepared for Mrs. Terence Comerford.

Mrs. Clinch, to whom the order was given, gasped.

"Mrs. Terence Comerford, ma'am?" she repeated.

"Yes: I hope you're not becoming deaf. My son was married, and Miss Stella is his daughter. He chose to keep his marriage a secret. I have only just learnt that his wife is living."

No more than that. Mrs. Comerford was not a person to ask questions of. She went her way serenely, with a queer air of happiness about her while Inch was swept and garnished. Of course Clinch and Mrs. Clinch debated these amazing happenings with each other; of course the servants buzzed and the news spread to the village and about the countryside with amazing swiftness.

Christmas morning saw the transference from the Waterfall Cottage to Inch accomplished. Stella was by this time able to sit up for the journey, and since there could be no proper Christmas festivity at Castle Talbot Terry O'Gara was to lunch at Inch. He was witness of the strange ceremonial air with which Mrs. Comerford laid down her seals of office, so to speak.

"Mrs. Terence Comerford will take the head of the table," she said.

Then she passed to the foot of the table while Mrs. Terence, flushed and half tearful, took the vacated place.

Terry was in the seventh heaven. There was no longer anything between him and Stella, who had accepted him as though their happiness had never been threatened. Stella, with that air of illness yet about her which made her many times more dear and precious to her lover, looked with shining eyes from her mother to her grandmother.

In the drawing-room afterwards, while Stella rested in her own pretty room, and her mother, rather overwhelmed by her new estate, sat by her, Mrs. Comerford talked to Terry.

"It is a long Winter here," she said. "I remember frost and snow in January when it was dangerous to walk across your own lawn because of the drifts. If the snow does not come it will be wild and wet. Stella was brought up in Italy. I should hurry up the marriage, young man, and take her away. Now that your father is going on so well there is no reason for delay. Besides, we want to get it out of her head that she was pursued by some ruffian the night she wandered and fell by the empty lodge at Athvara."

"Poor little angel," said Terry, "I am only too anxious, Mrs. Comerford. I shall be the happiest man alive if she will consent."

"Of course she will consent. She is an obedient child," said Mrs. Comerford, with an entire oblivion of Stella's marked disobedience in the not very remote past.

"It is adorably unselfish of you to be willing to part with her," said Terry, his face shining with happiness.

"For the matter of that I shall have my daughter-in-law," said Mrs. Comerford superbly. "She has never travelled. We shall probably do some travelling together. You had better resign your commission."

"Oh, must I? I might get a year's leave because of my ... Stella's health. I am very fond of the Regiment. But of course I should not put it before her."

"Of course not. I don't mind your sticking to the Regiment, as you say, for a bit longer. Your father and Stella's father each took their turn at soldiering. It is as well to be prepared, in case of need. There might be a bolt out of the blue sky. So much more reason for being happy while we may."

"You know that Susan Horridge, or Mrs. Baker, but she won't be called that, identified the dead man I found by the Admiral's tomb as her husband?"

"Yes, I heard so. A good riddance. I wonder if he was hunting for Susan and the boy when he met with that accident. He was 'warm' as the children say, close up against Waterfall Cottage. You are to make Stella forget that dream of hers of being pursued by some terrible creature that night."

"I will do my best," said Terry. "A pity some one does not take Athvara! It is a fine old house all falling to rack and ruin."

"I have heard a rumour that some Order is buying it for a boys' school. That would be best of all. A crowd of boys about would soon banish the ghosts. They would delight in the Admiral's tomb. My own boy and Shawn O'Gara, your father, made a cache there one cold Winter, pretending they were whalers in the North Sea. It was the time of Dr. Nansen. The tomb used to be open then. They had all sorts of queer things stowed away under the shelf that held the Admiral's coffin. Queer things, boys!"

She looked into the fire for a few minutes.

"Your father loved my boy," she said. "I believe he'd have died to save him. There was a time when I was angry against him, because he lived and was warm and my boy was cold, and because your mother had married him. I always looked to see her my Terence's wife. I was wrong. Terence had chosen his own wife."

The marriage was fixed for early in the New Year. Everyone seemed extremely happy. Terence had got his leave of absence for a year. Stella was making excellent progress and had begun to take a shy interest in the preparations for the wedding and the details of the wedding journey. She had seen Sir Shawn, lying on the invalid couch which had the very latest improvements to make his invalid's lot as easy as possible. He had drawn down her face to his and kissed it, saying something inexplicable to Stella.

"You are the dove with the olive branch to say that the floods have retreated."

He was very happy about the marriage, and Lady O'Gara, watching him as though he were a beloved and delicate child, smiled at his saying, a bright brave smile which made Stella say afterwards to Terry that his mother's smile was like Winter sunshine.

"It used to be so full of fun," said Terry, "her dimples used to come and go, but she is troubled about my father, though she says she is the happiest woman alive, because she can keep him perhaps for a long time yet."

Patsy Kenny was painting and papering his house in the stable yard, in the intervals of his professional labours, whistling over his work. Mrs. Horridge, as she still called herself, was back at the South lodge with Georgie, and old Lizzie Brennan as her lodger.

"The old soul," she said to Lady O'Gara. "I'll always find room for her. She do take on so when it comes over her that she might go to the 'Ouse. I've promised her she shan't. Wasn't it clever of her, m'lady, to go off and find Miss Stella's Ma for her. I don't believe Miss Stella would be with us this day if it weren't for that. I never saw a young lady so set on her Ma. M'lady," she drew Lady O'Gara away from the gate by which they were standing talking, a little way along the avenue where no listener could hear, "I've told Miss Stella a lie, and I'm not sorry for it, although I'm a truthful woman. It was a big lie too. I told her that there terror she had of runnin' and runnin' from somethink dreadful was but the fever. I told her she dreamed it. But I'd never have got it out of her head if her Ma hadn't come."

She turned away and was silent for a minute. Then she spoke again in a low voice.

"It was the drink," she said. "The Lord forgive all the wicked!"

One of these days Lady O'Gara was saying to herself that she must read and answer all the letters that had come to her while Sir Shawn still claimed her constant attention. There was a heaped basket of them on the desk in her own room. It was a very chilly afternoon. Sir Shawn was asleep upstairs. Presently Reilly and Patsy Kenny would carry him down on his wonderful couch. Terry was over at Inch. He was to bring back Stella, and later on they were to be joined at dinner by Mrs. Comerford and Mrs. Terence.

"I'm afraid no one ever wrote to tell poor Eileen," Lady O'Gara said to herself, with a whimsical glance at the letter basket and the flanking waste-paper basket. The telling that was in her mind referred to the approaching marriage of Terry and Stella. Eileen had been notified of Sir Shawn's illness and had written expressing her concern. But Eileen never could write a letter. The formal and ill-constructed phrases conveyed nothing. Somewhat to Lady O'Gara's surprise Eileen had not offered to return. But after that formal letter another letter had come, quite a thick one, and it lay still unopened amid the accumulated letters.

"Poor Eileen! I wonder if there was anything in Terry's story about the lakh of rupees!"

The thought had but entered her mind when she heard, or thought she heard, the sound of approaching carriage-wheels. She listened. It might be Dr. Costello, who had a way of coming on friendly visits very often. Or perhaps Terry and Stella were coming earlier than she had expected them.

The door opened. In came a young woman wearing magnificent furs, bringing with her a scent of violets. Eileen!

She flung her arms about Lady O'Gara with an unaccustomed demonstrativeness. But she turned a cold satin cheek to the lady's kiss. It had been characteristic of Eileen even in small childhood that in moments of apparently greatest abandonment she had never kissed but always turned her cheek to be kissed.

"Since you wouldn't write, dearest Cousin Mary," she cried in a voice strangely affected to Lady O'Gara's ear, "I've come to see what is the matter. And I've brought my husband."

A shortish man with a keen, clear, plain face came from behind the shadow of Eileen and her furs. Lady O'Gara had a queer thought. She recognized Eileen's furs for sables. She had never attained to sables. The coat must have cost three hundred guineas. How quick Eileen had been about her marriage! And how soon she had begun to spend the lakh!

Meanwhile her lips were saying -

"I am very glad to meet you, Dr. Gillespie. But what a surprise! I did not think Eileen had had time even to get engaged."

"You see there was so little to be done," the lakh responded in a very pleasant voice, which at once secured Lady O'Gara's liking. Besides, his hand-clasp was very warm, so unlike Eileen's chilly cheek. She hoped Eileen was going to be good to him. "I was Eileen's slave always. She had refused me innumerable times. She only had to say she had changed her mind and I procured a special licence."

"You will take off your furs, Eileen. Of course you and Dr. Gillespie will stay. Sir Shawn is so much better. And you have to hear all our news. You have sent away your car?"

Eileen was taking off the sables, and flinging them carelessly to one side, as though three hundred guinea sables were things of common experience with her. The rose-silk lining fairly dazzled Lady O'Gara's amused eyes, so sumptuous was it.

"Only between two trains, dearest Cousin Mary. We are going to London on our way to Italy. We've been married a week and have been boring each other dreadfully at Recess. I am longing for Italy, but I felt I must see you and introduce Bobbin. We have till seven o'clock to stay."

Lady O'Gara glanced at the bridegroom to whom his bride had given so absurd a name. He was looking amusedly, if adoringly, at Eileen. He had a good strong chin, a firm mouth, which was sweet when he smiled: his grey eyes were quizzical. She thought the marriage would be all right.

"I am going to get warm in the sun," said Eileen with a little shiver. "You see Bobbin has to go back to work. He has taken a house in Harley Street and we wish to settle in as early as possible. There has been an article in the Medical Journal."

"In fact London can't wait till I put up my brass plate, Lady O'Gara," Dr. Gillespie said, with twinkling eyes.

Reilly came to ask if he should bring tea.

"Yes, please; Mr. Terry and Miss Stella will be here very shortly."

Lady O'Gara thought she had better prepare Eileen, who had always had the air of Terry being her property.

"Our great news, after my husband being so well," she said, "is that Terry and Stella are going to be married almost immediately. By the way, they too are going to Italy. Perhaps you may meet there."

Eileen opened her eyes wide and lifted her hands, with a side look at her husband.

"I am so glad," she said. "Do you know, Cousin Mary, the one drawback to my happiness, you see I always cared for Bobbin, since we were small children, was the dread that Terry might mind."

Katharine Tynan was born on January 23rd, 1859 into a large family in Clondalkin, County Dublin, Ireland to parents Andrew Cullen Tynan (1829-1905) and Elizabeth O'Reilly (1831- c1869).

The family business was cattle rearing and the farmhouse, set with the mountains for a back drop, was a wonderful world for a young mind to learn and imagine, set out with an orchard at the back, a garden with a sun-dial, a summer-house, a labyrinth of little flower-beds with box borders, a privet hedge, and a great walnut tree.

Initially the young Katharine was slow to learn. She was educated at the Dominican convent school, St Catherine of Sienna, in Drogheda. It appears Katharine had a stubborn streak which inhibited her ability to learn as easily as the school would wish. However she would learn on her own terms and soon began to take her 'forbidden literature', hidden in her clothing, to her loft in a stable hideaway.

Her reading covered everything from Aurora Floyd (her mother failed to approve of this type of book) to "The Mysteries of Paris," by Eugene Sue, some lurid romances of G. W. Reynolds, a set of Maria Edgeworth, "The Poets of the Nation"—eclectic at the very least.

Her father though let her read everything, from "The Wide Wide World" to "Tristram Shandy," from Faber's "Tales of the Angels" to "The Near and the Heavenly Horizons" of Madame de Gasparin. She had books of Longfellow, a Burns of the most complete and unexpurgated, a Milton, a Moore, of course, and the first two volumes of the Corn-hill, where she revelled in Owen Meredith, and "The Great God Pan" of Mrs. Browning.

However until she turned seventeen none of this appeared to point to a literary career. But now that would change and her first verse were written and then printed in a Dublin newspaper.

The good reception to them led to another sonnet being printed in the Spectator. Thereafter the Graphic published several others and even paid a half guinea for the privilege.

By twenty she began to form friendships among those in the Dublin literary circles. The first was Father Russell of The Irish Monthly, the brother of whom was afterwards Lord Russell of Killowen, Lord Chief Justice of England. Through him she made various literary friendships and associations. Lady Russell's sister, Miss Rosa Mulholland, now Lady Gilbert, was an initial object of the young girl's worship.

In 1884 Katharine dispatched herself to London for the first time, and made an abiding friendship when she met Mrs Alice Meynell.

Alice, of course, was an established poet and helped, with her husband Wilfred, to publish many other poets. The following year Wilfred arranged for the publication of her first volume of poems, "Louise de la Vallière" (1885). The book brought her new friends: William Rossetti, Christina Rossetti, Cardinal Newman, and Cardinal Manning.

At about this timer Katharine became a close friend of Gerard Manley Hopkins and also formed a growing attachment to William Butler Yeats (who, it is rumoured, may have proposed marriage and been rejected), and later she became friendly with the correspondent of the Irish Nationalist and excellent poet Francis Ledwidge.

Katharine published a further book of poems "Shamrock" in 1887.

Returning to Ireland, she found herself welcomed into a literary circle, of which W. B. Yeats, "A. E." Russell, and Douglas Hyde were members. They would meet at the houses of Dr. Sigerson, John and Ellen O'Leary (the old Fenian chief and his sister), and Johnson of Ballykilbeg.

In 1889 she was back in London with the Meynells. Katharine remembered an historic evening at Lord Russell's house in Harley Street, when Gladstone, Lord Randolph Churchill and Charles Stewart Parnell, a stalwart in the cry for Irish Home Rule, were met together (Parnell was recovering his career as leader of the Irish Parliamentary Party after a forger Richard Pigott had supplied forgeries to the Times implicating Parnell in murder. Parnell was exonerated and Pigott committed suicide). Mr. Gladstone buried himself in a corner with an elderly lady, an old crony of his, and Lord Randolph disappeared early, and Mr. Parnell turned from the adulation of the crowd to startled surprise at the sight of one young Irishwoman who worshipped him and always would.

As she gathered friends and contacts into her life her literary output began to gather pace. Katharine had begun to write prose for the Speaker and for the Scots and National Observer. The noted writer and poet William Ernest Henley was a great admirer and he praised her work, giving her an inscribed copy of his book The Song of the Sword, inscribed "Katharine Tynan, Sorori in Arte," and others of his books including Hawthorn and Lavender.

In 1892 she married happily to Henry Albert Hinkson, he was almost six years younger, a fellow writer and a barrister. They moved to England, records give their address as 9 Loughfield Road, Ealing, in London, where the marriage produced five children although two were to tragically die in infancy.

In her growing literary efforts she would now usually write under the name Katharine Tynan Hinkson, or a similar variation.

By 1894 her output was prolific and was ranged from poetry to novels to short stories. It would later include a biography and a large amount of editing including the four volume "Cabinet of Irish Literature," a new edition of which she prepared for Blackie's, of Glasgow. She was also a reviewer, and contributed to many magazines.

Katharine's later volumes of verse are those of a natural and spontaneous order characteristic of the Irish muse.

In reviewing "A Cluster of Nuts," (1894) a writer for the Athenæum wrote: "Mrs Hinkson is a lyric poet, and her prose, like her verse, is near to the heart of nature, sweet with the smell of fresh grass and flowering thorn, and warm with a tender sympathy that embraces all things that live and die; but that goes out more fully to trees and fields and summer skies than to men and women." This was doubtless true at the time, and as far as it went, but Mrs. Hinkson has written much since then; her human relationships have increased, and no one can read her child poetry without feeling that her human sympathy is keen, tender, warm, and constant. Many mother-hearts will find expression in "The Meeting," "The Mother," and "The Desire." Devotional feeling makes much of her verse religious in the best sense, and spirituality of thought often imparts the lustre which transfigures.

In 1912 the family returned to Claremorris, County Mayo, when her husband was appointed magistrate there a post he held until his early death in 1919.

She is now also sometimes grouped amongst the War Poets of the First World War. Her experience was not direct but as a Mother with one son serving in France and another in Palestine, the emotions, fears and doubts are expressed in a beautiful heart-felt way.

Involved in the Irish Literary Revival, Tynan expressed concern for feminist causes, the poor, and the effects of World War I in her work. She also meditated on her Catholic faith.

She is said to have written over 100 novels, 12 collections of short stories, plays and many volumes of enduring poetry. Katharine's talents also extended in total to five volumes of autobiography.

Katharine Tynan Hinkson died at age 72 on 2 April 1931 in Kensal Green, London.

Katharine Tynan – A Concise Bibliography

Louise de la Vallière (1885) poems
Shamrocks (1887)
Ballads & Lyrics (1891)
Irish Love-Songs (1892)
A Cluster of Nuts, Being Sketches Among My Own People (1894)
Cuckoo Songs (1894)
Miracle Plays (1895)
The Land of Mist and Mountain (1895)
The Way of a Maid (1895)
Three Fair Maids, or the Burkes of Derrymore (c.1895)
An Isle in the Water (1896)
The Golden Lily (1899)
The Dear Irish Girl (1899)
Oh, What a plague is Love! (1900)
Her Father's Daughter (1900)
Poems (1901)
A Daughter of the Fields (1901)
A King's Woman (1902)
Love of Sisters (1902)
The Great Captain: A Story of the Days of Sir Walter Raleigh (1902)
The Handsome Quaker, and other Stories (1902)
The Adventures of Carlo (1903)
The Luck of the Fairfaxes (1904)
A Daughter of Kings (1905)
Innocencies (1905) poems
For the White Rose (1905)
A Little Book for Mary Gill's Friends (1905)
The Story of Bawn (1906)
The Yellow Domino (1906)
Book of Memory (1906)
Dick Pentreath (1906)
The Cabinet of Irish Literature. (4 volumes) (1906) editor, expansion of work by Charles Read
The Rhymed Life of St Patrick (1907)
Twenty-One poems, selected by W. B. Yeats
A Little Book of XXIV Carols (1907)
Father Mathew (1908) biography of Theobald Mathew
Experiences (1908)
A Union of Hearts (1908)

The House of the Crickets (1908)
Ireland (1909)
A Little Book for John O'Mahony's Friends (1909)
The Book of Flowers (1909) with Frances Maitland
Mary Gray(1909)
A Girl of Galway
The Rich Man
A Red, Red Rose (c.1910)
Heart O' Gold or the Little Princess
The Story of Cecelia (1911)
New Poems (1911)
Princess Katharine (1911)
Twenty-five Years: Reminiscences (1913)
Irish Poems (1913)
The Wild Harp (1913) poetry anthology, editor.
A Mesalliance (1913)
The Daughter of the Manor (1914)
A Shameful Inheritance (1914)
The Flower of Peace (1914) poems
Mary Beaudesert, V. S. (1915)
Flower of Youth (1915) poems
The Curse of Castle Eagle (1915)
The House of the Foxes (1915) novel
Joining the colours (1916)
Lord Edward: A Study in Romance (1916)
The Holy War (Great War Poems) (1916)
The Middle Years (1916)
Margery Dawe (1916)
Late Songs (1917)
Herb O'Grace (1918) (Poems)
The Sad Years (1918) tribute to Dora Sigerson
The Years of the Shadow (1919)
The Honourable Molly (1919)
Denys the Dreamer (1920)
The Handsome Brandons (1921)
Bitha's Wonderful Year (1922)
The Wandering Years (1922)
Evensong (1922)
White Ladies (1922)
A Mad Marriage (1922)
Memories (1924)
Life in the Occupied Area (1925)
The Man from Australia (1925)
The Wild Adventure (1927)
Twilight Songs (1927)
The Face in the Picture (1927)
Haroun of London (1927)
Pat, the Adventurer (1928)
The Respectable Lady (1928)
The River (1929)
Castle Perilous (1929)

The Squire's Sweetheart (1930)
Denise the Daughter (1930)
Collected Poems (1930)
The Admirable Simmons (1930)
The Forbidden Way (1931)
Philippa's Lover (1931)
A Lonely Maid (1931)
The Story of Our Lord (1932)
The Other Man (1932)
An International Marriage (1933)
Londonderry Air (1935)
The Briar Bush Maid
A Little Radiant Girl
A Passionate Pilgrim
Maxims
A Girls Song"